Real Estate

Appraisal Desk Book

REAL ESTATE
APPRAISAL
DESK BOOK

ROBERT W. WINSTEAD

M.A.I.

PRENTICE-HALL, INC., ENGLEWOOD CLIFFS, N. J.

Second Printing.....October, 1970

A Word From The Author

Basic appraisal knowledge is essential to anyone who makes decisions related to real estate. Anyone having an interest in real estate is directly or indirectly concerned with appraisal problems and how to solve them. The appraisal process provides the methods and procedures to estimate value, best land use, best size of the project, and other complex problems involved. It covers a range of real estate from one or more dwellings to one or more skyscrapers. Many investors and speculators have become wealthy through the application of the principles involved in the appraisal process.

The field of real estate appraising has expanded greatly in the last few years due to the great need for, and realization of the necessity of, professional appraisal services. The appraisal profession offers the qualified professional real estate appraiser a relatively good income. As in any line of endeavor, a period of education, training, and experience is required.

Most professional appraisers have entered the field as real estate dealers, salesmen, managers, or mortgage company employees. Through on-the-job training, home study, or attending special appraisal courses sponsored by the American Institute of Real Estate Appraisers and the Society of Real Estate Appraisers, many have secured some professional standing in the field. By and large, direct experience is the real training necessary to produce a professional appraiser, although academic study will greatly reduce the period of apprenticeship. Unfortunately, most people engaged in real estate and allied fields do not have time to perform actual appraisals or to take formal courses of training. This book is designed to assist those people, as well as the practising appraiser, by providing the essential information in one volume.

The real estate operator will be particularly interested in Chapter 6, "Location Analysis and Appraisal of Urban and Suburban Land," and Chapter 7, "How to Estimate the Need for Shopping Centers and Individual Retail Establishments," which include helpful basic business data tables. He will also find Chapter 12, "Equity Valuation, Yield, and Leverage," of immediate value to him.

Robert W. Winstead

Dedicated

TO THOSE WHO MAKE DECISIONS

IN THE FIELD OF REAL ESTATE

Contents

PART II. ADVANCED APPRAISAL PROCEDURES

Table of Exhibits

PART I

BASIC

APPRAISAL INFORMATION

AND PROCEDURES

1

Appraisal Concepts,
Procedures,
Principles and Axioms

These are the three basic concepts underlying the appraisal of real estate:

(1) An appraisal is an opinion of an appraiser which is based upon an interpretation of facts and beliefs as of a given date.

(2) The real estate appraised normally includes land and all buildings and other improvements thereon of a permanent nature. Certain easily removable items of the buildings may be considered as part of the real estate, but this varies from one area to another. The land and buildings, of course, are physical things, but real estate is a term used to designate the rights of real estate ownership rather than the land and buildings themselves. It is actually the rights of ownership that are appraised. Different owners may own one or more of the rights. Accordingly, it is necessary to know the rights that are to be appraised.

(3) The value appraised is the value to the typical user or investor and not necessarily to the owner or any specific person or organization.

There are three basic procedures used in the appraisal of real estate:

(1) The physical estimate, commonly termed the cost or physical approach, and sometimes the summation approach.

3

(2) The market estimate, usually called the market approach.

(3) The economic estimate, commonly termed the income or economic approach.

There are many techniques involved in the different facets of the procedures, and if you expect to perform appraisals you should master them. It is generally considered highly desirable to use all three approaches if they are applicable and the necessary data is available.

You should know the basic legal aspects of real estate. The fee simple interest is the estate commonly appraised. It is the absolute ownership of real property which gives the owner and his heirs the full power of disposition, etc. It includes the following bundle of rights: the right to enter upon or into an interest thereof, to use or not, the right to sell or not, to lease or refuse to lease, to donate or give as a gift, and the right to enjoy peaceful possession. Quite frequently the appraiser will be called on to appraise properties where one or more of the rights have been sold, leased, or otherwise conveyed or limited. Restriction as to land use is a release of certain rights of ownership. The lease of the property or the placement of easements on the property amounts to another form or relinquishment of one or more of the bundle of rights. As a general rule, it is the fee simple ownership that is appraised, but the rights actually involved must be known.

Fee simple ownership is subject to certain basic powers and rights of government: namely, the power of eminent domain, the power of taxation, the power of escheat, and police power. The power of eminent domain is the right of the government to take property for certain uses but, of course, the owner must receive just compensation for the property taken. The power of taxation is self-explanatory. The power of escheat is the provision whereby the interest in land or property will revert to the state upon the death of an owner who leaves no will and has no heirs. This power of escheat is possessed only by the sovereign states. In addition to the usual conception of police power, it includes the power to provide essential traffic rules and regulations, which may be used to change or govern the flow of traffic.

Basic principles and axioms explained

The Principle of Cost: Replacement cost tends to set the upper limit of value. This is held to be valid in view of the law of substitution set forth below.

The Principle of Substitution: The value of an article does not exceed the value of an acceptable substitute, if the substitute is available. Value to the typical buyer is the basis of comparison. It is related to the law of supply and demand. This is one of the most important principles. It is basic to the market approach.

The Principle of Utility: Value is in proportion to the best long-term productive use of a property. This is a basis of the economic (income) approach. Its measure is the present worth of the right to collect the future net benefits from the property.

The Principle of Highest and Best Use: The highest and best use of a property provides the greatest net return in rent or amenities over the longest period of time.

The Principle of Balance: The parts of a property must be related and balanced in the proper proportion to obtain the highest and best use. This is a matter of efficiency where each component part provides a maximum of utility.

The Principle of Contribution: The value of a component part of a property is valued according to its contribution.

The Principle of Conformity: Vacant and undeveloped land should be developed according to the land use requirements of the neighborhood. Normally, in real estate one should not invest contrary to the trend. Over, under, or improper improvements do not normally render the highest and best return to the property.

The Law of Supply and Demand: Prices and values, as a general rule, rise and fall depending on the supply and demand of the properties involved. This is a basic law of economics.

The Law of Diminishing Returns: As an example, the larger the office building on a particular site, the greater the returns are up to a certain point. The returns then diminish gradually in proportion to the cost of increasing the size of the building.

The Principle of Competition: Excessive profits will increase competition to such an extent that in due time the supply will be increased in relation to the demand, and the price lowered accordingly. It is not wise to consider excessive rentals as being indicative of the future.

Typical User Concept: Normally, the appraisal of real estate involves the value of the property to a typical user or purchaser rather than to a specific user or purchaser.

General Price Level: It varies with supply and demand.

The Principle of Anticipation: When one buys real estate he expects future benefits. He expects to receive at least a reasonable return upon the investment during ownership and to be able to recover at least the depreciated balance of the investment when he sells the property. When a home is purchased for owner occupancy, the owner expects to receive the amenities of occupancy as a reasonable return during occupancy and at least the depreciated balance of the investment when he sells the property.

The Law of Change: This is considered to be basic to the law of nature. Everything is considered to change sooner or later, except perhaps the few absolute laws of the universe.

The Law of Integration and Disintegration: Everything goes through the process; that is, it is either born, built, or brought together in some form, and in due time it tends to start to wear or waste away and disintegrate.

People Tend to Act Rationally: An appraiser must assume that people in general tend to act rationally and tend to do that which is best for theirs and themselves.

Methods of valuation and premises involved

As mentioned before, there are three basic procedures used to formulate the final opinion of the value of real estate. They are the physical approach, the market approach, and the economic approach. They are preliminary estimates used to select the final opinion.

Underlying Premise of All Approaches: The premise of all three appraisal approaches is that of the law of supply and demand. The law of supply and demand tends to set the value of real estate. This basic law applies throughout all the processes involved in valuation and, of course, it is basic to our economic system.

The Physical (Cost) Approach and Its Premise: The premise of the physical approach is the same as the principle of cost: The replacement cost tends to set the upper limit of value. The physical approach involves an estimate of the replacement or reproduction cost, new, of the building and other improvements involved, less depreciation, if any, to which is added the estimated value of the land. Replacement cost is defined as the cost of a similar and comparable modern structure of the same size, but not the exact replica of the subject appraised. Reproduction cost is defined as the actual cost to reproduce an exact replica of the subject involved. Normally, the replacement cost is used, particularly when older properties are involved. It would be almost impossible to find some of the materials or equipment on the market today that were used many years ago. In appraising a new and modern structure which has no functional or economic obsolescence, the replacement cost and the reproduction cost should be the same.

The Market Approach and Its Premise: The basic premise of the market approach is the principle of substitution: The value of an article does not exceed the value of an acceptable substitute if the substitute is available as required. The value to the typical buyer is the basis of comparison. It is related to the law of supply and demand. This is one, if not the most, important principle in the evaluation of real estate. The basic procedure in estimating the value by this approach is that of comparing the appraised property with comparable properties that have been sold within a reasonably comparable time as well as with those that are currently for sale or may have been offered for sale recently. Great weight is given to the supply and demand of comparable properties, and to any trends that may have been occurring in the market that would influence the value of the property being appraised. After several properties have been compared with the property being appraised, the typically indicated value, adjusted by the indicated trends, is accepted as the market value of the property. The supply and demand situation at the time of the appraisal and the possibility of new construction must be considered in formulating the estimate.

Economic Approach (Income Approach) and Its Premise: The premise of the economic approach is: Value is in proportion to the best long term productive use of a property over the longest period of time. Its measure is the present worth of the right to collect the future net benefits from the property. This approach tends to indicate the lower limit of the value. To have value, any property, of course, must have the ability to provide future net benefits. The procedure used to estimate the value under this approach involves the capitalization of the net income of the property. Capitalization as used here is the mathematical process of estimating the present value of the expectable net benefits from a property. It is the method of determining the present worth of the real estate through the use of a capitalization rate. The capitalization rate used is that considered to represent the proper market or desired yield relationship between the value of the real estate and the net income that it provides. The rate represents its percentage of the present value. For instance, a $10,000 annual net income [1] is a 10 per cent annual return on $100,000. The $10,000 represents 10 per cent of the present value of the property, so dividing $10,000 by .10 converts it to 100 per cent of the present value.

Correlation and Its Premise: The premise of the correlation is: The procedures, techniques, and computations of the approaches used to estimate the preliminary values are applicable, accurate, and interrelated,

---

[1] Before provisions for recapture of the investment or payment on the mortgage indebtedness.

and provide a sound basis on which to form a final conclusion of value. Correlation as used in the appraisal process is the procedure used to form the final conclusion of value. Until the premise is fulfilled, we cannot properly form the opinion of value. You must realize, of course, that the appraised value is a matter of opinion, but that it must be the appraiser's opinion.

The following publications will be found to be quite useful as reference works:

Questions and Answers on Real Estate: Fifth edition, Robert W. Semenow, 1966. Prentice-Hall, Inc., Englewood Cliffs, N.J.

Encyclopedic Dictionary of Real Estate Practice: Second edition, 1960, Prentice-Hall Editorial Staff, Prentice-Hall, Inc., Englewood Cliffs, N.J.

Appraisal Terminology and Handbook, American Institute of Real Estate Appraisers, Chicago, Illinois.

Encyclopedia of Real Estate Appraising, revised and enlarged, 1967, Prentice-Hall Editorial Staff, Prentice-Hall, Inc., Englewood Cliffs, N.J.

SUMMARY

1. Real estate is a term used to designate the rights of real estate ownership rather than the land and buildings themselves. Ownership of real estate is considered to consist of a bundle of rights.
2. Fee simple ownership is subject to certain basic powers and rights of the government; namely, the power of eminent domain, the power of taxation, the power of escheat, and police power.
3. The three preliminary estimates used in appraising real estate are: The physical (cost) approach, the market approach, and the economic (income) approach.
4. Basic premise of the three approaches: Supply and demand tends to be the underlying factor of all approaches and the final value estimate.
5. Premise of the physical approach: It is the principle of cost. Replacement cost tends to set the upper limit of value.
6. Premise of the market approach: To the typical buyer the value of a property does not exceed the value of an available acceptable substitute property.
7. Premise of the economic approach: Value is in proportion to the best long-term productive use of a property. Its measure is the present worth of the right to collect the future net benefits from the property.
8. Premise of the correlation: The procedures, techniques and computations of the approaches used to estimate the preliminary values are applicable, accurate, and interrelated, and provide a sound basis on which to form a final conclusion of value.

2

Demand
for
Appraisals

Appraisals are essential to anyone making important decisions involving real estate. While, in most cases, people buying a home do not personally employ an appraiser, the mortgage company does. Even when an appraiser as such is not employed, it is necessary for all parties concerned to make a decision as to the value of the property when a transaction is to be made. The more information the individual can secure, the better judgment he can make. An individual purchasing property involving a large sum for investment normally does have an appraisal made by a professional appraiser. All business enterprises and governmental agencies associated in activities directly concerned with the value of real estate must of necessity have appraisals made and employ appraisers to provide the service.

SERVICES PROVIDED BY APPRAISERS

Appraisals involved with sales, purchases and exchanges

When an individual or organization decides to sell real estate, it is necessary that a decision be made as to the asking price. If the price is too high, naturally, the property will be left on the market for an unnecessary length of time before it is sold. This may mean considerable loss in money as well as time. Many real estate sales agencies will not accept a listing that is excessively over-priced, and that is one of the secrets of a successful real estate business. Frequently the agency does not have the necessary free time to adequately investigate the property to establish a proper listing price unless it is of the type that they sell very often and is located in a neighborhood they are very familiar with. Of course, under normal circumstances it is wise to place the property on the market for a somewhat optimistic price for negotiation purposes. Buyers expect to secure some reductions except, perhaps, in large-scale, moderately-priced developments where the price is established on a take-it-or-leave-it basis. The appraiser can offer a very valuable service in connection with the transactions discussed.

Before listing a property for sale, the seller should, in most instances, have made a decision based on an appraisal as to what price to actually sell at. This is usually termed the holding price. Where real estate is being offered for exchange, many problems may be involved. A normal situation is when each owner is trying to hide his actual holding price so that he can make a better deal. As a result of this, both parties and their agents are dealing with inflated prices, creating a rather unrealistic situation. Most real estate sales agencies find that exchange transactions are very difficult and time consuming, unless there is a situation existing where the parties are in a reciprocal position relating to an advantageous income tax situation. In any exchange situation, particularly one involved with income tax situations, very good appraisal information is required.

Generally, market value is the value estimated when sales or purchases are involved. Good information must be secured as to recent comparable sales that have occurred in the locality. To formulate the market value estimate, detailed comparison of the properties must be made in order to pinpoint the value. The market value estimate can be one of the most time-consuming processes in the appraisal of real estate if the complete procedure is followed in detail. To get the proper information and to compare it properly, good knowledge and experience is necessary.

When a person is thinking of buying a building, he is sometimes faced with the question as to whether it would be best to buy an existing one or construct a new one. This may be quite a difficult decision, particularly when commercial properties are concerned. An appraiser may be quite helpful in this respect.

There are many other decisions involved in the sale and purchase of real estate too numerous to mention here.

Appraisals involved with other transfers of title

There are many decisions involved in the division of the assets of an estate that require an appraisal. This may be necessary due to probate requirements or the terms of the will. All of a decedent's property must be appraised at its fair market value for Federal Estate tax and ordinarily within one year of the death. Division of estates before the death of the current owner require appraisals in many instances. Many decisions are involved with real estate in connection with receivership matters and with the reorganization of companies and corporations which require appraisals.

The merger of companies and/or properties may require numerous inventories and appraisals so that the mergers may be made in an equitable manner.

Partnership arrangements or dissolutions frequently require independent appraisals to establish an equitable basis of the transactions involved.

Divorce settlements require appraisals of much real estate.

Valuations for financing purposes

Building contractors normally require financing during the construction of a building. This is termed "interim financing." Before a bank can advance money to start the construction an appraisal is required.

An appraisal is necessary before a lending institution can make a real estate mortgage loan to the owner. Even individuals loaning money on real estate use appraisals, though they may perform the work themselves.

Appraisals are required of the real estate assets used in connection with bond or stock operations which may be offered by syndicates, trusts, stock companies, underwriting firms, banking houses, and others.

Appraisals are sometimes required to determine the current security in connection with existing loans, particularly when there is the possibility of foreclosure.

Real estate mortgage loan extensions may require some form of appraisal.

Bonding companies need an appraisal of the security offered for performance bonds.

Appraisals are sometimes used by banks and others in connection with the verification of real estate assets claimed in financial statements.

Services to ownership or management

Inventory and condition reports are required of real estate assets by wealthy individuals, corporations, governmental agencies, and so forth. The realty appraiser is especially qualified to make these.

When lease or rental rates and terms of any consequence are to be formulated, the prudent owner will require an appraisal.

Income tax and accounting requirements necessitate various appraisals, such as appraisals for capital gains, gifts, depreciation schedules, and estimates of depreciation.

Land development or disposition studies are required. Questions frequently arise as to what kind and/or size of building(s) should be constructed on a particular tract of land; that is, the improvement(s) that would return the most net income for the land. Those involved with the disposition of or development of real estate require periodic market surveys in order to make decisions properly. Knowledge as to the potential development possibilities is a "must" for those concerns involved in the development of real estate. These appraisals may become very complicated and time consuming and require expert appraisal assistance.

Many other decisions are required in deciding as to the feasibility of certain judgments concerning real estate operations. These are usually related to highest and best use, market surveys and development potentials.

The trust departments of banks need appraisals in connection with the disposition of trust account real estate as well as for real estate loans made from the trust accounts.

Determining the feasibility of proposed remodeling or repair projects frequently necessitate appraisals.

Many decisions are involved in the insurance of property, particularly to determine if enough, but not too much, insurance is carried. Appraisals are required in connection with property losses.

Most major corporations over the nation have established company employee assistance or reimbursement programs in connection with employee relocation from one geographical area to another. The companies generally require separate appraisals from two and sometimes three appraisers.

Appraisals for other decisions

Many appraisals are required by taxing authorities in making assessments for real estate taxation. The owners of property must make a valuation decision involving rendition of real estate for taxation; and, if they feel that the tax assessment is unjust, they must make decisions as to proper valuation of the property and present their case to the taxing authorities for consideration.

Special assessments by cities and other taxing authorities frequently necessitate appraisals. The appraisal of real estate that has a special assessment must receive special consideration as to the assessment and its effect upon the value of the property.

Investigations by governmental agencies, corporations, and others frequently require inventory and/or appraisal of any real estate assets involved in the investigation.

Condemnation of real estate for eminent domain proceedings by governmental or other authorities require many appraisals. The owners of the real estate being taken for public use frequently hire their own appraiser to estimate just compensation for the property taken and damage, if any, to the remainder of the property. Testimony as an expert in connection with the appraisals made are required in connection with those cases that are not settled out of court.

There are other requirements for real estate appraisals, but the above are the principal ones.

APPRAISAL REPORTING METHODS

An appraisal should always be submitted in written form, since the matters discussed are of sufficient importance to require documentary evidence. This is an essential protection to the appraiser and to the client. It is a business-like method which leaves no room for misunderstanding or distortion. There are four principal reporting forms: A letter of opinion, a certificate report, a standardized short form report, and a narrative report.

Letter of opinion

Frequently the appraiser is called upon to give an opinion of value without submitting a formal report. Clients requesting this may be trying to reduce the expenses of a formal appraisal, or they may be trying to save time and need the information quickly. When such reports are necessary and permissible, you may issue a letter of opinion subject to your final appraisal. You must make a preliminary appraisal and place it in your file for substantiation. You will probably need it; therefore, be sure to have it ready.

The letter of opinion is a written letter providing the following basic information:

(1) Identification of the property, type of value and property rights appraised

(2) Assumptions and contingent and limiting conditions of the opinion

(3) The age and condition of the property and estimated remaining economic life of any improvements involved

(4) The date the estimated value is to apply

(5) The stated opinion of value

(6) Any other information supplied is left to the discretion of the appraiser or the requirements of the client.

Certificate type of report

This type of report is generally a printed short form with a certificate above the appraiser's signature. The certificate used is generally similar to the following:

I certify that I have no personal interest, present or prospective [1] *in the above described property, and that my employment in making this valuation is not contingent upon the amount of the valuation.*

The report should provide all the basic data of a regular appraisal. If the form doesn't provide for it, you must add it.

Standard short form appraisal report

This is the type of appraisal reporting form used by many insurance companies, governmental agencies, and others. Ordinarily, it is a form consisting of approximately two or three pages providing for all essential information required in an appraisal. If it doesn't provide for all the essential information you must add it by using additional pages. It is generally printed more or less in the form of a questionnaire with blank spaces for the information. Typically it has a certificate above the space for signature.

It usually takes considerably more time to complete an appraisal on this type of form than might be expected. These forms usually have detailed questions involving most of the basic data and procedures used in the appraisal process. While the form may not take up much space, the information covered can be quite involved and time consuming to secure.

Narrative reporting form

The narrative report generally involves essentially the same data included in a standardized reporting form, but it may contain more details and, of course, it is in a narrative form. If the appraisal involves very

---

[1] If you have an interest in the property, you must divulge it and amend the certificate.

valuable property or complicated problems, the data involved will be considerably more detailed, the analysis will be more thorough, and the illustrations more numerous. This is the method of reporting that is customarily used for the more valuable properties and complicated appraisal problems. However, this method is quite versatile, in that it can be made very brief and tailored to the problem involved.

Appraisal knowledge today provides very practical methods of estimating real estate value and the effects of certain conditions, etc., on the value. These methods and techniques are discussed in the following chapters in detail. The methodical procedures involved in the appraisal process will influence one to approach important problems with care, and with the need to investigate, and to consider and weigh all factors before making an important decision.

SUMMARY

Real estate appraisals are a practical, everyday necessity in almost all transactions concerning real estate and generally involve the following:

(1) Decisions involved in sales, purchases, and exchanges
(2) Decisions involved in other transfers of title
(3) Valuations for financing purposes
(4) Operation and/or management decisions
(5) Other too-numerous-to-mention decisions.

No attempt should ever be made to submit a verbal appraisal report.

There are four basis reporting methods, which are:

(1) Letter of opinion
(2) Certificate report
(3) Standard short form report
(4) Narrative report.

3

The Appraisal
Process

Essentially, the appraising of real estate falls within the field of economics, embracing its principal rules and laws as they affect free private enterprise. A real estate appraisal is the application of these laws and rules in a most practical manner. The principal data and procedures involved in the appraisal process are as listed below. It is the function of the appraiser to provide much of the data and solve the appraisal problems for the client. As one can see, the subject is wide and the problems may be numerous and quite varied.

APPRAISAL DATA

Identification of Property Appraised

Legal description and street address
Neighborhood map, plats, photographs, and so forth
Type of property.

Purpose of the Appraisal

> Rights to be appraised
> Use of the appraisal
> Type of value to be estimated
> Date appraisal obtains, if different from date prepared.

Assumptions, Contingencies, and Limiting Conditions

Physical, Social, and Economic Data as to Location

> Description of the city and/or area
> Description of the neighborhood
>> land use, zoning and restrictions, and so on.

Description and Data as to the Site

> Area and dimensions
> Zoning and restrictions
> Physical description (including street frontage, topography, water drainage, soil and subsoil as appropriate)
> Present use and highest and best use of the land.

Description and Data as to the Buildings and Land Improvements

> Structural outline
> Electrical outline
> Mechanical outline
> Drawings as appropriate (include essential dimensions)
> Quality of materials and construction
> Design and functional analysis
> Construction costs, if available
> Age and condition
> Present use and highest and best use.

Income and Expense Data (including charts if available)

Maps, Photographs, Construction Plans, and so on.

PRELIMINARY ESTIMATES OF VALUE

Physical Approach

> Land valuation
> Estimate of reproduction or replacement cost new of the improvements [1]

---

[1] "Improvements" as used in this context includes all buildings and land improvements on the site. The word is quite generally used in this manner by appraisers.

       Amount of accrued depreciation: physical, functional, economic
       Summation of the cost, less depreciation.

Economic Approach

       Current and recent income and expense data
       Present tenant, lease, or rental rate and terms
       Comparable rental rates
       Estimated future gross income
       Estimated vacancy and collection loss
       Estimated future expense
       Reserve for replacements
       Net income
       Assumed remaining economic life of the building
       Capitalization rate
       Estimated productive (capitalized) value.

Market Approach

       Comparable offerings and sales
       Comparison with comparable offerings and sales
       Supply of and demand of comparable properties
       Availability of competing sites for new construction
       Trends
       Estimated market value.

Correlation of the Estimated Values

       Check for correlation and accuracy
       Comparison of values and adjustments
       Bracketing of values
       Plausibility.

FINAL OPINION OF VALUE

DISCUSSION

The following is only intended as a very brief discussion of the appraisal procedures involved, as each item will be discussed more fully in later chapters.

Identification of the property

The appraiser must know the exact location of the property that he is to appraise—not only the street address but also the legal description of the property which describes its location in relation to recorded maps on file in the county map record or similar official record. The dimensions of the tract of land should be verified from the official record or survey plat. If there is any question as to location, area involved, or boundaries, it is highly desirable for the appraiser to secure a survey plat or an official map, for he is not ordinarily prepared nor expected to do the work of a surveyor. Perhaps the owner will have an official survey of the tract, which will save considerable time. Good photographs of the property from different positions will be very helpful in describing it, and can save hundreds of words of description.

Purpose of the appraisal

It is essential that the appraiser know the intended purpose of the appraisal in order that the report may be prepared and written in a form consistent with its intended purpose or use.

The appraiser must know the rights that are to be appraised. He must know if the rights of the fee simple estate or only limited rights are to be appraised. Ordinarily, those to be appraised will be those of fee simple. The appraiser may be called upon, from time to time, to appraise the rights of the ownership of leased property (leased fee), or the rights of the tenant leasing the property (leasehold). You must know the rights that you are to appraise.

The type of value or price required and date of the appraisal

The valuation sought may be the market value, the depreciated replacement cost, the productive value, the estimated sales price, the value of the leased fee, the value of the leasehold, and so on. Usually, the type of value sought depends on the use of the appraisal. The appraiser may be of assistance to the client in determining which type of value should be estimated. It must be known if the appraisal is to be of the current value or the value of some past date. As a general rule, it is for the current date.

Assumptions, contingencies, and limiting conditions

Such conditions are usually involved and they must be listed in detail in the appraisal since they are an integral part of the valuation.

Physical, social, and economic data as to location

If the client is not familiar with the city or area in which the property is being appraised, it will be necessary to provide a brief description of the major factors of the city or area. Ordinarily, it is not wise to go into a lengthy discussion—a brief description based on Chamber of Commerce information is adequate. The description of the neighborhood is basic to all appraisals and should include the important physical, social, and economic data involved. It should be appropriately described as to basic population characteristics, special hazards, nuisances, natural physical features and landscaping, kind and condition of neighborhood buildings, sufficiency of public utilities, street surfacing, transportation, and economic conditions as appropriate. When a residential appraisal is involved, special consideration must be given to schools, churches, shopping and employment centers. Data as to tax rates may be discussed as well as any information as to special assessments.

The typical income range of the neighborhood is a very basic element not only for residential appraisals, but also for retail properties. Of course, the price range of residences in the neighborhood is usually quite closely related to the income range of the occupants. Consideration must also be given to the stage of development of the neighborhood, the likelihood of new construction, and the amount of owner occupancy and of vacant properties. Consideration must be given to any important trends discovered. Particular attention should be given to amenities for residential properties and to income data for commercial properties. Land use zoning and restrictive covenants as to land use should be considered and listed.

It is quite important to know this information; obviously, the value of the property will be highly influenced by it.

Description of the site

The property owner or the appraisal client may have a survey plat which will provide full information as to the dimensions and area of the site. It is a good idea to always inquire as to the availability of a survey plat as it may be the most available source of information as to the exact position and dimensions of the land and buildings. If unavailable, some data may be secured from the public records of the city or county. The survey plat should be checked to see that it has the same legal description as the property being appraised. If the owner has a copy of his deed to the property, it may be helpful in this respect. Buildings may have been added after the survey. The appraiser must inspect the site and describe the topographical features, drainage conditions, and so on. He must observe and report all pertinent physical features of the property and the streets and utilities which serve the property.

Highest and best use

The "highest and best use" of the site is one of the most important factors in an appraisal. This estimate is of tremendous importance, not only to the value of the property but also to the amount of time involved to appraise it properly. Unless the appraiser starts with the correct assumption as to the highest and best use, the complete appraisal report will be out of focus and incorrect. As a general rule, the highest and best use for the land will be obvious; when it is not, it will be necessary to investigate the situation more thoroughly. The appraiser may assume certain best uses, estimate the annual net income available for each such use, and then capitalize the net income from the property, using the land residual technique to find which use gives the highest return to the land. The computations may become quite time-consuming, especially when the land is of high value. These are the methods used for land development or disposition studies.

Description of the improvements

The physical inspection of the improvements is one of the most basic tasks of the appraisal. If the building is to be constructed, you must secure the information from the plans and specifications. If possible, the appraiser should secure a copy of the plans, specifications, and a survey of existing building improvements, as they will be of considerable benefit. The exterior dimensions must be measured, as changes may have been made since original construction. As the measurements of the outside are being taken, *the foundation should be checked very thoroughly* for cracks or evidence of settlement or shifting. A good diagram of the interior of the property should be drawn, portraying all rooms and areas. This should be done on graph paper. The different materials, components, and equipment used in the construction, as well as the spacing of the framing material, and so on, should be listed on an appropriate form.

Information should be secured from the owner or others as to the actual age of the property. If the age is unknown, it will be necessary to estimate it. Care must be taken to draw a neat floor plan and to write a legible list of the building materials used. In the case of large properties, it may be necessary to make several trips to the property in order to make a thorough inspection. Even in the inspection of a small property a second inspection may reveal items that were not observed on the first. Adequacy of the electrical outlets and fixtures should be noted. All mechanical equipment should be listed on the inspection form. The drawings will ordinarily indicate items of functional obsolescence that were not observed during the inspection of the property. Economic obsolescence, which is the result of influences outside of the property itself, should be observed during the inspection of the neighborhood.

PRELIMINARY ESTIMATES OF VALUE

Physical approach

Land Value: It is difficult to discuss land value without mentioning the highest and best use. The estimation of the highest and best use of the land is one of the most important items in the appraisal of commercial land, and particularly of potentially commercial land. If, in estimating the best use, it is necessary to use the land residual process, a good start has been made toward the estimation of the land value. If available, sales and asking prices of comparable land should be secured and compared to the subject land to estimate the comparative market value. Asking prices as well as sales prices must be analyzed as to their indication of value. In the older residential neighborhoods, where land sales are non-existent, the best alternative is to estimate the land value by selecting several typical properties that have sold recently, and then deducting the depreciated value of the improvements to find the indicated value of the typical site. In some areas, the land value may vary from about 15 per cent to 20 per cent of the total sales price for modest homes, depending on the locality involved. In a neighborhood where there are sufficient vacant sites that have sold recently, the market value should be based on the typical sales prices. If the land has a higher use than that for the present improvements, there is a rather complex problem involved which is discussed in a following chapter.

Replacement or Reproduction Cost of the Improvements: An accurate estimate must be made of the replacement or reproduction cost of the improvements. If the appraiser is not qualified by experience or training to estimate the cost, it will be necessary for him to employ a cost estimator or an engineer to do so. The cost estimate may be made by the quantity survey method (an estimate of the cost of each item of material, labor, and so on), by the unit in-place method (the cost of a square-foot area of each component plus lump sum estimates for other items), or it may be based upon the square-foot or cubic-foot area of the gross floor area of the structure, plus lump sum estimates for other items not considered in the basic price; or a combination of these methods may be used. In any event, the estimate must include all of the costs involved in placing the structure and other improvements in place on the ground and to market the property. This, of course, includes overhead, profit, and any other actual costs required.

Accrued Depreciation: Any depreciation involved in the improvements must be estimated. Depreciation is divided into three categories: That for physical deterioration, that for functional obsolescence, and that for economic obsolescence. Of course, physical deterioration is self-explanatory. The dollar amount of accrued physical deterioration may be estimated by computing the cost to cure the observable items that are worn, plus 1 per cent per year of age of the cost of the unobservable items of construction. The dollar amount of functional obsolescence is estimated either on the basis of cost to cure or by capitalizing the loss in net income if incurable. You may also estimate the loss of value by market comparison. Functional obsolescence involves a reduction in the optimum utility or appearance and is the result of a deficiency in the property itself. It may be stated as the loss in value due to inherent features of the improvements themselves, such as appearance, antiquated design, over- and under-improvement,[2] excessively small or large rooms or high or low ceilings, super-adequacy of equipment, or unusual design offering market reaction, and so on. Economic obsolescence is not concerned with the physical features or utility of the property but with the influences from outside the property itself. Such effects generally affect all similar properties in the neighborhood. Frequently this is due to a change in neighborhood occupancy, changing business conditions, or a decline in employment opportunities. Sometimes, it is due to a neighborhood nuisance such as an odor or sound. Normally, economic obsolescence is not curable. It may be estimated by market comparison or by the capitalized value of the net income loss.

Summation of Replacement or Reproduction Cost: The summation of the cost is the sum of the estimated cost of the improvements (less depreciation) and the value of the land.

The economic approach

In this approach, the income is the yardstick of value. The potential future net rental income of the real estate (not the business) is the value

---

[2] If a building is too large or small for the location, the maximum land value is not attained. This loss in land value developed is the difference between that for the highest and best use and the improper use. This method is described later.

normally measured. Capitalization is the procedure used to estimate the productive value by this approach, and it involves the conversion of the future anticipated net income into present productive value. If the property has a long-term lease by a financially responsible individual or organization, the future net income stream based on the lease should be discounted into present worth by use of annuity tables. If the property is not leased, it is necessary to estimate what the future income will be. This should be based on the income rates of comparable properties. If, however, the property is rented for all it is worth, it should be valued on that basis. Basic to the problem of estimating the future income from the property is the determination of the highest and best use, which has been discussed in the preceding pages. This is basic to all of the procedures used in the appraisal of real estate. If there is any question as to the highest and best use, it must be resolved.

It is customary to use the gross monthly rent multiple method to estimate the value of one and two family dwellings by the economic approach. The gross monthly rent multiple is found by dividing the gross sales price by the gross monthly rental rate, thus finding the individual gross monthly multiple. The multiple to be used to estimate the value of such properties is the typical rent multiple in the neighborhood. Occasionally, the rent multiple process is used for a quick estimate for other income properties. The gross annual multiple is normally used for other income properties, and it is computed by dividing the gross sales price by the gross annual income.

Market approach

This is frequently the most important approach to be used, since it is the most direct method to estimate market value.

The law of substitution is basic to this approach. No property is worth more than it costs to substitute an acceptable property. This is based on the desires and needs of the typical purchaser or investor and not as to one particular purchaser or one particular owner. The principle of substitution applies to both the physical approach and to the market approach. The law of supply and demand affects all approaches to the value, but it particularly affects the market approach. The law of diminishing returns is involved when the land is improperly improved; that is, when the structure is too large, too expensive, overequipped or vice versa, or just an improper improvement. It is generally understood that a house which is much larger than those in the neighborhood will usually sell for less than the cost of reproduction. This also applies to super-adequacies of equipment.

The market approach is concerned with the comparison of the appraised property with acceptable substitute properties, and with the reaction of the typical purchasers interested in the neighborhood. In the comparison process it is necessary to consider sales that have occurred as recently as possible. Generally, three or four sales are considered sufficient for the average residence and four or five for commercial properties, but you may use more when appropriate and available. Ideally, only sales will be considered which have occurred within the last 12 months. Of course, if none have occurred in the immediate neighborhood during that time, it is necessary to go into the general neighborhood or competing neighborhoods to find those that have sold within the required time. Sometimes the market may be such that older sales are used, but it is not as desirable. The type of property involved makes a great difference. Some types of commercial and industrial properties sell so seldom it is necessary to consider sales as much as five years old. The relative desirability of the property should be compared on a standard blank form for the purpose, in terms of per cent or dollars, using plus or minus adjustments. Commercial structures are generally compared on the basis of factors contributing to the income from the property, while residential properties are usually compared on the basis of the amenities offered. After inquiring into the sales that have been made in the neighborhood over the appropriate period of time and checking as to asking prices of properties for sale and as to probable new construction, the appraiser is in a position to consider the supply and demand of property in the neighborhood.

The appraiser should have a good file of sales and other related data on properties in the neighborhood of his operation. The Multiple Listing Service of the local Board of Realtors is a good source for residential and some income type properties. If the M.L.S. has a commercial service, it should be quite helpful. Newspaper clippings provide a good source for data concerning income properties in general. Usually for other than residential properties it is necessary to employ the services of an abstracter to search the public records, such as county deed records, for recorded sales data. If acreage sales (or metes and bounds descriptions) are involved, it is advisable to have the abstracter indicate the location of the properties on a map. The comparable market data should be listed on a standard blank form for this purpose and after use it should be filed carefully for future use. The better the appraiser's file as to sales data, the better he is prepared to complete the market estimate.

It is very important to know the trend in the neighborhood and general area. The appraiser should know, of course, whether prices are increasing or decreasing and other information that may indicate a trend affecting the value of the properties in the neighborhood. For instance, is the available supply of similar properties increasing or decreasing? Based on the supply and demand situation, what appears to be the outlook for similar properties?

After completing the procedure suggested above, the appraiser should be in a position to complete the estimate of the market value. The choice should be the typical indicated, considering the supply and demand position and the trends indicated.

Correlation

After the values have been estimated by the approaches used, it is necessary to reconcile the differences, if any, insofar as practical. First, it is necessary to review the approaches used as a check for possible errors. A review may indicate errors or misconceptions. Make the necessary corrections or adjustments to the approach. It is necessary to review the approach quite thoroughly after making adjustments, since a new error may be made unless all related items are adjusted. In reconciling the approaches, use a standard of comparison, such as the indicated value per square foot, and so forth. By using three approaches, the appraiser is, more or less, sighting at the target for the proper value. Generally, the closer the estimates are to each other, the more accurate the appraiser has been in the approaches. If there is too wide a spread between the high and low values indicated, they should be reviewed closely. Normally, the physical approach sets the upper limit of value and the economic approach the lower limit of value. Frequently, a closer review will substantiate one or the other by bringing two of the three together.

Final opinion of value

The final opinion of value should be the final conclusion reached as the result of the correlation. It is not mandatory that the final estimate be exactly the same as one of the approaches used, but it should be within the indicated bracket.

APPRAISAL

STAPLE PICTURE HERE

PURPOSE: Mortgage __X__ Insurance _____ Collection _____

Request by: Mr(s) _(Illustrative Case)_
　　　　　　　seller—attorney—buyer—broker

Phone _____ Date _____

To inspect Mr(s) _____
Contact ____ Phone/Key at _____

Owner's Value: $ _15,000._ Name ____—____

For general use:

Ins. Value, 100% $ ....
Ins. Value "As Dep." $ ....—....
No. of dwelling units _One_
Masonry..... or Frame. _X_.

Loan Number .... _1_
Loan Date ....—....

$ _14,500._
Final Estimate of Value

ADDRESS: _(Illustrative Case)_
CITY/COUNTY: ____—____
SUBDIVISION: ____—____　　BLK ─ LOT ─

INDICATE NORTH

(Omitted for this purpose)

SKETCH EXTERIOR PLAN—SHOW DIMENSIONS

SQ. FT. AREAS
HSE: _1232_

NEIGHBORHOOD DATA

PROXIMITY OF PROPERTY TO:	Less ¼ mi.	¼ to 1 mi.	1 mi. +	Trans. to
Downtown Area	X		8.5	
Local Shopping	X			
Grammar School	X			
High School		X		
Expressway Access	X			
Other:	X			

TYPE OF DEVELOPMENT: ONE BUILDER _____ FEW BUILDERS _____ MANY BUILDERS _X_

TRENDS:	INC.	DEC.	STAB.
Income Level	X		
Population	X		
Housing Units	X		
Density Pop./Unit			X
Avg. Prop. Values	X		
Ethnic Compos.	changing		
% of Development	80 %		

GENERAL ECONOMICS:

TYPICAL RESIDENT'S GROSS INC. $ _6,000._ $/yr.

TYPICAL OCCUPATION. _Office & Jr. Exec._

TYPICAL PROPERTY VALUES: $ _14,000._　Avg.

$/Age: $ _17,000. /5-7 yrs._　High
$/Age: $ _13,000. /5-7 yrs._　Low

TYPICAL FINANCING CONV. ____　INS. _FHA_

TYPICAL LOAN/VALUE RATIO _90-95_ %

SITE DATA

LOT SIZE	68' x 120'			Corner	Inside X
ZONING *	1 family res	Present X	or		
IMPROVMTS.	HIGHEST AND BEST USE OF SITE				

IMPROVMTS.	Asphalt St. X	Conc. St. X	Curbs X	Sidewalks X	Driveway Conc.
UTILITIES	Gas X	Elect. X	Water X	San. Sewer X	Alley
				Storm Sewer X	Well
			Party Wall	Driveway	Septic
				Sidewalk	Other

EASEMENTS (DETRIMENTAL TO VALUE):

Describe Easements: 5' utility easement at rear of lot.

BUILDING DATA

EXTERIOR

		Good	Avg.	Poor
FOUNDATION	Conc. X	Block	Brick	X
	Bsmt.	Crawl	Slab	
WALL CONST.	Frame X	Veneer	Block	X
WINDOWS	Metal X	Wood	Type S & S	X
ROOFING	Asphalt X	Wood	Type	X
SIDING	Wood X	Alum.	Stucco	X
GAR.-CAR PT.	Det'd.	Att'd. X	Blt.-in O'H Door	X
# Cars	Frame X	Veneer	Block	X
OTHER	Gutters	Porch X	Patio	X

REMARKS: Aluminum windows. Has 2-1 ton window air conditioning units. Flowers over tub.

INTERIOR

TYPE Modern   AGE 5 yrs

				Good	Avg.	Poor
WALLS & CEIL.	Drywall X	Plaster	Wood	X		
FLOOR	Conc. X	Tile	Wood	Carpet X		
CENT. HTG.	Air X	Water	Steam	SPACE		X
FUEL	Gas X	Oil	Elect.	Coal		X
FUR./BOIL.	Age 5 yrs	HWH	40 Gals.	A/C X		X
ELECT.	100 Amps	Fuse	Cir. Br. X	O/S X		X
BATH(s) #1½	Age 5 yrs	FLR/Walls Ceramic X		Other SR		X
BATH FIX(s).	Lavs. 2	W.Cs 2	Tub(s) 1	Shwr(s). 1		X
KITCHEN	Age 5 yrs	Cb. & St.	Adq. Adq	Inadq.		X
OTHER	O/R Oven	Dishw.	Disp. X	Ex. Fan X	Flr. Plan △	X
		Firepl. Attic fan				X

Rooms

FLOOR	ROOMS	LIVING	DINING	KITCHEN	#BEDRM	CLOSETS	BATHS #/FIX	#APTS.
BASEMENT								
1st FLOOR	1	Space 1	3	8	1½ 6			Den 1
2nd FLOOR								
3rd FLOOR								
ATTIC								
TOTAL	1	Space 1	3	8	1½ 6	No. Units 1		

DEPRECIATION

PHYSICAL DETERIORATION   IF NOT TYPICAL, DESCRIBE   Typical

FUNCTIONAL OBSOLESCENCE   "

ECONOMIC OBSOLESCENCE   "

Exhibit 3–1.   Demonstration Appraisal Report.*

* Not zoned, but restricted.

DEFINITION OF MARKET VALUE:* "Market value contemplates the consummation of a sale and the passing of full title from seller to buyer by deed, under conditions whereby:

1. buyer and seller are free of undue stimulus and are motivated by no more than the reactions of typical owners;
2. both parties are well-informed or well-advised and act prudently, each for what he considers his own best interest;
3. a reasonable time is allowed to test the market; and
4. payment is made in cash or in accordance with financing terms available in the community for the property type in its locale."

*Society of Residential Appraisers

COST APPROACH TO VALUE:

LAND VALUATION—(ZONED: _Residential_ _per. no._): _66_   F.F. or x $45.50(-) $/F.F. or = $3,000.

+ SITE IMPROVEMENTS: "AS IS" driveway, landscaping, etc. .... + 505.

other: _Patio (10' x 12')_

TOTAL .... $ 3,505.

BUILDING VALUATION—REPLACEMENT COST

BLDG.	AREA	UNIT COST	COST NEW	ACT. AGE	EFF.	PHY.	FUNC.	ECON.	TOTAL	DEP. VALUE
MAIN	1232 S.F.	$8.40	$10,349.	5 yrs.		$700.				$9,649.
Garage	469 S.F.	3.10	1,454.	"		75.				1,379.
Porch	56 S.F.	2.50	140.	"		10.				130.

+ 11,158.

INDICATED VALUE from COST APPROACH ⟹ _Rounded to_ $ 14,663.
$ 14,650.

MARKET DATA APPROACH TO VALUE:

ADDRESS OF COMPARABLE SALES	A 100 _Jones St._		B 101 _Montil St._		C 150 _Doe St._	
SALE PRICE OF COMPARABLE	1	$15,900.	6	$13,250.	8	$17,700.
DATE OF SALE ADJUSTMENT	(-)	$ (+)	(-)	$ (+)	(-)	$ (+)
AGE & OVERALL CONDITION		_Newer_ 300.	_Older_	500.	_Older_	600.
SIZE & UTILITY	_Larger house_ 300.		_Smaller house_	250.	_Smaller house_	200.
MODERN KITCHEN, BATH, HEATING	_Older 2 baths_ 250.		_Larger 2 bad_			
GARAGE & PORCHES						
SITE & LOCATION	_Larger lot_ 100.		_Smaller lot_	200.		750.
OTHER	_Better appearance_ 500.				_Better appearance_	800.
SUB-TOTALS	(-) $1,150.	(+) $	(-) $	(+) $ 950.	(-) $ 750.	(+) $
TOTALS		$14,450.		$14,200.		$14,750.

INDICATED VALUE - from MARKET APPROACH $ _14,500._

INCOME APPROACH TO VALUE: (if applicable)

ESTIMATED MONTHLY RENTAL: $ _125._   × GROSS MONTHLY MULTIPLIER (_115_) =

INDICATED VALUE from INCOME APPROACH $ _14,375._

MARKETABILITY "AS IS": Good _____ Average _X_ Fair _____ Poor _____

REMARKS: _The market is somewhat slow now._

CORRELATED ESTIMATE OF VALUE,   AS OF _8 - 1_, 196_4_: $ _14,500._

I (We) certify that to the best of my (our) knowledge and belief the facts and data used herein are true and correct, and that I (we) personally inspected the property from the inside and the outside, and that I (we) have no undisclosed interest, present or prospective therein.

_____   _____
field appraiser   reviewing appraiser

MARKETABILITY "AS REPAIRED": Good _____ Average _____ Fair _____ Poor _____

NEEDED REPAIRS:	CURABLE ITEMS	EST. COST
None		

COR. ESTIMATE OF VALUE............ $ _____

EST. CONTRIBUTION TO
VALUE   FROM REPAIRS............. + _____

CORRELATED VALUE ESTIMATE, AS REPAIRED: $ _____

17-PRA PROFESSIONAL RESIDENTIAL APPRAISAL—   ACCOUNTING DIVISION

Exhibit 3-1 (continued).

Reprinted with permission of the Accounting Division, *17-PRA Professional Residential Appraisal* (blank form), 221 North La Salle St., Chicago, Illinois 60601. You may order the blank forms direct from the firm listed.

Demonstration appraisal report

Refer to Exhibit 3-1 for a demonstration of a residential appraisal report made on a standardized form, reprinted with the permission of the Accounting Division, American Savings and Accounting Supply, Inc., 221 North La Salle Street, Chicago, Illinois 60601. You may order a supply from them.

SUMMARY

1. Appraisal of real estate is essentially a field of economics.
2. Real estate appraisals are necessary to solve a wide range of problems.
3. Broadly speaking, the appraisal process involves the following:
   a. Appraisal Data
      Identification of the property appraised
      Purpose of the appraisal
      Assumptions, contingencies, and limiting conditions
      Physical, social and economic data as to location
      The site
      The buildings and other land improvements.
   b. Preliminary Estimates of Value
      Physical approach
      Economic approach
      Market approach.
   c. Correlation of the Preliminary Estimates.
   d. Final Opinion of Value.

4

Inspection
and Description of
Building Improvements

INSPECTION OF BUILDINGS

Exhibit 4-1 is an illustration of the items and basic nomenclature involved in residential buildings. This is basic to most buldings. If you are not familiar with the structural details of buildings, it is recommended that you secure a copy of *Minimum Property Standards,* published by the Federal Housing Administration, as residential construction is a basic type of construction. It provides some good information and illustrations and can be obtained from your nearest Federal Housing Administration office.

Foundation

The foundation should be inspected very carefully, since it is so important to the structure it supports. If a concrete slab. foundation fails to carry its load properly, it may not be possible to repair it sufficiently to continue to use the building. If vertical cracks have appeared in a concrete slab foundation, this probably indicates it has settled. However, if they are only hair-width this may be due to volume changes and may possibly have no particular significance if the foundation is steel reinforced. Foundations other than the concrete slab type can generally be

33

COMPONENT PARTS OF A BUILDING *

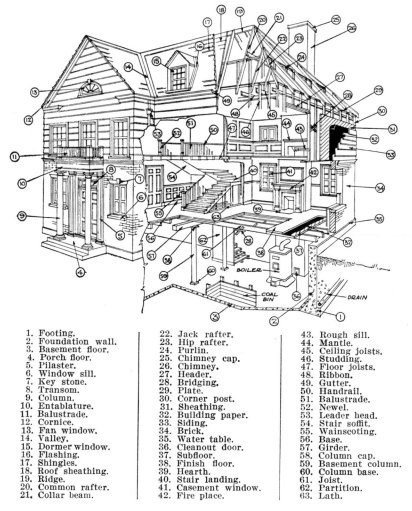

1. Footing.	22. Jack rafter.	43. Rough sill.
2. Foundation wall.	23. Hip rafter.	44. Mantle.
3. Basement floor.	24. Purlin.	45. Ceiling joists.
4. Porch floor.	25. Chimney cap.	46. Studding.
5. Pilaster.	26. Chimney.	47. Floor joists.
6. Window sill.	27. Header.	48. Ribbon.
7. Key stone.	28. Bridging.	49. Gutter.
8. Transom.	29. Plate.	50. Handrail.
9. Column.	30. Corner post.	51. Balustrade.
10. Entablature.	31. Sheathing.	52. Newel.
11. Balustrade.	32. Building paper.	53. Leader head.
12. Cornice.	33. Siding.	54. Stair soffit.
13. Fan window.	34. Brick.	55. Wainscoting.
14. Valley.	35. Water table.	56. Base.
15. Dormer window.	36. Cleanout door.	57. Girder.
16. Flashing.	37. Subfloor.	58. Column cap.
17. Shingles.	38. Finish floor.	59. Basement column.
18. Roof sheathing.	39. Hearth.	60. Column base.
19. Ridge.	40. Stair landing.	61. Joist.
20. Common rafter.	41. Casement window.	62. Partition.
21. Collar beam.	42. Fire place.	63. Lath.

Exhibit 4-1.

repaired more successfully. If concrete is porous, or is mixed unevenly, and edges have broken off, it may be due to insufficient cement being used and, as a result, it may be a poor foundation. Where possible, check to see if the foundation wall is sufficient in width and depth. The beam and/or pier type foundation can be more thoroughly inspected than other types. There should be crawl space under the floor of structures having piers or wall type foundations.

* U. S. Department of Commerce, *How to Judge a House,* Washington, D.C.: Government Printing Office, page 17.

If there is any indication of possible severe damage to the foundation, it should be inspected by a foundation engineer. Where proposed construction is involved, the foundation should be designed by an engineer.

Exterior walls

The walls, of course, should be in proper vertical and horizontal alignment. This may be checked by sighting down the walls from the corners. If the walls are made of brick, notice the joints and, if there is a question, test the mortar with a knife or other instrument for hardness. See if the mortar crumbles easily; if it does, this is a sign of poor quality, indicating an improper mixture. Does the brick fit snugly around windows and doors? Are there any cracks in the brick wall indicating possible settlement? If so, frequently there will be cracks at nearby windows indicating a separation from the window frame. If the walls are cracked the foundation is probably weak and damaged. The joints between wood or metal and masonry should be properly caulked. The sills of all windows should be set to drain out. Check to see that all exterior areas have proper drainage for water. You can check through a window or door to find the thickness of the wall. All exposed brick of a brick masonry (all brick construction) wall should have two header bricks (bricks joining two parts of a wall together) to about every square foot of brick area. Twelve inch or wider brick walls generally have concealed "headers," that is, concealed from the exterior, and you can hardly check this on such walls.

Perhaps the wall is a brick veneer or stone veneer wall; that is, one having approximately a 4 inch veneer of brick or more of stone on the exterior and having wood studs for framing to carry the load of the building. The brick or stone veneer is decorative and is not supposed to carry weight in this use, but offers good weather protection as well as decoration.

In the case of a frame type of building, the vertical supporting members should be spaced according to the load imposed. Normal spacing of wood studs for one-story structures is generally 16 inches to 24 inches, depending upon the quality of construction and the species of lumber used. The wood studs should have, approximately, a 1 inch wood or other approved sheathing material applied for extra strength and weather protection when veneer construction is employed. Unless the sheathing is weatherproof, 15# felt asphalt-treated paper should be applied over it, and in all instances there should be approximately 1 inch of air space between the sheathing and the brick or stone veneer. After the construction has been finished, in the case of brick or stone veneer, you can check the spacing of the studs from the inside walls by use of a magnet indicator or by soundings. The brick or stone veneer should be well tied to the framework by metal ties but, of course, you can hardly check this after construction. Occasionally, when the ties are not used, the veneer wall will crack in places where stresses occur. In checking brick walls be on the lookout for a white efflorescence. As a general rule, this is due to moisture in the interior of the brick, which is dissolving soluble salts and carrying them to the surface, where they are deposited by evaporation. If the building is new, this may be due to careless handling of the bricks, and if this is the case, the white deposits may be washed off and not reappear. On older structures, or when it occurs again on new structures, this may indicate a leakage of water into the wall from some source, or it may indicate bricks that were not baked enough. Soft brick should be waterproofed, particularly in humid climates.

Where wood siding is used, examine the walls for the condition of the paint and evidence of any rotted wood. Naturally, the siding should be even and uniformly overlapped. Joints should butt tightly and be waterproof. You can scrape some paint off and determine the kind of wood used but, as a general rule, you can tell if cypress or white pine or other high-quality material has been used by the smooth, uniform appearance of the boards. Use of a poor grade or unseasoned wood will show up in about one year by warping and expansion, loss of paint, and so on. Noncorroding nails should be used to fasten the wood to the studding, otherwise, unless they are specially treated, they may rust through the paint.

If wood shingles or shakes are used for wall siding, non-corroding nails should be used also. Since the walls do not receive the weather that the roof does, they do not necessarily require as good a grade of shingles. The shingles should be at least three-eighths of an inch thick at the bottom. They should be double course or applied over an approved sheathing.

If the exterior walls are stucco, check for cracks and see if water has seeped through the stucco. If so, it must be corrected. Window sills should be constructed to drain water away from the wall.

If wood or shingle siding is used, check to see that there is metal flashing over all exposed windows and doors. This is important to keep water from seeping into the wall and causing damage in a number of ways.

Anywhere that wood is involved near the ground, check for termites. Look around to see if there are any sheath-like, tube-like tunnels which termites build to crawl within. If they exist, it is best to require inspection by a termite inspector. Termites live in the ground. They are blind and shun sunlight. Lumber properly impregnated for this will generally be undamaged. Metal shields are generally a must on foundation walls or piers (but not the integral concrete beam and slab type) when wood is involved in the structure.

Basement

If the structure has a basement, this gives you a splendid opportunity to inspect the foundation and the floor framing. Continue the inspection of the foundation there. Examine the basement for water leakage. Examine the floor joists or beams and girders and sills to determine if they are sagging or warping, which may indicate they are insufficient for the load. If wood is used, notice the grade used. If not obvious by looking at the wood, the appraiser should check for grade marks. Check to see if there is a wood sub-floor. Check the exposed walls and foundation for evidence of settlement and water seepage.

Interior walls and floors, equipment, and so on

If there are cracks in the interior walls, beware and look for settlement of the house. If there are no cracks in the foundation, yet the building seems awry, try opening and closing the doors and windows. If any doors cannot be opened and closed, check further to see if the building is settling. If new, the doors may have expanded as a result of unseasoned lumber. Go through and inspect all details of the house. Especially if it is a condemnation appraisal, write down the condition of all major items of the improvements. This will serve you in good stead, not only in estimating the depreciation, but also as evidence of your thorough appraisal. It will save you some embarrassing moments while being cross-examined. Be sure to list all the built-in or attached equipment as to brand and condition. Try to find out when major repairs or replacements were last made. Be sure to list all "extra items," paying particular attention to special cabinets and unusual items.

Evidence of unseasoned lumber used in the construction of a building may be indicated by wall cracks, gaps between the baseboard and the floor, uneven floors, creaking stairs, sticking doors and windows. Joints in the wood mould around the doors and windows will increase to a noticeable width if unseasoned lumber was used. Excessive vertical cracks in the plaster or sheetrock over doors and windows are indications of sagging framework of the window and door heads, or settlement of the foundation.

The finished floors should be level and smooth; the joints should be tight when wood is used. If the floor joints are adequate and if a sub-floor has been included, they should not squeak or spring under your weight. Of course, this would only be an adequacy test for dwelling purposes.

Wainscot

Check for cracks and other indications of settlement. Many times open joints may exist in tile. If not due to poor tile setting, it may be an indication of settlement.

Roof structure

The engineering and design of the roof structure is beyond the scope of this text. Refer to the F.H.A.'s *Minimum Property Standards* for residential properties and to a good construction manual for other type structures.

If the roof appears to sag or is otherwise obviously weakening it will be necessary to check the structure for adequacy. If you are not qualified to determine this you should have it inspected by someone who is. You are not expected to be an engineer, so call for assistance when necessary.

Roofing

In case any information herein conflicts with special instructions of the manufacturer, the latter should normally apply. As a matter of information, it is usually not necessary for the appraiser to climb onto the roof of a house. An inspection of the ceilings of most structures will generally indicate whether a roof is leaking, unless they have been refinished since the last rain.

Wood shingles: The best type of wood shingle is one of edge grain, western red cedar, cypress, or redwood. A large exposure to weather in the lapping of the shingles naturally results in a thinner and less enduring roof. The first course of shingles at the eaves should be at least two plies. The shingles should be at least one-eighth inch apart for expansion when wet. Rust-proof nails should be used. No more than two nails to a shingle should be used. No nails should be visible, as the shingles should cover them. The nailheads should not be driven into the shingles, as this destroys the fiber and results in decay. The age and condition of the shingles will be indicated by their appearance.

Asbestos shingle roofs: Observe for quality of workmanship, damaged shingles, adequate flashing and evidence of weathering. Non-corrosive nails should be used for the application of the shingles.

Composition shingles and roll roofing: These are of asphalt and felt. Non-corrosive nails should be used. Observe the quality of workmanship and look for evidence of any shingles coming loose due to wind, and so on. This type of roof must have a solid sheathing base and at least 15# felt between the sheathing and roofing. If the sheathing is not solid, you can well imagine the effects of the sun and any weight which might be placed on the shingles.

Slate roofs: Observe to see if loose, broken, or cracked too near the joint in the slate below. The break should not be closer than 3 inches to the joint. If there are any raised surfaces of the shingle, this may be an indication that nails are working through below. Light, gray lines across the slate are possible indications of inferior slate, so check to see if they are soft and crumbling. A slate roof requires a solid sheathing base laid tightly and covered with heavy felt paper.

Tile roofs: This roof must also be laid on a solid sheathed roof base with felt paper between. This type of roof is quite heavy and requires strong roof framing. Check the roof for broken tile or loose or irregular courses.

Built-up roofs: These are limited to low-pitch roofs, when shingle type roof covering cannot be used, and require three or more plies of hot-mopped (with asphalt) and lapped felt paper and a base of solid sheathing. The finish surfacing may be with pea gravel, slag, crushed brick, rock, or marble. Particularly notice whether there is enough of the surfacing material and check for any leakage and necessary repairs.

Metal roofs: These roofs may be used on very low pitch. Non-galvanized metal, other than copper, and zinc, should be kept painted, of course. Copper and zinc are very durable for roofing, but quite expensive. Check the seams to see if they are properly crimped to make them watertight. Non-corrosive nails should be used, but zinc should not be used in contact with other metals, with the exception of iron, because of electrolysis.

DESCRIPTION OF BUILDING IMPROVEMENTS

Extent of description

This section describes the extent of the building and other improvement details that you should record for your file and for preparing the appraisal report. Ordinarily it isn't necessary to provide such detailed description in the appraisal report itself, but generally it is wise to have the details available in your file for eventualities. Information is provided later in the book as to typical reporting forms. A detailed description is generally quite essential when court testimony will be involved, and an occasional client may want detailed information provided in his report. Occasionally a client will call later for more detail than is provided in the typical appraisal report.

You may use a form similar to that in Exhibit 4-2. It is designed to cover most types of structures, and it is contemplated that a separate sheet will be used for each structure. The form follows the order of the FHA-VA inspection form, which is considered a very suitable arrangement both for residential and commercial properties, and for the average light industrial building. In using the form, complete it in the detail appropriate to your appraisal. Some clients are more concerned with your opinion of the quality of the construction than the minute details of construction.

Detailed instructions

The following assumes you are inspecting a wood-frame dwelling. Under "Structure or Other Improvements Described," merely list general information, such as the number of stories, type of building, the number and types of the various rooms, areas, baths, and the general quality of the structure as to materials and workmanship. Complete the status information. Refer now to the "Construction" items on the blank form. Item "1" will not normally be completed for existing structures. The other items should be completed in detail as required or as appropriate to your appraisal, along with an indication of the condition *of the item.* Indicate the type of foundation, such as concrete beam and slab foundation, concrete pier foundation or concrete beam and pier foundation, whatever the case. Indicate whether it has a chimney and fireplace.

Describe the exterior walls by indicating the type, such as wood frame, brick veneer, brick masonry, etc. If the wall is not a completely masonry wall, indicate the type of framing members used for perpendicular support, which in the case of typical wood frame are termed "studs." Indicate how far apart the members are, measuring from the center of each. Check from the nailheads, if observable, otherwise you can check from sounding or with a magnet on the inside wall finish. Also, if wood, indicate the size, specie and grade, if observable. Most wood frame studding is 2 × 4 inches and normally is spaced anywhere from 16 to 24 inches on

DESCRIPTION OF THE BUILDING IMPROVEMENTS

Structure or Other Improvements Described: (enclose photographs)

Status: Proposed _____ Existing _____ Under Construction_____

Construction:

1. Excavation:	14. Interior Wall and Ceiling Finish:
2. Foundation:	15. Interior Decoration:
3. Chimneys:	16. Interior and Exterior Doors and Trim:
4. Fireplaces:	17. Windows:
5. Exterior Walls: (including painting)	18. Entrances and Exterior Detail:
6. Floor Framing:	19. Interior Detail: (Including built-ins)
7. Subfloor:	20. Stairs and Elevators:
8. Finish Flooring:	21. Special Floors and Wainscots:
9. Partition Framing:	22. Plumbing:
10. Ceiling Framing:	23. Heating and Air Conditioning:
11. Roof Framing :	24. Electric Wiring:
12. Roofing :	25. Lighting Fixtures:
13. Gutters and Downspouts:	26. Insulation:

27. Miscellaneous: (Porches, terraces, walks, drives, garages, landscaping, etc.)

Observed Condition of the Improvements:

Present Use of the Structure:

Estimated Age and Remaining Economic Life of Structure:

Comments:

Exhibit 4-2.

center. ("On center" means the distance from center to center of the framing member.) Various species of lumber may be used. If you are not familiar with lumber, I suggest you secure literature from a local lumberyard concerning the most common species used locally. If southern yellow pine, the grade is generally #2, but it may be #1 or #3. The lower the grading number of yellow pine, the better. Discuss or mention the condition of the painting, if any, of the exterior walls and the general condition of the walls. If the house is not built on a concrete beam and slab foundation, there should be some kind of floor framing which, typically, is 2×8, 2×10, or 2×12-inch wood members spaced anywhere from 16 to 24 inches on center. If there are floor framing members, there will probably be a sub-floor. This may be determined by looking under the house. Normally the sub-floor is made of 1×8 or 1×6-inch wood (usually ship-lap), or it may be plywood, nailed to the floor framing members. State the kind and grade of finish flooring, such as oak, pine, etc. Indicate the framing used in the partitions, ceiling, and roof.

Indicate the kind of roofing. Be sure to complete the condition for each item. Indicate the extent of gutters and downspouts. As to interior wall and ceiling finish, indicate whether the walls and ceilings have sheetrock, plaster, or wood ship-lap, etc. As to interior decoration, indicate the type of painting or whether it has wallpaper, etc. Indicate the type of doors, such as slab or panel doors, and the species of wood doors, if possible. Inspect the windows to determine the kind and condition. Indicate whether the frames are wood, steel, or aluminum. Also indicate whether there is wood trim around the interior side of the windows. If there is any special entrance or exterior detail involved, such as an unusually decorative colonial entrance, window shutters, and so forth, so indicate. Indicate the type of cornice under entrance and exterior detail. In an open cornice, the rafters extend over the eave of the house and are exposed. Rake cornices are those where a covering is applied directly on the rafters under the eaves. A cornice is termed a box cornice if the underside of the eaves is covered horizontally, the underside in this case being at a right angle to the house wall.

Under *Interior Detail* indicate the amount of kitchen cabinets or vanities in the bathrooms by lineal feet of counters, and describe the type of counter top. Indicate any other special cabinet work or paneling that may not be described elsewhere. Stairs and elevators are self-explanatory. Merely list and describe. Of course, ordinarily elevators are not involved in single-family dwellings, but if you do find one, list it by make and condition. Under *Special Floors and Wainscots,* indicate floors different from main floor, such as in baths and kitchens. Also list any wainscoting found. Under *Plumbing,* indicate the number of bathrooms and the quality and condition of the plumbing fixtures. Indicate the kind of piping used for water pipes, such as galvanized or copper tubing. Under *Heating and Air Conditioning,* indicate the size, type, and brand of equipment, if any. The fuel used by the heating system should be listed. This may be found on the unit. Under *Electric Wiring,* describe the type of wiring used, such as knob and tube, non-metallic sheathed cable, flexible metal sheathed cable, or metal conduit, as the case may be. Indicate the adequacy of electrical outlets and switches. Indicate any 220-volt outlets found. Under *Lighting Fixtures,* describe the quality and condition. Under *Insulation,* indicate whether there is any insulation in the walls [1] or ceilings, and the thickness and kind.

Under *Miscellaneous,* you should briefly describe the garage, porches, terraces, walks, drives, etcetera, and indicate their general condition. Briefly describe the landscaping in very general terms. Under *Observed Condition of the Improvements,* describe the general condition of the total structure.

The *estimated remaining economic life of the structure* is usually about the same as the balance of the *usable* physical life of the structure, for all practical purposes. This period cannot exceed the physical life or endurance, and generally is shorter. It is usually estimated in multiples of five years. The economic life of a common wood-frame dwelling is considered around 40 years, a brick-veneer dwelling 50 years, and a masonry dwelling 55 years or more. If the best materials and construction are used, and the property and the neighborhood are well maintained, the economic life may be much longer. If you know the age you can deduct that, and the remainder would about indicate the estimated remaining economic life of the structure. But that is not necessarily always so. The property may not have been maintained as well as it should, and the physical life could cause the economic life to end prematurely. In such a case, estimate the effective age based on appearance, so that you may more properly estimate the remaining economic life. There may be an economic obsolescence of the neighborhood that will effect the economic life, which should be considered.

Necessary photographs

While at the site, take the necessary photographs. There should be a

---

[1] Unless you have plans and specifications of the building, you probably cannot determine this as concerns the walls.

front view, or one for each front side view of the property, and a street view showing the property, which should include the street and the neighboring properties. Generally, it is wise to take a rear-view photograph also and any other special views that are necessary or would be helpful. Include the photographs on a page as an attachment or enclosure of the appraisal. Even though all the photographs may not be required by the client, they may be quite valuable to you. They may save you making a return trip for rechecking an item you may have forgotten and failed to write about in the inspection report. A complete set of good photographs is very helpful with condemnation appraisals, particularly if the court case is held one or more years later or after the buildings have been removed. Close-ups should be taken where the building is seriously damaged or special situations exist. Views of the interior of the structure are frequently quite helpful in condemnation cases.

STRUCTURAL MEASUREMENTS

In order to compute the areas required in the physical approach we must have full information as to the dimensions of the building or buildings. If a proposed structure is involved, it is essential to have the plans and specifications. The plans must be in sufficient detail to permit the area computations. Normally, of course, if they are prepared by architects or qualified designers, they will be accurate and usable. Exhibit 4-3 is an illustration of the most detailed appraisal drawing generally required for appraisal of an existing dwelling. It should be drawn on ten-line graph paper. If an existing structure is involved, it is a good idea to ascertain from the owner or his agent if the actual construction drawings or a survey of the property are available. Quite frequently they are. It's a good idea to check the survey or blueprints with the buildings, as there may have been some changes made. If the blueprints or a survey are not available, you must measure the building, and you should do this very carefully. As a general rule, it is advisable to draw the rooms or other areas involved within the structure. The usual drawing prepared by the appraiser himself is based on single lines representing walls, and only show the room arrangement and functional utility of the property as necessary to the valuation. In taking the measurements of a dwelling you will need a measuring tape 50 or more feet in length. Either a light metal tape or a waterproof linen tape is usable for this. Of course, if you are going to be around areas where there might possibly be open electric wires it is advisable to use a non-metallic cloth tape instead of metal or metallic cloth tape. Unless the cloth tape is indicated as non-metallic, it

Exhibit 4-3.

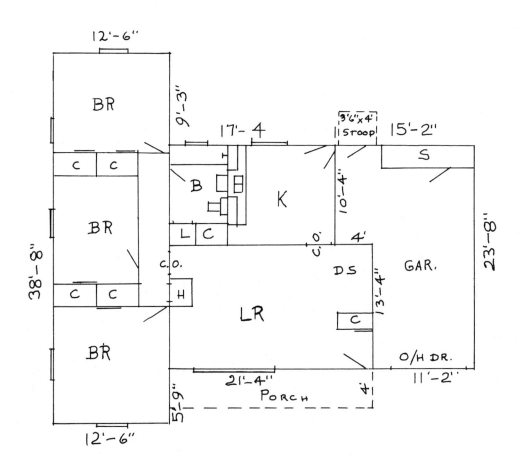

(ADDRESS)

is generally metallic and conductive of electricity. The tape used, of course, must be divided into feet and inches or tenths of a foot. The tapes divided into the tenths of a foot are quite useful in computing the areas. It is advisable to convert the portions of a foot shown in inches to decimal equivalents for ease of computation.

Exhibit 4-4 provides three examples of building shapes and methods of computing the building areas and their perimeters. Building area measurements are generally based on the foundation perimeter and the floor area of each floor is added to arrive at the total square feet in the floor area.

AREA AND
PERIMETER CALCULATIONS

(Note difference in perimeters for same amount
of area)

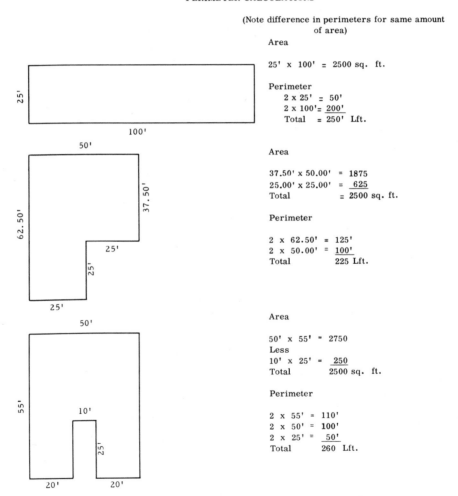

Area

25' x 100' = 2500 sq. ft.

Perimeter
   2 x 25' = 50'
   2 x 100'= 200'
   Total   = 250' Lft.

Area

37.50' x 50.00' = 1875
25.00' x 25.00' = 625
Total   = 2500 sq. ft.

Perimeter

2 x 62.50' = 125'
2 x 50.00' = 100'
Total   225 Lft.

Area

50' x 55' = 2750
Less
10' x 25' = 250
Total   2500 sq. ft.

Perimeter

2 x 55' = 110'
2 x 50' = 100'
2 x 25' = 50'
Total   260 Lft.

Exhibit 4-4.

Computation of the area of the building sites may offer some problems in this respect as, quite frequently, the angles at the site corners are not 90° angles. However, it is not usually necessary to compute the areas of moderately-priced residential sites for valuation purposes, as they are commonly valued on the basis of front footage, that is, the actual number of lineal feet fronting upon the street. In this case, the value is quoted on the basis of so much per front foot. In the case of high-value sites when the land area is required, unless the appraiser has an accurately drawn survey indicating the degree of the angles involved and is qualified to compute such areas, he had best require that the area be calculated by the surveyor. Some land areas are very difficult to compute even with all the necessary information unless one has specialized in surveying.

POINTERS

✔ The appraiser must become familiar with the nomenclature of the structural components of buildings that he expects to appraise.

✔ The foundation is the most essential thing that the appraiser checks. Any type of foundation that has structural defects will cause loss in value, but a concrete slab foundation may be damaged so severely as to seriously impair the use or marketability of the building. If the appraiser finds evidence of structural deficiency in the foundation and he is not qualified to pass judgement on it, he should secure someone who is qualified to do so for him, whether it be another appraiser, a builder, or an engineer. As a general rule, frame buildings do not offer the many problems that masonry, brick veneer, or stone veneer construction may involve. The masonry or veneer type of construction must be inspected more closely.

✔ Quite frequently an inspection of the interior can offer better evidence of defects in the foundation than can be found by inspection of the outside, for often the grass, shrubs and flowers hide much of the foundation from inspection. Any large cracks in the interior walls or ceilings, particularly over and under windows and above doors should be investigated very carefully, as these defects may be evidence of foundation settlement. A discussion with the occupant of the building will quite frequently bring out information not otherwise readily available to you. You are only in contact with the building a short time, while the building occupant may know of repairs made to the structure or may have observed deficiencies that might not be apparent during a brief inspection. A second inspection of a building may indicate items overlooked the first time. Of course, if the building is occupied, many portions of the interior will be hidden behind furniture, making a visual inspection rather awkward. Usually, it is unadvisable or impractical for an appraiser to move much furniture, particularly if the house is occupied, but you must if it appears necessary.

✔ Regardless of the type of appraisal that is being prepared, it is necessary to inspect the building thoroughly insofar as practical. This is necessary even if only a letter of opinion is involved. The building improvements should be described adequately. Normally, a detailed description is provided only in narrative reports. In most cases it is only necessary to outline the basic structural, electrical, and mechanical items; otherwise, the report will be too voluminous even for the narrative type of report.

✔ If proposed construction is involved, the appraiser must be provided with the plans and specifications and they must be in sufficient detail to make the necessary calculations as well as to portray the proposed construction.

✔ If an existing building is involved, secure the plans and the survey of the property, if at all possible, as these will not only save time (if they are readily available), but will allow you to make much more complete computations. If you must draw the floor plan of the building from your own measurements, more time will be taken. You cannot afford to make complete architectural drawings, even if you are qualified. Ordinarily, it is not required that the interior partitions of a dwelling be located with exactness. In fact, many appraisers step them off, but I would recommend the use of a small measuring wheel for this.

✔ In preparing the drawings of an existing building, do so very carefully and recheck the dimensions before leaving the site to be sure that they are accurate, as this may save a return trip. It is a good idea to add up and compare the opposite sides of the building to see that they essentially agree before you leave the site.

SUMMARY

1. The appraiser must be knowledgeable as to the structural details of buildings.
2. He must closely inspect all the exposed portions of the building to ascertain the materials used, the type and quality of the construction and the present condition.

3. He will find that a blank form designed for building inspections will be very useful.

4. The appraiser should briefly list the type of materials and equipment used and their current condition.

5. The general condition of the total structure should be indicated.

6. The apparent age of the structure should be given.

7. The present use of the building, particularly if it is other than the designed one, should be indicated.

8. All necessary photographs of the property should be taken.

9. In order to compute the areas required in the physical approach, the appraiser must have full information as to the outside dimensions of the building. If available, this can be secured from a surveyor's plat, but the data should be checked, as changes may have occurred.

10. If the blueprints are available for existing structures, they should be used in drawing the floor plan of the building, but the data should be checked.

11. Unless a land tract involves plain shapes which are easy to compute without special equipment or training, it is wise to require that the land area be computed by a surveyor, particularly if the land is high value. This is not ordinarily required on small modestly-priced home sites priced on a front foot basis.

5

Physical
Approach

Premise: The value indicated by the physical (cost) approach tends to set the upper limit of value.

Definitions

The physical approach involves an estimate of the replacement or reproduction cost of the building and other improvements involved, less depreciation, if any, to which is added the value of the land. *Replacement cost* is defined as the cost of a similar and comparable modern structure of the same size, but not an exact replica. *Reproduction cost* is defined as the actual cost to reproduce an exact replica of the subject structure. Normally, replacement cost data is used in the appraisal procedure, particularly when older properties are involved, as it would be almost impossible to find some of the materials or equipment on the market today that were used many years ago. In some instances, however, it may be desirable to use the reproduction cost of a building. This is sometimes necessary in condemnation appraising because the court may be quite technical as to the appraisal methods used and may tend to lend more credence to the reproduction cost of the building. When you are appraising a new and modern building, the replacement cost and reproduction cost should be almost the same, however.

METHODS OF COST ESTIMATING

There are several methods. The principal ones are: The square-foot, the cubic-foot, the quantity-survey, and the unit-cost-in-place methods. These may be titled differently, but the important thing is to know the methods and to be sure all costs are included. There are many costs involved in construction, including the following:

CONSTRUCTION COSTS

A. Direct Costs

   (1) Preliminary costs such as: planning studies, consulta-tations, test boring, surveys, permits, and recording fees
   (2) Professional fees such as for: engineers, architects and appraisers
   (3) Cost of the building and its equipment
   (4) Other land improvement costs (on and off site) such as for: drainage, sidewalks, utilities, grading, land-scaping, fences, walls, driveways, parking areas, ter-races, permanent recreational facilities, roads and pylons
   (5) Contractor's overhead and profit.

B. Indirect Costs of Owner

   (1) Miscellaneous costs during construction
   Taxes and insurance
   Administrative expense
   Financing charges (interest and fees)
   Interest on equity investment
   Legal expense for construction and contract matters
   (2) Tenancy costs, such as: improvements made for ten-ant; leasing expense (including broker's fee); promo-tion and publicity; loss of fair return on investment until normal occupancy is attained, or until the prop-erty is sold if it is not rental property.

C. Management and Administrative Costs

(1) Management expenditures or the amount equivalent to the value of the service

(2) Administrative costs such: as salaries for accounting, promotion and other overhead staff personnel; office expense, insurance, taxes, and legal expense not otherwise paid; travel and entertainment.

Several cost manuals are published that apply to most U. S. cities and their neighboring communities. These manuals may not be as accurate as locally developed costs, but they provide much more detailed and varied information than is generally available to an appraiser unless he is also a professional cost engineer, contractor, or builder. When using any cost method you should ascertain what costs are included. Generally, published data does not include all of the preliminary items of direct cost, indirect cost, or the management and administrative costs. It is probably not possible to include the data. Accordingly you must check the data, regardless of the source, and adjust it for any item that should be included. Such costs may not be of great importance to very small structures, but when a project of much cost is involved they can be considerable.

DISCUSSION OF THE METHODS OF COST ESTIMATING

Square-foot method

This is a commonly used method. It is the most rapid and, in many instances, the most foolproof. Local, or nationally published costs adjusted for local use, are employed. They are based on known square-foot area costs. Refer to the cost manual as to the building area to be included in the square-foot cost involved. The total floor area normally includes the total area of each floor within the building and is generally based on the foundation perimeter. Different square-foot prices will be quoted for the different kinds of construction involved in the same building. Computations should be in accordance with the manual's classification. For instance:

Living area	2000 sq. ft. @	$10.00	$20,000.00
Porch	100 sq. ft. @	3.00	300.00
Garage	600 sq. ft. @	4.00	2,400.00

Compute the square-foot content of the building as instructed in the manual and price it accordingly. Normally square-foot prices are adjusted for differences in building perimeters, corners and height, then the adjusted square-foot price is quoted in the appraisal report. This method can be used with most types of property. Costs based on actual recent local experience with the type of building appraised are usually the best if you can secure sufficient reliable data. Whether local or nationally published cost figures are used, adjustment is made for any differences involved in the structures. The square-foot cost basis is the most rapid, and can be quite accurate, as it eliminates many individual estimates which are sources of error. Separate cost data is used (also on a square-foot basis where appropriate) for other items such as terraces, sidewalks, driveways, and so on, that are outside of the exterior walls of the building. Other items are generally priced on an appropriate unit or allowance basis.

Cubic-foot method

This procedure is basically the same as the square-foot method except the cost is based on the cubic-foot building content. Compute the cubic-foot content of the building in accordance with the method employed by the cost manual used. Other basic data and costs are secured as mentioned for the square-foot method. This method has advantages and disadvantages quite similar to the square-foot method.

The unit-cost-in-place method

The basis of this method is the complete cost per unit of measure of each of the following areas: foundation, floors, ceilings, walls, roof, etc. This cost data is not as available as that for square-foot or cubic-foot methods and is not as commonly used. The appraiser may, if he is so qualified, compute these costs for his own use; however, the time involved is quite consuming. The Marshall and Stevens Publication Company publishes a very good variation of this method.

The quantity survey method

This is the oldest method, and probably the most reliable if the estimator is fully qualified. It is used by many building contractors. It involves an individual cost estimate of the amount of labor, lumber, bricks, mortar, nails, and other expenses involved in the construction of the building. The use of this method produces the estimated reproductive cost of the structure. The disadvantage is that it is the most time-consuming. While it might take two hours to estimate the replacement cost of, say, the normal residence by the square-foot or cubic-foot method, it might well take eight hours by the quantity survey method. However it is usually more accurate than the others if the estimator is sufficiently trained, experienced, and informed as to current costs. Otherwise, it is quite hazardous to use. The appraiser may use the square-foot or cubic-foot method without actually being qualified in construction methods and techniques. Even the qualified cost engineer may overlook enough items in the quantity survey method to make it somewhat risky. Few appraisers use this method because of the required qualifications and the time involved.

Other methods of estimating costs

A similar method to the unit-in-place method is a combination lineal-foot and square-foot method. The walls are estimated on a lineal-foot basis and the foundation, floor, roof, and ceiling on a square-foot basis. While this is a variation of methods, it can be quite accurate if the basic figures are correct. It is a most uncommon method, but one that has been used for mill-type construction. Another method used involves the known actual total cost of a building when it was constructed. Reference is then made to historical cost indices and the original cost is adjusted to the new time. This method does have the considerable advantage that it is a most rapid procedure; however, it has the disadvantage that the building may have been changed since original construction or the owner may have been over-charged, and this may not be known. When the method is used you should have the original plans, specifications, and building contract. Local historical cost indices should be used. Some chambers of commerce maintain the indices. Several nationally published cost manuals include national indices that are adjusted for regional areas.

SOURCES OF COST DATA

If you do not have reliable cost data or you are not sufficiently experienced to use the data, it will be necessary for you to have a cost estimator or other qualified person to assist you in the estimate. In the appraisal of commercial and other high-cost structures, appraisers frequently employ cost estimators, engineers, builders, or contractors to calculate the cost for them. There are several cost manuals on the market which offer considerable assistance. Marshall and Stevens Publication Company, 1645 Beverly Boulevard, Los Angeles, California 90026, publishes the Marshall Valuation Service which is an exceptionally good cost service that covers most types of structures that the appraiser will encounter. It provides costs by the cubic- and square-foot method, two variations of the unit-in-place method, historical indices, and special supplemental costs.

TYPICAL SUMMATION OF THE ESTIMATE

Regardless of the cost method used, the estimate is usually summarized as follows:

PHYSICAL VALUE ESTIMATE

Estimated replacement cost new:		
Main building: 10,706 sq. ft. of floor area @ $11.25		$120,442
Other improvements (these may be listed separately)		14,107
Subtotal		$134,549
Less estimated depreciation:		
Physical deterioration:	6,727	
Functional obsolescence:	None	
Economic obsolescence:	None	6,727
Estimated replacement cost of the improvements		$127,822
Estimated land value (approximately 14,895 sq. ft. @ $1.85)		27,556
Subtotal		$155,378
Other costs (indirect, management and administrative)		10,000
Estimated total physical value		$165,378

(The value estimate is generally rounded to the nearest multiple of $50, $100, $250, $500, or $1,000 as appropriate to the amount of the valuation. This is discussed in Chapter 10).

It must be understood, of course, that the physical approach is only one indicator of value. It is highly desirable to use the other two approaches if they are applicable. If a special-purpose property is involved, such as a church or public school, the physical approach is usually the only one that can be used. Of course, such buildings are normally used only for that purpose and have no rental income of consequence. Generally when properties of this type cannot be sold for the designed use, the selling price is much less than what the depreciated cost would be.

DEPRECIATION

Definitions

There are three types of depreciation, namely: (1) physical deterioration, (2) functional obsolescence, and (3) economic obsolescence. Physical deterioration is a loss in value due to the effects of age, the elements, use, improper maintenance, and so forth. Functional obsolescence involves a loss in value as a result of the design and arrangement of the facilities of the structure itself. This obsolescence may be due to over-improvement, super-adequacy, inadequacy, or to a change in styles and designs. It is a condition existing in the property itself. Economic obsolescence is concerned with those factors outside of the property itself that may reduce its value. Factors that create economic obsolescence include: adverse use encroaching into the neighborhood, obnoxious odors permeating the air, loud and disagreeable sounds, changes in optimum land use, governmental actions that reduce the property rights, a supply and demand situation, etc. It is a situation outside of the property that tends to reduce the general value of all similar properties in the neighborhood as well as the value of the appraised property.

COMMON METHODS OF ESTIMATING DEPRECIATION

Estimating combined physical deterioration and functional obsolescence

Age-Life Method Based on Internal Revenue Service Tables: This method is based upon the age or estimated age of the structure concerned. To estimate by this method, select the rate per year for the structure from the table in Exhibit 5-1 for Composite Rates. Multiply the rate per year by the age or the effective age (whichever is applicable) of the structure and multiply the building cost (new) by the product. The effective age is based on appearance rather than the actual age and depends on how well the property has been maintained and the quality of the construction, and so on. This is not a very accurate method to use since it includes an allowance for both physical deterioration and functional obsolescence which may not apply to any particular property. If you use this method, you should use the effective age of the property and use the table only as a guide. Certainly you wouldn't use the table indiscriminately.

Estimating physical deterioration only

Combined Observed Condition and Age of Materials Method: This method first includes an estimate of the cost to put the observable part [1] of the structure in new condition, and second, an estimate of the physical deterioration of those structural materials concealed by the walls, ceilings, and so forth. This concerns those items that cannot be observed except by considerable expense or damage to other parts. The best way to estimate the observable physical deterioration is to secure an estimate from a contractor as to the cost to place the structure in as-good-as-new condition; however, ordinarily you must make this estimate yourself.

Of course, the appraisal of the structure will not ordinarily require the removal of any part of the building. For the unobservable items we must assume that, due to the passage of time, a percentage of the structural material involved will have depreciated a proportionate amount. The wood framing members commonly used in the construction of the ordinary residential structure may normally be expected to last 100 years or more, unless the weather elements are permitted to infiltrate, causing a more rapid deterioration. Therefore, if the structure is, say, 10 years old, perhaps approximately 10 per cent or less (depending on their quality) of the value of the framing members will have been reduced. Since most foundations of buildings are of concrete or masonry, their normal life expectancy might be as much as 200 years if properly constructed, and a relatively small percentage of their life expires each year. A similar estimate is made for all other unobservable materials of the structure. The equipment depreciation may be similarly estimated.

This method of estimating physical deterioration is the most time-consuming method, and it is quite unusual for it to be used. It is not recommended, as it would be rare for the fee to be sufficient to justify its use. When it is used, the appraiser should have a complete list of the life expectancy of all the building materials and equipment involved.

Combined Observed Condition and Structure Age-Life Method: This method of estimating physical deterioration is based on an estimate of the cost to place the observable items of the property in new condition, plus 1 per cent of the cost of the balance of the structure. This method is about as accurate as estimates of depreciation can be. It is the most common method used by appraisers today. Ordinarily, there is not as much deterioration in the early years, so the percentage may be varied as appears appropriate.

---

[1] The exposed portions of the walls, ceilings, floors, roof, foundation, cabinets, windows, doors, etc. where you can see evidence of deterioration.

Functional obsolescence

Curable Conditions: The most practical method to estimate functional obsolescence is the cost-to-cure method. It is estimated by computing the cost to remodel or alter the building to eliminate the element creating the obsolescence, such as a poor floor plan or outmoded design. The best method to determine this is to secure an actual bid or estimate from a reliable contractor. The qualified appraiser may estimate the cost if it is impractical to secure the information from a contractor. The estimate should be based upon what contractors typically charge. If your building cost estimate is based on replacement instead of reproduction costs, you must consider whether the replacement costs have automatically adjusted for functional obsolescence for style, outdated equipment, etc. so that you will not be depreciating for the same item twice. You may also estimate this type of obsolescence by estimating the loss in market or rental value.

Incurable Conditions: If an over- or under-improvement which is not feasible to cure exists on the site, the maximum possible land value may not be developed. An over-improvement exists if the building is too large for the location, and if the building is too small it is an under-improvement. The most accurate way to estimate this loss is to estimate the land residual value of the site for its highest and best use, and then for its actual use. The loss will be the amount of over- or under-improvement involved. Other incurable forms of obsolescence may be estimated in ways similar to the method described below.

Economic obsolescence

Normally, the best method to estimate economic obsolescence is to find out the typical reduction in price paid by a typical buyer for a property having obsolescence. The way to make this estimate is to prepare two lists of sales of similar properties, one for properties having the same economic obsolescence and one in a neighborhood that does not, and then compare them. The typical difference in value should indicate the typical amount of economic obsolescence involved. Generally, this obsolescence affects both the land and improvements. Both land and building values should be reduced proportionately.

DEPRECIATED VALUE OF THE PROPERTY

Deduct the total of the three kinds of depreciation from the total cost, new, of the improvements to find the depreciated value of the property.

POINTER

✔ You must certainly use a lot of common sense and good judgement in matters of depreciation as in all matters of appraisal. After you have completed the preliminary estimates for the approaches involved and start the correlation of the estimates, you will have a better perspective of the depreciation involved.

Helpful guidelines for depreciation rates

FOR DEPRECIATION RATES

The following chart is for the combined building and its equipment and the rates are the per cent per year. The rates contemplate that the cost of new equipment will be capitalized, and that the cost of the equipment replaced will be charged to the replacement reserve. The equipment includes normal fixtures, elevators, and so forth.

Composite Rates (percent)* Type of Construction		
	Good	Average	Cheap
Apartments	2 1/2	2 1/2	3
Banks	2	2	2 1/2
Dwellings	2	2 1/2	3
Factories	2 1/4	2 1/2	3
Farm Buildings	2	2	2 1/2
Garages	2	2 1/2	3
Grain Elevators	1 1/2	2	2 1/2
Hotels	2 1/2	2 1/2	3
Loft Buildings	2	2	3
Machine Shops	2	2 1/2	3
Office Buildings	2	2 1/2	3
Stores	2	2	2 1/2
Theaters	2 1/2	3	3 1/2
Warehouses	1 1/2	2	2 1/2

* Internal Revenue Service, *Bulletin F. Tables of Useful Lives of Depreciable Properties,* Washington, D.C.: U.S. Government Printing Office, Page 7.

Exhibit 5–1.   Composite (Depreciation) Rates.

If you use the above, your estimate of the remaining economic life should agree, viz, 2 per cent indicates 50 years.

TOTAL (USEFUL) LIFE (YEARS) FOR BUILDING LESS EQUIPMENT

If the equipment depreciation is not included in the building depreciation rate, as it is in Exhibit 5-1, the appropriate rate should be based on the following total life years for only the structure:

(Example of rate computation, 100% ÷ 50 years. = 2% per yr.)

Total Life (years) *

Apartments . . . .·.50	Hotels . . . .·50
Banks . . . .·67	Loft buildings 67
Dwellings 60	Machine shops 60
Factories 50	Office buildings 67
Farm buildings 60	Stores . . . .·67
Garages . . . .·60	Theaters 50
Grain elevators 75	Warehouses 75

---

* Internal Revenue Service, *Bulletin F. Tables of Useful Lives of Depreciable Properties,* Washington, D.C.: U.S. Government Printing Office, Page 7.

Exhibit 5–2.   Total Useful Life for Buildings Exclusive of Equipment.

See page 62 for average useful life of various items of equipment.

DISCUSSION OF THE PHYSICAL APPROACH AND VALUATION OF SPECIAL-PURPOSE PROPERTIES

Institutional type special-purpose properties

This approach is about the only one to be used for institutional type special-purpose properties that do not have rental income and are not marketable in the usual sense. This applies to all such properties that are not generally rented, bought or sold. As a general rule, this type of special-purpose property can only be used economically for the primary use the building is designed for.

BUILDING EQUIPMENT

If the equipment and other items listed are depreciated separately, you may use the following indicated useful lives as appropriate.*

Average useful life (years)

Air conditioning:
    Air conditioning systems
        Large - over 20 tons 20
        Medium - 5 to 15 tons 15
        Small - under 5 tons 10

Elevators:
    Freight 25
    Passenger 20

Fire equipment:
    Fire alarm systems 25
    Movable equipment 20
    Sprinkler system (Life of building)

Heating systems:
    Boilers and furnaces 20
    Burner equipment--
      Gas 16
      Oil 10
    Radiators 25

Heaters, electric 10

Heaters, gas 15

Lighting systems:
    Conduits and fittings (Life of building)
    Wiring 20
    Fixtures 15

Telephone equipment:
    Conduits and fitting (Life of building)
    Wiring and fixtures 20

Wells and well pumps 25

Miscellaneous facilities:
    Awnings 5
    Doors, Louvre,
      Ventilating 15
    Incinerators 14
    Safes and vaults (Life of building)
    Screens, window 10
    Shades 5
    Venetian blinds 8

Plumbing:
    Faucets and flushing
      valves 15
    Bath tubs, lavatories,
      toilet bowls, etc. 25
    Pipes --
      Brass or copper (Life of building)
      Iron, cold-water 25
      Iron, hot water or
        steam 20
      Sewer, cast-iron
        or vitrified (Life of building)
    Valves --
      Brass body, water
        or steam (Life of building)
      Iron body, water
        or steam 20

Roofs:
    Asbestos 25
    Asphalt and tar (prepared)15
    Galvanized Iron--
      Light or cold dipped 15
      Heavy or hot dipped 20
    Tar and gravel (5-ply) 20
    Tarred felt 10
    Copper   (Life of building)
    Slate   " " "
    Tile   " " "
    Tin   " " "

---

* Internal Revenue Service, *Bulletin F, Tables of Useful Lives of Depreciable Properties*, Washington, D.C.: U.S. Government Printing Office, Pages 7-9.

Exhibit 5-3. Average Useful Life of Building Equipment.

General

The main purpose of the physical approach is to estimate the depreciated value of the property. It has great weight for new properties or those to be built. They probably would not be constructed if they weren't worth at least the cost of construction, but of course this may occur. It is very unusual that a property is worth more than its replacement cost. It probably only occurs when the demand is greater than the supply of the property—a situation that is usually temporary in the United States.

The land value used in connection with the physical approach should be that as estimated by the instructions given in the chapter pertaining to land value. In estimating the replacement cost of constructed buildings when no blueprints or specifications are available, you must determine the area of the building and the actual construction materials used. Even if the plans are available you must check them for accuracy. You must be very careful to include all of the costs involved. It is very easy to overlook such costs as service charges for financing, interest during construction, administrative expense, insurance and taxes during construction, legal expense, title and recording expense, real estate commissions, surveys, permits, architect's and engineer's fees, a reasonable profit due the builder for his risks and work in creating the finished product, and the advertising and other costs involved to secure normal occupancy of rental property. In using any cost data it is necessary to know if an allowance has been provided for these expenses; if a reasonable allowance is not provided, it must be included. Usually personal property is not included in the appraised value of the real estate; however, certain items which would otherwise be classed as personal property but which are permanently affixed to the building are customarily considered as real estate. Venetian blinds and wall-to-wall carpeting which are affixed to the building are considered as a part of the real estate in many localities. Frequently, whether or not an item of personal property may be included is dependent upon local custom and legal interpretation. The free-standing refrigerators and ranges which are provided in many apartment buildings are not includible in most areas as real estate. Where personal property is furnished the tenant, the income for it should not be considered in the gross income unless an allowance for its amortization is provided in the economic approach.[2] When the

---

[2] Ordinarily, if personal property is included in the same appraisal with the real estate, it is deducted from the total value and the two value estimates are shown separately.

building is to be constructed and it is necessary to provide an estimate of the value for the personal property, it should be fully described in the plans or specifications, otherwise an allowance should be provided subject to inventory and documentation of the actual cost.

The depreciation estimate is one of the most hazardous estimates that can be made because it is something that cannot be directly measured as such. An appraiser can normally secure or compute estimates for this within a reasonable range. Estimating physical depreciation that is unobservable may require considerable time to estimate in detail. Some of the cost manuals indicate the percentage costs of the main components involved in the construction of a building and these percentages may be used to compute the quantity of unobservable items. Functional obsolescence is relatively easy to compute if it is curable, for then all that is necessary is to make an estimate of the actual cost to remodel the structure to overcome the functional obsolescence. Those items of functional obsolescence that cannot be economically cured usually are best estimated by measuring the loss in rental value or market reaction and its effect upon the sales price of a property. Economic obsolescence is somewhat more difficult to estimate because it involves influences outside of the property itself and not on the site. There may be a nearby plant that exudes disagreeable odors sufficient to make an adverse market reaction to properties within range of the nuisance. There may be a railway switchyard nearby that creates a great deal of noise, or the property may be so located that auto traffic or lights from automobiles on the street or parking area make the site less desirable for residential use. In situations similar to these about the best method to use is to compare several similar properties having the same obsolescence with several not having any obsolescence.

The physical approach is very closely related to the economic and market approaches. Actually, the physical approach is basic to the other approaches. In the comparative procedures used in estimating the market value of a property, it is necessary to have on hand much of the data computed in the physical approach in order to make the comparisons involved in the market approach. The same is true for the economic approach. In estimating the stabilized income of a property you must compare it against the rental rates of comparable properties, and to do this you must know the size of the rental units involved as well as the relative difference in costs. The economic approach, of course, normally has a direct relation to the depreciated value of the property since rental rates tend to be based upon a return necessary to pay for any mortgage payments and expenses involved, as well as to provide a profitable return on the equity. When supply and demand are relatively equal, the depreciated cost will tend to be equal to the market value. Of course, if all the approaches are computed absolutely correctly, the indicated values of all three will be very close. To do this is much easier said than done.

Due to the basic importance of the physical approach, it is standard procedure to complete it before any other. It naturally follows the analysis of the location and building data.

SUMMARY

1. The value indicated by the physical (cost) approach tends to set the upper limit of value.
2. The principal methods of building cost estimation are: the square-foot, cubic-foot, quantity-survey, and the unit-cost-in-place methods.
3. There are three types of depreciation: physical deterioration, functional obsolescence, and economic obsolescence.
4. The best method to estimate physical deterioration is the combined observed condition and structure age-life method.
5. The best method to estimate curable functional obsolescence is the cost to cure method. If incurable or not feasible to cure, the use of land residual estimates based on the present improvement as compared to an improvement not having the obsolescence is the best procedure.
6. The best way to estimate economic obsolescence is usually the comparative market method.
7. The physical approach is usually the only approach to be used for special-purpose properties that are not typically rented, bought, or sold.
8. The physical approach is basic to the other approaches for most properties because it includes much data essential to the others.

PART II

ADVANCED APPRAISAL

PROCEDURES

6

Location Analysis
and Appraisal of Urban
and Suburban Land

LOCATION ANALYSIS

It is generally agreed that the three most important factors in the appraisal of real estate are: (1) location, (2) location, (3) location! It is very important to realize that in the appraisal of urban and suburban real estate, its value is generally in proportion to the usefulness of its location to people, assuming any improvements involved are the highest and best use of the land. People create value. If land is advantageously located in relation to an urban area, a developer may buy it, subdivide it, build houses and sell them to people who then require shopping centers and other community, civic and social facilities. Raw land which had only acreage value would have then been converted to a higher use, thus increasing its productivity manyfold and, accordingly, multiplying its worth many times the original value. As the land is developed and occupied for residential use, certain sites become the logical locations for other more valuable uses. The higher the best use of a site, the more valuable it becomes.

Neighborhood data

Since the location is such an all-important factor in real estate, it is most important that we analyze a property's neighborhood. All-important

69

neighborhood elements affecting the value of the property must be considered. Exhibit 6-1 on page 71 is similar to the neighborhood section of the typical short standard appraisal reporting form which is sufficient for many uses; however, the appraiser must analyze the neighborhood in much more detail even though he lists only the brief information required in the short form report.

Residential neighborhood data

In preparing a detailed or narrative report for residential property, particularly for an apartment project, the neighborhood analysis may be expanded to include the list as shown below.

NEIGHBORHOOD DATA (RESIDENTIAL)

Physical and Related Data
> Location of the Neighborhood
> Topography; Drainage; Soil
> Street Surface; Curb and Gutter; Sidewalks; Street Lights
> Utilities
> Type; Typical Size; Status as to Age, Condition, and Functional Obsolescence of Neighborhood Properties
> General Price Range; Typical Price, etc.
> Built-Up Percentage of the Neighborhood
> General Appeal

Economic and Related Data
> Population; Occupations; Income
> Ownership; Rental Occupancy Per Cent; Rental Rates; Vacancies
> Sources and Distance to Employment Centers
> Comparative Marketability of Competing Neighborhoods

Civic, Social, and Community Facilities
> Shopping; Schools; Churches; Public Transportation

Governmental and Legal Data
> Taxes and Special Assessments
> Zoning and/or Restrictions as to Land Use
> Provisions for Architectural Control and Maintenance
> Police Protection
> Fire Protection

General
> Adverse Influences and Economic Obsolescence
> General Enhancement Features
> Trends
> Comparative Appeal
> Other

Even though you do not actually list all of the details involved, you will probably consider all of them in the appraisal.

DISTANCE FROM CENTER OF METROPOLITAN AREA _____ DIRECTION _____ SECTION IS APPROXIMATELY _____% BUILT UP

USES OF PROPERTIES IN IMMEDIATE NEIGHBORHOOD _____

IMMEDIATE NEIGHBORHOOD PRICE RANGE $ _____ TO $_____ AGES _____ TO _____ YEARS

TREND OF NEIGHBORHOOD _____

TYPICAL STRUCTURE TYPE _____ VALUE $ _____ AGE _____ YEARS

COMMENTS: _____

_____

_____

_____

Exhibit 6-1.

Basic Neighborhood Data Form.

Particular attention should be noted as to the following: Uses of the neighborhood properties: availability of all utilities; surface water drainage; general condition and functional obsolescence of the neighborhood properties; occupancy data; location of shopping facilities, schools, churches, bus transportation; special assessments, if any; zoning and/or restrictions and provisions for architectural control and maintenance; sources and distance to employment centers; adverse influences, economic obsolescence; general and comparative appeal; general enhancements and trends. Any trend affecting the value should be seriously considered since this will greatly influence the value of the property.

Commercial locations

Most of the data listed on page 72 will normally be considered in the appraisal of commercial property; however, some of the items may not be actually listed in the appraisal report, depending upon the type of report involved. If a narrative report is being prepared, most of the information will probably be included.

Particular note should be taken of the built-up percentage in the neighborhood; status of obsolescence and maintenance; drainage conditions; street surfacing and conditions; availability of all utilities; and comparative importance and desirability of the neighborhood. Other very important features are: Lease and rental information; typical employment and income of the trade area occupants; pedestrian and vehicular traffic; and parking facilities in the neighborhood. The direction of commercial and residential growth is very important. Any zoning and/or protective covenants as to land use should be particularly noted. Note whether local tax rates are unusually high or low. Any adverse influences or trends affecting value should be thoroughly investigated.

NEIGHBORHOOD DATA (COMMERCIAL)

Physical and Related Data
General Location; Built-up Percentage
General Description of the Neighborhood Structures
Status of Functional Obsolescence and Maintenance in the
    Neighborhood
Topography; Drainage; Soil
Streets and Public Utilities
Length of Blocks; Street Surfacing; Traffic Signals; Side-
    walks; Street Lights

Economic and Related Data
Trade Area Involved
Population of Area; Family Size and Ages
Typical Employment and Income of Area Occupants
Comparative Importance and Desirability of Neighborhood
Lease and Rental Information
Local Economic Conditions and Status of Competition
Pedestrian and Vehicular Traffic; Parking Facilities
Public Transportation and Shipping Facilities
Direction of Commercial and Residential Growth

Governmental and Related Data
Zoning and/or Restrictions as to Land Use
Local Taxing Policies
Fire and Police Protection

General
Adverse Influences and Economic Obsolescence
General Enhancement Features
Trends
Other

Industrial neighborhood data

In the appraisal of large industrial properties most of the following
information will be required. (In the appraisal of small properties not
involving many employees, little if any information as to amenities will
be required.)

Metropolitan or Area Data
Manpower
        Availability and Quality
Amenities of Location for Personnel
        General Appeal as Location of Employment

Accessibility to and Desirability of:
　　　　Housing
　　　　Civic, Social, and Community Centers
Water and Power Sources
Public Transportation and Shipping Facilities
Zoning, Land Restrictions and Architectural Control
Streets, Freeways and Railroads
Market for Products and/or Services and Accessibility
Availability of Raw Materials
Location of Competitors
Tax Rates and Basis of Assessments
Other

Data of this nature can become quite voluminous, and care must be taken not to supply a lot of extraneous material, but to indicate the important and essential points in detail. The Metropolitan Data should be based on the latest data for the area as influenced by the nearest city in the area. Frequently there will be several cities and towns in the metropolitan area. The *Amenities of Location for Personnel* are very important in the employment of the personnel involved. The item under *Market for Products and/or Services* is quite a technical subject about which the appraiser might not be expected to know or at least not fully informed. If the appraiser has inadequate information along this line, he should omit the item. Undoubtedly, the industrial concern involved will have made technical studies in this respect and the appraiser should ask to see the data. Under *Other*, list any other required information. The modern industrial parks are providing very desirable sites. Many are providing attractive and appealing locations not only for the operation of the activity as such, but appealing to the employees and operators as well.

Site or land data

The location of the site in relation to the neighborhood is very important for all kinds of properties. The following Exhibit 6-2 is similar

SIZE _____ x _____ x _____ x _____ x _____ x _____ CORNER _____ INSIDE _____

PUBLIC WATER _____ WELL _____ SEWER _____ SEPTIC TANK _____ ELECTRICITY _____ GAS _____

CURB & GUTTER _____ SIDEWALK _____ STREET SURFACING _____

COMMENTS: _____

Exhibit 6-2. Basic Site Data Form.

to the site section of the typical short standard appraisal reporting form. While it is sufficient documentary data for many appraisals, many other elements must be considered and most of them must be listed and discussed in the narrative report.

The following is a list of the items that should be considered in the appraisal of a site whether or not they are included in the report:

For Residential Sites:

Site

    Location in the Neighborhood
    Dimensions
    Shape and Area
    Corner—Inside
    Topography and Drainage Conditions
    Soil
Availability of Utilities
    Public
    Private
    Other
Right-of-Way Improvements
    Street Surfacing
    Curb and Gutter
    Sidewalk
    Surface Water Drainage
        Storm Sewers
        Swales
        Ditches
Land Use Zoning and/or Restrictions
Encroachments
Highest and Best Use
Special Assessments
General Comments

For Commercial Sites:

Site

    Location in the Neighborhood
    Dimensions
    Area
    Corner—Inside
    Topography and Drainage Conditions
    Soil
    Sub-Soil
Public Utilities

Right-of-Way Improvements
   Street Surfacing
   Sidewalks; Curbs; Street Lights
   Parking Facilities Off-Site
   Traffic Lights and Cross-Walks
   Surface Water Drainage
   Other
Orientation of Site
   Position
      Physical
      In Relation to Potential Customers
      In Relation to Major Concerns and Heavy Advertisers
      Compatibility with Neighborhood Concerns
   Forenoon and Afternoon Sun
   Natural Light and Ventilation
   Visibility and Situation for Advertising
   Accessibility
Other
   Pedestrian Traffic and Type
   Vehicular Traffic and Type
   Transportation Facilities
   Fire and Police Protection
   Zoning and/or Restrictions as to Use
   Adverse Influences
   Highest and Best Use of Site and Present Use
   Special Assessments
   General Comments

For Industrial Sites:

Dimensions, Area and Shape of Site
Topography, Drainage, Soil and Sub-Soil
Water and Power Sources
Accessibility
Streets and Roads
Transportation and Shipping Facilities
   Trucking Facilities
   Railway Facilities
   Marine Facilities
Zoning and/or Land Use Restrictions
Special Assessments
Other

Special elements as to site analysis

All details of the site analysis should be included as appropriate. In most localities there are very few special assessments, but where they do occur they must be considered in the appraisal. All pertinent data as to the assessment should be shown. Special assessments may be for the construction of streets, and other public improvements. If you encounter a special assessment against the property appraised, determine whether it is prepayable or not. In any event, it will have to be considered in the value of the property. If it is prepayable, the purchaser may require the seller to prepay the assessment. If the seller has not contracted to prepay it, the appraiser must consider the effect of the outstanding balance of the special assessment on the value of the appraised property. If the improvements obligated by the special assessment have not been constructed, the appraiser must consider the obligation, list the facts in the appraisal, and consider the effect in the opinion of value.

As a general rule, highly desirable residential neighborhoods are either restricted, zoned, or both, to a use appropriate to the neighborhood. Information as to restrictions may be secured by talking to the owner or a neighborhood real estate dealer and they may be verified by the abstract or title policy or other documents involved with the property. The title or abstract company can supply copies of recorded documents. Information as to zoning may be secured from the zoning authorities. If there are any special economic factors to be considered that affect the value of the property, they should be discussed in detail. Be sure to consider any adverse influence or general enhancement features that exist in the neighborhood which will affect the marketability of the property being appraised.

HIGHEST AND BEST USE OF LAND

This is most important. The highest and best use is the basic feature of consideration by land owners, developers, land planners, planning commissions, zoning boards, and so on. It is difficult to discuss land value without first mentioning its highest and best use. The highest and best use is considered to be that which is most productive in terms of rent or amenities for the longest period of time. The land must be adapted, needed, and available for the use. If the site is zoned or restricted to a certain use, normally no other use will be considered unless it is reasonable to assume the zoning or restrictions will be changed. Any such assumptions must be listed in the appraisal. If the site or the land is unrestricted or unzoned, and the highest and best use is not apparent, there may be a difficult problem involved. If the best use must be estimated, it will be necessary to make a test of the likely uses. The one that indicates the highest return to the land for the longest period of time is considered the highest and best use. The following paragraphs indicate the procedure involved.

Sites for rent producing properties

When rent producing properties are involved, we may estimate the highest and best use and estimate the productive land value by the same computations. For that purpose, refer to Exhibit 6-3 on a following page, which provides an example of the procedure involved. Generally, the procedure is self-explanatory. The most apparent best use for the land should be selected. The estimated cost of the improvements for the use involved should be obtained or computed. Ordinarily, to estimate the highest and best use of land or the land value by the land residual proc- ess (illustrated in Exhibit 6-3) new improvements should be used. After a study of comparable properties and local experience, the estimated annual income and expenses should be computed. The more familiar one is with the type of property involved, the more rapidly the estimate may be completed. Unless you are familiar with the type of property being considered, it will be necessary to secure the income and expense data from experienced owners or operators of similar properties, or from reliable statistical sources. We are concerned with typical income and expense for the type of property involved. A quick method of estimating an approximate total for the expenses, including a reserve for replace- ments, is by the use of known and proven local expense to income ratios of such property. In using the form in Exhibit 6-3 you must be sure to include in the expense ratio a typical allowance for loss due to vacan- cies and collections, as it is not generally included in local ratios. Be sure a reserve for replacement for all major building items, such as roofing and equipment that require replacement as the years go by, are included. The reserve for replacements is normally included in the local expense ratios, but it may not be in those quoted in national publica- tions. In any event be sure that all items are included.

You should be knowledgeable as to the expense ratios for your locality. Good local data will certainly expedite the calculations. A list of current

PRODUCTIVE LAND VALUE COMPUTATION

Land Area: _____ 76,000 Sq. Ft. _____

ASSUMPTIONS AS TO A HYPOTHETICAL USE:

Type of Improvements _____ 70 Unit Garden Apartment Project _____

Estimated Cost of Improvements_____ $655,500.00 _____

Estimated Economic Life of Improvements ____ 40 years _____

Annual Income and Expenses:

Gross Income . . . . (A rental schedule may be provided) . . . . $ 124,656 _____

Less all expenses of operating the property* ___(46%)**____ . . . . $ 57,342 _____

Net income to the property . . . . $ 67,314 _____

Less income for improvements:

____$655,500_____ X____9%_____ . . . . $ 58,995 _____
(Cost of improvements)   (Cap. rate: Interest 6 1/2% + Recap.   2 1/2% ***)

Net income to land . . . . $ 8,319 _____

COMPUTED PRODUCTIVE LAND VALUE: (Capitalized value of land earnings)

_$8,319_____divided by 6 1/2%_____ . . . . $ 127,985 _____
(Net income to Land)   (Interest Rate)
                                           Rounded to $ 128,000

_____

Comments: The rental schedule contemplates that the apartments will be rented unfurnished, but with all utilities to be paid by the owner.
          Since the land area amounts to 76,000 S.F., the productive land value is indicated as approximately $1.68 per average sq. ft. of land.
          The net income of $8,319 is a 6½% annual return on a value of $127,985.

   *Including vacancy and collection losses.
  **Percent of the gross income. Also, see footnotes 1, 2, 3 and 4 for helpful expense estimates.
 ***Based on estimated economic life, viz., 100%/40 yrs. = 2½%.

Exhibit 6-3.

typical lease or rental rates applicable to income type property should be maintained. This should be based on the net rentable area of the building concerned, if it is rented to several tenants, or the gross area of the building if to one tenant. The local method of computation should be used. *The Office Building Experience Exchange Report*,[1] the *Apartment Building Experience Exchange Report*,[2] *The Dollars and Cents of Shopping Centers*,[3] and *Expenses in Retail Business*[4] provide helpful information for those properties.

Continuing with the computation of the highest and best use, complete the necessary entries to arrive at the net income for the property. Estimate the capitalization rate. Compute the product of the cost of the improvements and the capitalization rate and deduct the product from the net income to the property as noted in the illustration. This will leave the income attributable to the land, which is then capitalized (divided in this case) by the appropriate interest rate (be sure *not* to include the recapture part of the capitalization rate in this computation) to find the productive land value. After such a computation is made for several different hypothetical new buildings, the one that provides the greatest return to the land for the longest period of time should be the highest and best use for the land involved. At the same time the indicated productive land value will be indicated.

Acreage suitable for development

The highest and best use of this type of land should be estimated by using the market approach where possible, or the method described for "Land Valuation of Rent Producing Properties," if the land is of a rental income producing nature.

---

[1] *Office Building Experience Exchange Report* published annually by the National Association of Building Owners and Managers, 134 South LaSalle St., Chicago, Illinois. Appraisers of office buildings should secure a copy.

[2] *Apartment Building Experience Exchange Report* published annually by the Institute of Real Estate Management, 36 South Wabash Ave., Chicago, Illinois. Appraisers of apartments should secure a copy.

[3] *The Dollars and Cents of Shopping Centers* (a study of receipts and expenses) published by Urban Land Institute, 1200 – 18th St., N.W. Washington, D.C. Appraisers of shopping centers should secure a copy.

[4] *Expenses in Retail Business* published by the National Cash Register Co. (Merchants Service) Dayton, Ohio.

Other land

The highest and best use is indicated by what the demand is willing to pay in rent or purchase price for the site. Use the procedure described above which is most applicable.

APPRAISAL OF URBAN AND SUBURBAN LAND

How to estimate comparative market value of land

Ordinarily the market approach is the best method to estimate the value of urban and suburban land. It involves a comparison of the appraised properties with comparable properties that have been sold or leased. From this the comparative value is derived. Comparable sales [5] may be scarce or non-existent in the neighborhood of the appraised, and you may have to search other competing neighborhoods to secure sufficient data. You must have good comparables to properly estimate the comparative value of the appraised. Other things being equal, the most recent sales should be used. In comparing the properties to the appraised, it is necessary to compare each comparable with it, item for item, making the necessary adjustments to find the comparative value based on that sale. The price, time of sale, utility, relative location and conditions of the sale are most important factors to consider. If the sale was made under unusually impelling or distressing circumstances, involving either party, it would not be usable for comparison.

An orderly procedure must be used in the comparative process. The procedure described below (illustrated in the combined use of Exhibits 6-4, 6-5 and 6-6) is recommended. You will find an orderly procedure such as this will assist in making more rapid and better estimates.

Instruction in the use of land sales analysis forms

Please refer to Exhibit 6-4, Market Transaction Form. The form is generally self-explanatory. The *Transaction No.* is for use as a convenient reference number. *Type* in this case refers to whether the transaction was a sale or lease. List the street address and legal or other description under *Land Description*. Describe any improvements under *Improvements*. Under *Consideration*, provide full information as to the total consideration, indicating the amount of cash, vendor's lien, mortgage lien or other evidence of any loan involved. If a lease, indicate the rental rate and terms. The blank for *Document Stamps* is for listing the amount of

---

[5] In using the word "sales" in the comparative process, it is customary to include leases of comparable properties. The present worth of the lease is used in lieu of sales price.

MARKET TRANSACTION

Transaction No. ___1___   Type _____Sale_____   Date __12-1-61__

Document Record: Vol. 1000   Page: 25   Type of Document:_____

Grantor:* Ben Goodman   Grantee:* John Doe

Land Description:
     1.24 acres out of J. J. Jones Survey, Abstract 255, fronting on west side of Better Street, about 500' south of Easy Street, Great City, Best State.

Improvements:

     None

Consideration: $54,000

Comments: Document Stamp**

     Mr. Goodman confirmed the above.

_____
* Lessor and Lessee respectively if a lease.
** For areas where required.

Exhibit 6-4. Market Transaction Form.

Exhibit 6-5.

ANALYSIS OF COMPARABLE LAND SALES*
As of 12-1-62

SALE NO.	PROPERTY	DATE OF SALE	AREA OF LAND	INDICATED PRICE	TIME	SITE (2) ANALYSIS	IMMEDIATE (3) NEIGHBORHOOD	GENERAL (4) NEIGHBORHOOD	OTHER (5) ITEMS	ADJUSTED VALUE**
					ADJUSTMENTS (Adjusted up or down to subject)					
1	John Doe Tract on Better Street	12-1-61	1.24 Acres	$1.00 per S.F.	plus 5%	minus 10%	plus 10%			$1.05 per S.F.
	(1) Time adjustment for 1 year. (2) This site better than the appraised. (3) This immediate neighborhood not as good as the appraised.									
2	J. J. Day, tract on Jay Street	11-1-60	2.00 Acres	$0.80 per S.F.	plus 10%	plus 15%				$1.00 per S.F.
	(1) Time adjustment for two years. (2) Site is about same except for size, and utility.									
3	G. Gay tract on Bay Street	10-1-61	1.50 Acres	$0.90 per S.F.	plus 5%		plus 5%			$0.99 per S.F.
	The immediate neighborhood is not quite as good.									
4	A. Jones tract on Park Street	10-1-62	1.50 Acres	$0.95 per S.F.					plus 5%	$1.00 per S.F.
	The price appears somewhat low.									

Based on the above, the indicated value for the subject appraised is about $1.00 per average sq. ft. of land.

FORM NO. 6-C, WINSTEAD APPRAISAL SERVICE

* Winstead Appraisal Practice Course, Houston, Texas, Winstead Appraisal Service

** Indicated value of subject appraised, compared to this sale.

stamps (if any) placed on the transaction document. Under *Comments,* list down any other important information relative to the transaction which would be useful in the comparison.

Analysis of Comparable Land Sales, Exhibit 6-5, is designed to be used in connection with the *Market Transaction Form.* Adjustments are made on the form as required. Under *Sale Number,* The Market Transaction number of that used in Exhibit 6-5 is entered in the first column of this form. A brief of the address and/or owner of the property should be shown under *Property.* Under *Indicated Price,* the amount confirmed should be shown. You should contact the necessary parties to confirm the sale if the details are not shown in the deed or document concerned. In the columns under *ADJUSTMENTS,* indicate by plus or minus the percentage that in your opinion you consider should be made to indicate the comparative value of the appraised property. After indicating the plus or minus adjustment by percentage or, if you prefer, by dollar amounts, indicate on the line below a word description indicating briefly the reasons for the adjustment and number the reasons by the column number of the adjustment. The *Adjusted Value* is found by adjusting the *Indicated Price* by the net amount of *ADJUSTMENTS* involved. When this procedure has been followed for each comparable sale, the approved procedure is to find the simple average or arithmetic mean, or to select the typical value indicated by the adjusted values. If you have statistical background, you may carry the process further. In any event, indicate your calculations at the bottom of the page, as well as the preliminary value indicated.

A word of caution should be given. In comparing properties, particularly vacant land, it is necessary to compare properties that have the same highest and best use. Properties having a different highest and best use are not comparable. Of course, if the property is zoned, the comparables should have similar zoning or possibility of change.

Land valuation for rent producing properties

The market value is generally the value estimate required. If there aren't sufficient comparable sales to estimate the market value you may estimate its income or productive value. The client will probably be interested in this computation. Productive value of the land as used here is the same as that produced by the income or land residual process. It is computed by the same procedure involved in estimating the highest and best use, as illustrated in Exhibit 6-3.

If the land is already improved with its highest and best use, the computation should be based on that use. If the improvements do not constitute the highest and best use of the land you should estimate the land value based upon its proper use and adjust it for its present use. This may be accomplished as follows: Estimate the probable value of the land when the present building's economic life will end, then refer to the table, "Present Worth of One Dollar" (Reversion Table), and compute the present value of the land reversion. Add to that value the present worth of the land income (computed by discounting its annual net income by use of the table, Present Worth of One Dollar Per Annum) for the improper use period. This is a realistic approach to the valuation of land that is improperly improved, if there is no excess land involved. If excess land is involved it should be valued separately. You may have to increase your appraisal fee when such calculations are required.

Valuation of speculative suburban acreage

"Speculative suburban acreage" is used to describe land that is more valuable for investment use than for farming or ranching, etcetera, but for which there is no other immediate demand for the land. It is land that will be in demand for a higher use in the foreseeable near future. It may be raw acreage in the path of city growth or industrial expansion. This is land that at long last is starting the first phase of suburban use. The best way to value this type of land is by the market approach. It will be necessary to check sales in the area until you find several good comparable sales. In the event there are no good comparables nearby it will be necessary to go into adjacent competing areas to find the next best comparable sales. The procedure illustrated in Exhibit 6-5 is about the only procedure that can be used for this type of land.

You may recognize land in this speculative situation by checking recent land sales and asking prices. When nearby farm or ranch land is consistently selling much higher than its value for farming or ranching purposes, and there is no other reason involved, such as mineral or oil discoveries, land speculation is the probable reason. Of course, any land that is nearby a city would appear to be in this situation, but until speculators or investors are actually buying nearby land, it may not be required for some time. Most nearby usable and available land surrounding the growing cities of the United States are in this position today. If the land has been zoned, this will most certainly have to be considered. If the zoning is proper it provides for the development of such land to its highest and best use, otherwise part of the owner's rights in the land may actually be denied him without recompense unless he can get the matter corrected.

Land valuation for development purposes
(estimation of potential land value)

If land development is premature, considerable money may be lost. Great waste in both land and money has occurred in this manner. I am sure most everyone has noticed land that has been subdivided and offered on the market prematurely. The streets may be graded and a few signs put up, but no utilities are provided. The sites are offered on the market for little or nothing down and with very low monthly payments. It frequently happens that only enough sites are sold to stymie the proper use of the land when it does become ready for development. Even if the tract is ripe for development, if insufficient improvements are made in the way of streets and utilities the land may never be properly developed. Over the years there have occurred many instances when too much land was subdivided and improved at one time with the result that many developers and land owners went bankrupt or lost large sums of money. More orderly development procedures are generally practiced today, but we will probably always have premature subdivision of raw land. When land that has been prematurely subdivided does become ripe for development and is still mostly unimproved, the next developer is faced with the time-consuming and expensive task of attempting to locate and buy out the lot owners, who have perhaps moved thousands of miles away.

Assuming that the land is ready for development and a developer is interested in knowing the potential value of the land and the maximum price he would be warranted in paying for it, we may proceed as follows:

Please refer to the example in Exhibit 6-6. The illustrated form is designed to expedite the calculation of the potential value of the land while it is still in the raw land category. Generally, I believe you will find the form self-explanatory. If the proper development is unknown, you will have to make several estimates using the form, until you arrive at the highest and best use. If you are not familiar with subdivision development, it will be necessary for you to secure the assistance of a colleague who is, as well as to study the matter quite thoroughly and consult with developers or land planning specialists. This will be necessary in order to arrive at the proper conclusion regarding the many problems involved in developments of this nature. Special matters of consideration are:

ESTIMATED POTENTIAL LAND VALUE FOR DEVELOPMENT PURPOSES*
(commercial, industrial, and residential tracts, or acreage)

Land Appraised: 31.181 acres of land out of the B. B. Better Survey,
_____ Abstract 100, City of _____ , _____ County, State
_____ of _____ ,
Estimated time to develop and market the land: 5 years _____

Land Data:

Potential land use considered: Single family residential subdivision _____
  development. This tract is ripe for development at this time. _____
_____
_____

Proposed lot size 11,138.5 S.F. (average) _____ Net lots per acre _____

Gross land area involved: Acres 31.181** , or sq. ft. ___ 1,358,244 **
Less area for streets, etc.: _____ , " " " ___ 355,766 **
Net land area for valuation: _____ , " " " ___ 1,002,478 **

Improvements considered: (indicate whether in-place or proposed)
Street surfacing Concrete (proposed) _____ Curb and gutter: Conc. (proposed)
Sidewalks Conc. (proposed) _____ Drainage system Storm Sewers (proposed) _____
_____

Street lights: (proposed) _____ Utilities _____ (proposed) _____
_____

Other: _____
_____

Calculations:
Corner lot premium - 14 at $500.00   7,000
Forecasted gross land sales: 1,002,478 S.F. at $1.00 $1,002,478 _____
                            (area or lots)   (price)
Total gross land sales..$1,009,478
Less estimated expenses and profit: ***
        Development costs $ 140,000 _____
        Marketing expense   42,000 _____
        Overhead and profit   353,000 _____
        Deferred expense   **** _____
        R.E. taxes and estimated interest on _____
        outstanding investment for 5 years   237,000 _____
        Total expenses and profit $ 772,000 $ 772,000 _____
ESTIMATED POTENTIAL LAND VALUE......................... $ 237,478
(Indicated potential value per acre of gross land $7,616.)

Comments: The development contemplates homes in the price range of $35,000 to $60,000. Nearby comparable sales indicate
_____ that the forecasted land sales will be obtainable.

  * Winstead, *Appraisal Practice Course I*, Houston, Texas: Winstead Appraisal Service, © 1961, Page 104.
  ** As indicated on the proposed development map.
  *** To be based on comparable cost data.
  **** Adjustment included in other listed items.

Exhibit 6-6.

>Expensive drainage problems
>Highest and best use
>Most readily marketable lot size
>Land to be reserved for streets, churches, schools, shopping
>   facilities, parks, etc.
>Underground pipelines, mines, or fills
>Unusable land
>Quantity of land that should be sub-divided at this time
>Required investment and term of investment
>Probable development cost
>Probable sales prices

From these questions you can see the complexity of the problems involved. Fortunately, the appraiser is not expected to provide the answer to all of them personally, but he must know where to secure the information so that he can make the necessary computations.

After securing the necessary information required in the first part of Exhibit 6-6, you should make a market survey on which to base your forecast of gross land sales. In preparing the survey you should secure comparable sales information from the official records, from developers, and from real estate dealers in the neighborhood. In estimating the net land area for valuation, be sure to allow for the street right-of-ways, unusable land and other land that is not marketable as such. See Exhibit 6-7, "Land Area Required For Residential Development." Estimate the assumed expenses and required profit as indicated in the form and any other involved in the development. Developers, land planning specialists, surveyors and engineers will be able to provide you with the probable development cost per acre. Complete the form as indicated to compute the estimated potential land value.

Land valuation of acreage suitable for development as a community unit

The community unit for our purpose here is defined as several acres of land under one ownership or control which have an indicated highest and best use for development as a residential area with required shopping facilities, churches and so on. The best method of estimating such land value is by the market approach, if at all possible. If that is impossible, or you are making a feasibility survey or highest and best use study, it will be necessary to estimate the potential land values involved by using a procedure similar to that illustrated in Exhibit 6-6 as described in a preceding paragraph, and also, when appropriate, the procedure shown on the form titled Productive Land Value Computation, illustrated

LAND AREA REQUIRED FOR RESIDENTIAL DEVELOPMENT*

Table E

Lot Areas and Dwelling Densities

Dwelling Unit Type	D.U.'s per Net Acre	Assumed Average Sq. Ft. of Lot per D.U.
Single-family	1	40,000
Single-family	2	20,000
Single-family	3	12,500
Single-family	4	10,000
Two-family	6	6,000
Row house	15	2,600
Garden apartment**	25	1,600
Multi-story apartments**	50	800

* Community Builders' Council, *The Community Builder's Handbook,* Executive Edition, Washington, D.C.: Urban Land Institute, © 1960, Page 315.

** The more intensive the use of land, the greater need there is for recreation space, wider streets and sidewalks, shorter blocks, and off-street parking. In multi-family development careful consideration must be given to land coverage and open space needs. High density, multi-family intrusions into single-family residential development must be avoided. Apartment buildings must be spaced and located within the project so as to provide transition between residential land uses. The developer of multi-family areas has a responsibility in making such sections of his city fitting, appropriate and serviceable to his community.

Exhibit 6–7. Land Areas and Dwelling Densities.

in Exhibit 6-3. If there are many acres involved or the possible development is complex, an exhaustive study of the area and a large quantity of computations will be required. In an appraisal of this type, it will be well to consult in detail with developers familiar with this type of property as well as land planners, architects, and engineers. Such an appraisal is very time-consuming and very expensive. You should have a contract for your services and the fee should be commensurate with the expense, time, and responsibility involved.

Land value of individual residential sites

The best method to appraise individual residential sites is by the market approach. However, when the area is largely built-up and there are no good sales of comparable vacant sites that have occurred, you may select several recent sales of comparable properties nearby or in competing neighborhoods and deduct the estimated depreciated value of the improvements (computed by the physical approach) from the total sales price. The typical land residual price indicated should be a fair estimation of the land value. You must be sure that all applicable costs are included with the depreciated value of the building to be sure of a proper indication of the land value.

The residential land value computed above may be used in several different ways. We may reduce the data to a front foot (street frontage) value, to an average square-foot value based on the site area, or to a ratio of land price indicated to total property sales price. The ratio may be computed as follows. If a dwelling sold for $21,000 and the land residual price is $4,200: $4,200/$21,000 = 20%. If the ratio so found is 20% and the total market price of the appraised property is $22,000 we may compute .20 × $22,000, which is $4,400, the indicated land value. The square-foot and front price computations, of course, are computed by dividing the indicated land price by the front feet or square feet involved in the particular land residual computed. You then merely multiply the front footage or square foot area of the appraised land by the rate involved to compute its value. Be sure to use the typical price or rate indicated for the neighborhood. Also be sure to use properties having sites essentially the same size and shape.

In case of rental property, the land value may be estimated as illustrated in Exhibit 6-3, which was discussed previously.

Land value for industrial sites

The market approach should be used for industrial sites if possible. Otherwise, estimate its productive value.

SUMMARY

1. It is the general consensus that the three most important factors in the appraisal of real estate are: (1) location, (2) location, (3) location!
2. The value of real estate is generally in proportion to the usefulness of its location to people, assuming any improvements involved are the highest and best use for the land.
3. Since location is such an all-important factor in real estate, it is most important that we analyze its neighborhood.
4. The highest and best use is considered to be that which is most productive in terms of rent or amenities for the longest term of use. The property. must be adapted, needed, and available for the use.
5. Usually the highest and best use and the productive land value may be estimated by the same computations.
6. In comparing properties, it is important to use a detailed worksheet on which to consider the main elements of the properties.
7. If it is not possible to use the market approach, then it will be necessary to find the value of the land based on its productive return. The productive land value refers to the net earnings value of the land.

7

How to Estimate the Need for Shopping Centers and Individual Retail Establishments

This chapter provides basic information for real estate appraisal planning concerned with estimating the highest and best use of suburban land, and for estimating the resultant land value for the various retail and service business uses. It may also be used for the downtown areas of cities having a population of approximately 100,000 or less.

Before proceeding with a detailed estimate as to the need for a shopping center you should complete the location analysis of the neighborhood and site in order to judge the probable trade area that the proposed shopping center can logically serve. The following discussion assumes that the site being appraised is the logical location of a shopping center, but the question is: "What size should it be?"

There are two Basic Business Data Tables at the end of this chapter which are provided for illustration (Exhibits 7-5 and 7-6). One is for retail establishments and one for service establishments. The tables were computed from selected S.M.S.A. statistics of the *U.S. Bureau of Census, Census of Business, 1963 Retail Trade and Selected Services.* Secure copies of the publications concerning the location being appraised and compile your own Basic Business Data Tables.[1] (An S.M.S.A. is the abbreviation for "Standard Metropolitan Statistical Area" and concerns an area of such closely related economic interests that the entire area so designated can be considered as a single economic unit in compiling and reporting federal and other statistics. They generally include one or more counties.) Most service and retail businesses encountered in shopping centers are included in the tables.

Secure a suitable map and recent aerial photograph of the area involved for use with the following estimates.

USE OF THE BASIC BUSINESS DATA TABLES

1. Delineation of the trade area involved

Assuming you have a tract of land that is suitable as a shopping center, and your problem is to determine the size, tentatively outline the area that the site would appear to logically serve. Secure the Census Report for your area, and data from the chamber of commerce, the school district, the post office, and so on, as to the total population in the area involved. If the information is out of date you may count the houses in an aerial photo for the area and then multiply by the known median family size in order to make a reasonably good current population estimate. If there is any significant amount of the area that is still to be developed for residential uses, it will be necessary for you to estimate the probable population that will live there within about two years. Ordinarily, it would be inappropriate to consider a time beyond two years for your current estimate since you are primarily concerned with the feasibility of a large current investment. Any land that is to be reserved for development beyond that time should be handled separately and its value estimated entirely on its comparative market value. For the land that will be developed within two years, see the exhibit titled "Land Required For Residential Use" for assistance in estimating the probable dwelling density for undeveloped land. Of course you must consider the limitations of any zoning or restrictions, and the market involved. Multiply the dwelling density involved by the median family

---

[1] Since the enclosed Basic Business Data Tables were prepared, the Bureau of Census has released similar statistics for many central business districts and major retail centers in publications titled, "Major Retail Centers." Where appropriate and available, deduct the central business district data before compiling your tables.

size for the probable income range group to estimate the future population for the undeveloped land. If the undeveloped land area involves a very significant percentage of the population to consider in the trade area, proceed with caution and conservatism.

The delineated trade area should be divided into two areas if it is larger than required for a neighborhood center. The primary area should be the area within a close walking distance and/or about a 5-minute driving range. The primary area is concerned with the potential trade for daily convenience stores such as food and personal service businesses, and the total of the areas is concerned with the other businesses needed to serve the area. The population estimates should be divided accordingly.

PROJECTED RENTAL INCOME FROM HYPOTHETICAL ESTABLISHMENTS						
Kind of Business	Potential Gross Sales	Competitive Gross Sales Estimate	New Establishment Sales Potential	New Establishment Area Required*	Probable Lease Rate Per Year**	Establishment's Annual Gross Rent
Drug Store	$608,000	$397,000	$211,000	3,600 S.F.	$2.40	$8,640

* Square feet of gross leased area.
** Per square foot of gross leased area.
  You may use the form in Exhibit 7-1 to list the pertinent entries. The computations used for the data should be documented for further use, as you will probably want to recheck and revise the computations.

Exhibit 7-1.

2. Preliminary selection of the needed establishments

Use a form similar to Exhibit 7-1 for the following computations.

A. *Potential Gross Sales (for the Area Considered)*

Refer to both types of Basic Business Data Tables that you have previously prepared, then scan the column "Average Population Per Establishment" and, based on the population of the delineated area or sub-area involved, make a tentative selection as to the new businesses that could reasonably be located there in relation to the data.

Referring now to the column "Average Sales Per Person" [2] of the Basic Business Data Tables, multiply the amount shown in the column times the projected population of the section involved to arrive at the potential gross sales for the kind of business considered. If you have any establishments to consider that will draw from a larger area than delineated, you will have to base their estimates on the applicable larger area. Be sure that the estimates for the daily convenience businesses are based on the primary area, as adjusted by a consumer survey which is discussed later in this chapter.

We are now concerned with adjusting the "Average Sales Per Person" to coincide with the consumer expenditures for the income group concerned. The best generally available data or criteria for this adjustment that I have found is *Supplement 3-Part C, BLS Report 237-38 July 1964 to Consumer Expenditures and Income, Urban United States 1961* [3] which provides some usable data for the expenditures mentioned in its "Table 29A, Family Expenditures. . . . All Urban Families and Single Consumers—United States 1961." [4] If you do this type of work you should secure a copy from the Bureau of Labor Statistics for your region. Using Table 29A you may adjust the Potential Gross Sales of Exhibit 7-1 above or below the average indicated by the Basic Business Data Tables, as appropriate. Use the applicable price range column (of the reference) opposite the heading "Money Income after Taxes and Other Money, Receipts."

If the above does not provide for sufficient adjustment you should secure the information during the spot check of the neighborhood as contemplated below. After you become very knowledgeable of the trade area considered you may make judgement adjustment as appropriate.

B. *Computation of the "Competitive Gross Sales Estimate"*

The quickest method to estimate this (and perhaps as good as any) is through the use of the "Average Sales Per Employee" [5] column of the Basic Business Data Tables. First adjust the "Average Sales Per Em-

---

[2] Hereafter, when used, this also refers to "Average Receipts Per Person" as applicable to the business involved.

[3] Special reports are issued every few years for selected cities having over one million in population. Houston, Kansas City, Milwaukee, Minneapolis-St. Paul, and San Diego were covered in the 1963 survey.

[4] To adjust the publication to-date you should refer to consumer price index reports of your chamber of commerce or you should subscribe to Consumer Price Index of the Bureau of Labor Statistics. It is published for the U.S. and 50 selected cities.

[5] Hereafter this reference also applies to "Average Receipts Per Employee" as applicable to the service involved.

ployee" by the same adjustment factors discussed in paragraph "A" above. After the adjustment, make a count of the employees of the competitive stores for the business involved and multiply the total figure by the adjusted "Average Sales Per Employee" to arrive at a preliminary estimate for the "Competitive Gross Sales Estimate." If you are a member of Dun and Bradstreet they can probably secure much of the employment data for most individual businesses in your city.

You may check the gross sales estimate as follows if you can secure the gross leased area of the competitive stores. Most city tax assessors maintain a file showing the area of all buildings on each separately owned tract. When you secure this data you may refer to *The Dollars and Cents of Shopping Centers* as mentioned in paragraph "D" below and use the adjusted "Sales Per Square Foot" for the type of establishment to arrive at a somewhat comparative estimate.

The computations discussed above must be adjusted for purchases made in other trade areas, including the central business district if it has not already been considered. If the Bureau of Census hasn't published "Major Retail Centers" statistics for the city concerned, about the only other way this can be done with any relevancy is to make a spot check of the consumers in the trade area being analyzed. The trade area should be divided into sections for this purpose. The sections should include the same number of dwelling units in so far as possible and then a prescribed number of dwelling units should be selected at random in each. An interview should then be made with the housewife of each selected dwelling in order to determine the family shopping habits for each kind of business concerned. From this survey you may also estimate the potential convenience center sales that may be made to the occupants in the secondary area. See Exhibits 7-2 and 7-3.

A special mimeographed form should be prepared for the survey which should include the following among any other applicable items:

After completion of the consumer survey mentioned above tabulate the information and adjust the Competitive Gross Sales Estimate in Figure 7-1 as appropriate.

C. *New Establishment Sales Potential*

By deducting the "Competitive Gross Sales Estimate" from the "Potential Gross Sales" we arrive at the "New Establishment Sales Potential."

D. *New Establishment Area (Gross Leased Area) Required*

If there is an indicated need for a new establishment, we need to know what size building will be required to handle the sales. You may refer to *The Dollars and Cents of Shopping Centers* published by the Urban Land Institute, 1200 18th Street, N.W., Washington, D. C. It provides tables as to the sales per square foot of the gross leased area. You may

---

CONSUMER SURVEY

1. Approximately what percentage of your purchases from the following listed type business establishments are made in areas outside of the ___(subject)___ area? (Secure an answer for each kind of establishment if possible and list on Exhibit 7-3)

2. If the following new establishments were located at _____(subject)_____, what percentage do you think you would continue to purchase elsewhere? (Secure an answer for each kind, if possible, and list on Exhibit 7-3)

3. Is there any other business you think should be located at the appraised site?

4. What do you think about the quality of the merchandise and service now offered by the establishments serving this area?

5. Is the price range of merchandise too high or low?

6. Do the present stores handle a complete line of merchandise?

7. How many people are in your family?

8. What are your children's ages and sex?

9. What are the approximate ages of the parents?

Exhibit 7-2.

Estimate of Family Purchases Outside the Subject Trade Area
(Before and after the location of the proposed project)

Kind of Business	Other Area Expenditures	
	Before	After
(List each proposed establishment)	List by percent	

Exhibit 7-3.

use these tables to compute the approximate size of the needed establishment by dividing the "New Establishment Sales Potential" by the sales per square foot [6] indicated in *The Dollars and Cents of Shopping Centers.* The publication not only indicates the sales per square foot but the following also: rate of percentage rent, total rent as a percentage of sales, and total charges per square foot—all as to range, median and average for the kind of business and the U. S. region.

E. *Probable Lease Rate Per Year (Per S.F. of the Gross Leased Area)*

Estimate the probable lease rate per year on the basis of the comparable rates in the area. You can use the publication referred to above for guidelines. If you cannot secure sufficient guideline information from it, the publication *Percentage Leases,* published by the National Institute of Real Estate Brokers, 36 South Wabash Ave., Chicago 3, Ill. and *Expenses in Retail Businesses* published by the National Cash Register Co. Merchants Service, Dayton, Ohio may be of considerable help to you.

F. *Establishment's Annual Gross Rent*

When you have estimated the "Probable Lease Rate Per Year," multi-

---

[6] The amounts shown should be adjusted to current prices by use of the Consumer Price Index.

ply the "New Establishment Area Required" by it to arrive at the "Establishment's Annual Gross Rent."

3. Final selection of the new establishment(s)

Check the establishments as to their compatibility if this has not already been considered.[7]

After making any necessary adjustments indicated, you then proceed by selecting the most profitable group of establishments as to rent-producing ability. You may need considerable technical assistance to decide what the best combination is. If you haven't had experience in making the estimates described in this chapter you should employ a specialist, at least for consultation.

Remember, the establishments require a certain minimum amount of land for parking, driveways, etcetera above that required for the buildings, so if you are limited as to land you will also be limited as to the number and size of establishments. Refer to the Exhibit 7-4, "Shopping Center Parking Areas." You will note the recommended parking ratio for planning purposes is three square feet of parking area to one square foot of gross floor area for shopping centers; therefore, to compute the total land area required, multiply the total building area by four. Also see Exhibit 7-4 for value of parking space.

When you finally arrive at the best grouping and size of establishments after considering all pertinent factors, total the column "Establishment's Annual Gross Rent" for those you have accepted to secure the "Projected Income from Hypothetical Establishments." You may then proceed with the estimate of the indicated productive land value as discussed heretofore. Be sure to make adjustments as necessary for the current price level.

Suggested Reference Works:

The Selection of Retail Locations by Richard L. Nelson, F. W. Dodge Corp., N.Y., 1958.

The Dollars and Cents of Shopping Centers and *The Community Builders Handbook* published by the Urban Land Institute, Washington, D.C. They have other fine publications relative to shopping centers.

Part I in *Shopping Towns, U.S.A.—The Planning of Shopping Centers* by Victor Guen and Larry Smith. Reinhold Publishing Corp., New York, N.Y.

Shopping Centers, Design and Operation, Progressive Architecture Library, Reinhold Publishing Corp., New York, N.Y.

---

[7] *The Selection of Retail Locations* by Richard L. Nelson, F. W. Dodge Corp., N.Y., 1958, provides compatibility tables, etc. that are quite helpful.

SHOPPING CENTER PARKING AREAS *

VALUE OF A PARKING STALL

It may be useful to find a value for each parking stall to indicate its relationship to the sales volume of the center <u>after it is in operation</u>.

The value of a parking space can be determined by taking the average unit sale and multiplying it by the average number of passengers arriving per car, times the number of turnovers per stall per day. The result will give the dollar amount sold to the people who park in a stall each day. By multiplying this amount by the number of shopping days per year, you know the value of the stall in terms of annual sales volume. For example, take this hypothetical case:

A – average unit sale (in dollars)	$5.10
C – customers per day	1.5
M – minimum daily turnover per space	3.1
P – percent of customers arriving by car . . .	60%
N – number of shopping days per year	300

A (5.10) x C (1.5) x M (3.1) = $23.72, the hypothetical value per day of each stall. N (300) x $23.72 = $7,116.00 the value of one parking stall per annum in retail volume. - - -

THE PARKING RATIO

. . . Based on its long period of experimentation and experience in shopping center <u>planning</u>, the Community Builders' Council recommends a ratio of 3 square feet of parking area to 1 square foot of gross floor area be used for <u>planning</u> calculations. This method provides a workable measurement for the site's parking capacity. It takes into account the area allocation for the car stall, the moving aisles, access drives, planting spaces, pedestrian walkways--the appurtenances of parking.

---

* Community Builders' Council, *The Community Builder's Handbook,* Executive Edition, Washington, D.C.: © 1960, Page 315 and Page 303, respectively.

Exhibit 7-4.

Exhibit 7–5. BASIC BUSINESS DATA TABLES FOR RETAIL ESTABLISHMENTS *

Kind of Business	DAYTON SMSA** (Consists of Greene, Miami, Montgomery, and Preble Counties, Ohio)			LOS ANGELES-LONG BEACH SMSA** (Coextensive with Los Angeles County, Calif.)		
	Average Population Per Establishment	Average Sales Per Employee***	Average Sales Per Person	Average Population Per Establishment	Average Sales Per Employee***	Average Sales Per Person
LUMBER, BUILDING MATERIALS, HARDWARE, FARM EQUIPMENT DEALERS						
Lumber Yards	16,910	$32,897	$ 20.18	22,788	$48,746	$ 21.98
Building Materials Dealers	14,839	33,641	13.79	22,617	45,139	11.90
Heating, Plumbing Equipment Dealers	30,297	22,911	2.49	75,485	27,876	1.67
Paint, Glass, Wallpaper Stores	14,257	22,293	5.33	14,378	31,703	8.62
Electrical Supply Stores	80,791	12,296	1.20	79,458	20,488	1.25
Hardware Stores	7,990	26,958	18.57	12,150	23,836	10.49
Farm Equipment Dealers	19,135	42,717	10.57	97,400	37,352	1.65
GENERAL MERCHANDISE GROUP STORES						
Department Stores	29,085	18,984	176.65	44,079	24,594	197.62
Limited Price Variety Stores	10,538	13,527	22.18	11,818	14,487	22.75
General Merchandise Stores	29,085	15,150	13.08	16,277	27,980	21.12
Dry Goods Stores	90,890	14,692	.53	26,486	20,627	3.70
Sewing, Needlework Stores	103,874	9,524	.28	43,759	12,961	.82
FOOD STORES						
Grocery Stores, Including Delicatessens	1,085	39,794	305.82	1,562	50,135	360.49
Meat Markets	27,966	20,516	2.62	10,613	34,328	11.82
Fish (Seafood) Markets	181,780	****	.37	88,805	25,418	.90
Fruit Stores, Vegetable Markets	29,085	21,433	1.77	29,895	25,837	3.14
Candy, Nut, Confectionery Stores	16,525	7,836	1.78	25,917	13,090	2.47
Dairy Products Stores	60,593	17,451	1.22	30,654	18,189	2.72
Retail Bakeries, Manufacturing	12,119	10,053	5.23	10,340	8,736	5.91
Retail Bakeries, Nonmanufacturing	45,445	12,464	1.18	20,752	19,456	2.25
Egg and Poultry Dealers	103,874	****	1.07	61,612	24,467	.97

* Computations shown are by the author, based on the U.S. Bureau of Census, Census of Business, 1963, Retail Trade, (for the State of California and for the State of Ohio); U.S. Government Printing Office, Washington, D.C.

** For 1963.

*** Or nonemployer proprietor.

Kind of Business	DAYTON SMSA* (Consists of Greene, Miami, Montgomery, and Preble Counties, Ohio)			LOS ANGELES-LONG BEACH SMSA* (Coextensive with Los Angeles County, Calif.)		
	Average Population Per Establishment	Average Sales Per Employee**	Average Sales Per Person	Average Population Per Establishment	Average Sales Per Employee**	Average Sales Per Person
AUTOMOTIVE DEALERS						
Passenger Car Dealers, Franchised	6,992	$63,717	$231.69	9,998	$68,249	$289.16
Passenger Car Dealers, Nonfranchised	8,358	42,288	12.33	8,578	53,391	25.18
Tire, Battery, Accessory Dealers	10,853	23,615	12.15	6,901	25,766	18.58
Home and Auto Supply Stores	36,356	27,196	3.63	91,497	31,541	2.72
Household Trailer Dealers	242,374	***	.15	43,444	63,283	7.84
GASOLINE SERVICE STATIONS						
Gasoline Service Stations	955	25,167	108.44	1,013	26,000	126.79
APPAREL, ACCESSORY STORES						
Men's, Boys' Clothing and Furnishing Stores	15,148	20,766	11.85	7,832	25,736	23.05
Custom Tailors	181,780	18,250	.20	30,044	11,574	1.21
Women's Ready-to-Wear Stores	11,728	16,803	16.06	4,045	19,258	33.51
Millinery Stores	121,187	10,188	.22	113,939	14,677	.31
Corset, Lingerie Stores	***	***	***	73,644	15,842	.81
Hosiery Stores	727,121	***	***	464,521	23,939	.19
Apparel, Accessory, Other Specialty Stores	80,791	20,340	1.31	18,467	16,325	4.42
Furriers, Fur Shops	145,424	***	***	58,629	27,293	1.71
Family Clothing Stores	29,085	18,820	14.78	19,996	20,820	11.31
Men's Shoe Stores	145,424	29,833	.49	74,553	23,051	1.41
Women's Shoe Stores	90,890	21,371	1.82	35,945	25,275	5.50
Children's, Juveniles' Shoe Stores	727,121	***	***	90,131	22,868	.89
Family Shoe Stores	11,361	***	***	10,048	27,704	11.84
Children's, Infants' Wear Stores	103,874	***	***	26,486	18,284	3.12

Exhibit 7-5 (continued).

* For 1963.
** Or nonemployer proprietor.
*** Basic data unavailable.

Exhibit 7-5 (continued).

Kind of Business	DAYTON SMSA* (Consists of Greene, Miami, Montgomery, and Preble Counties, Ohio)			LOS ANGELES-LONG BEACH SMSA* (Coextensive with Los Angeles County, Calif.)		
	Average Population Per Establishment	Average Sales Per Employee**	Average Sales Per Person	Average Population Per Establishment	Average Sales Per Employee**	Average Sales Per Person
FURNITURE, HOME FURNISHINGS, EQUIPMENT STORES						
Furniture Stores	5,771	$33,028	$ 34.52	4,133	$33,949	$ 44.03
Floor Covering Stores	33,051	34,165	4.56	16,233	33,976	12.53
Drapery, Curtain, Upholstery Stores	23,456	14,689	2.08	19,417	16,118	3.29
China, Glassware, Metalware Stores	363,561	***	.06	64,242	27,347	2.59
Miscellaneous Home Furnishings Stores	363,561	***	.01	29,033	16,373	1.90
Household Appliance Stores	8,170	27,515	11.47	10,861	34,358	14.66
Radio, Television Stores	17,312	26,360	7.14	13,156	34,785	13.55
Record Shops	66,102	16,682	.50	39,469	22,016	1.60
Musical Instrument Stores	33,051	26,479	4.41	24,749	24,065	4.42
EATING, DRINKING PLACES						
Restaurants, Lunchrooms	1,570	8,378	54.90	1,050	8,823	93.76
Cafeterias	23,456	7,783	6.51	26,486	8,922	6.48
Refreshment Places	3,446	9,399	12.77	3,359	8,385	16.30
Caterers	14,542	7,551	5.18	6,762	13,385	10.77
Drinking Places (Alcoholic Beverages)	1,687	10,710	30.59	1,933	10,608	26.91
DRUG STORES, PROPRIETARY STORES						
Drug Stores	4,131	21,027	41.41	4,490	26,101	64.44
Proprietary Stores	51,937	9,833	1.38	95,854	24,403	1.52

* For 1963.
** Or nonemployer proprietor.
*** Basic data unavailable.

Exhibit 7-5 (continued).

Kind of Business	DAYTON SMSA* (Consists of Greene, Miami, Montgomery, and Preble Counties, Ohio)			LOS ANGELES-LONG BEACH SMSA* (Coextensive with Los Angeles County, Calif.)		
	Average Population Per Establishment	Average Sales Per Employee**	Average Sales Per Person	Average Population Per Establishment	Average Sales Per Employee**	Average Sales Per Person
OTHER RETAIL STORES						
Liquor Stores	6,551	$43,193	$ 22.07	2,801	$40,892	$ 57.55
Antique Stores	45,445	***	.26	37,508	15,611	.77
Secondhand Stores	9,443	***	3.33	7,320	21,219	8.39
Book Stores	145,424	20,667	.77	32,999	18,459	3.20
Stationery Stores	45,445	14,305	1.36	22,039	17,360	4.35
Sporting Goods Stores	20,775	***	3.49	16,821	24,560	5.56
Bicycle Shops	145,424	***	.14	45,404	22,888	1.26
Hay, Grain Feed Stores	23,456	55,015	15.13	68,622	89,437	7.86
Other Farm Supply Stores	51,937	41,567	1.71	134,195	20,725	1.22
Garden Supply Stores	30,297	19,048	2.72	42,527	21,600	2.75
Jewelry Stores	10,538	17,772	6.33	8,139	26,701	13.81
Coal and Wood Dealers	51,937	16,308	1.46	335,487	22,310	.26
Ice Dealers	363,561	***	.08	241,550	11,674	.09
Fuel Oil Dealers	55,932	34,690	2.00	402,585	39,923	.67
Bottled Gas Dealers	72,712	23,682	2.15	262,555	28,409	.60
Florists	13,220	13,782	4.34	10,539	13,389	4.45
Cigar Stores, Stands	42,772	15,214	.59	40,258	24,580	1.40
News Dealers, Newsstands	30,297	14,808	1.59	25,480	16,415	1.96
Camera, Photographic Supply Stores	66,102	22,800	1.57	24,155	31,491	7.17
Gift, Novelty, Souvenir Shops	30,297	9,786	.75	13,449	13,141	2.46
Optical Goods Stores	13,983	17,607	4.19	10,358	16,386	4.17
Typewriter Stores	103,874	20,368	.53	125,808	20,667	.78
Luggage, Leather Goods Stores	121,187	***	***	90,131	18,709	.62
Hobby, Toy, Game Shops	38,270	19,262	1.11	20,895	16,623	3.17
Religious Goods Stores	727,121	***	***	116,130	16,912	.45
Pet Shops	60,593	***	.21	29,033	14,737	1.11

* For 1963.
** Or nonemployer proprietor.
*** Basic data unavailable.

Exhibit 7-6.

BASIC BUSINESS DATA TABLE FOR SELECTED SERVICE ESTABLISHMENTS*
HOUSTON SMSA
(Coextensive with Harris County, Texas)

Kind of Business	Average Population Per Establishment	Average Receipts Per Employee** (Per Year)	Average Receipts Per Person (Per Year)
Self-Service Laundries	4,010	$ 6,750	$ 2.89
Cleaning, Dyeing Plants, Except Rug Cleaning	4,440	6,314	13.22
Self-Service Drycleaning	124,316	***	***
Beauty Shops, Including Combination Beauty, Barber	972	4,537	12.15
Barber Shops	1,522	4,673	6.24
Cleaning, Pressing Shops	7,674	6,883	1.47
General Auto Repair	1,804	11,118	16.17
Radio, Television Repair	2,932	8,892	4.82
Motion Picture Theaters, Except Drive-In	31,876	10,330	5.47
Drive-In Motion Picture Theaters	77,697	10,080	1.91
Bowling Establishments	35,519	7,875	4.31
Amusement Parks, Kiddie Parks, Theme Parks	155,395	20,938	.27

* For 1963.
** Or nonemployer proprietor.
*** Basic data unavailable.
Note: Computations shown are by the author, based on the U.S. Bureau of Census, Census of Business, 1963, Selected Services, (For State of Texas); U.S. Government Printing Office, Washington, D.C.

SUMMARY

1. Prepare "Basic Business Data Tables" from the Retail Trade, Selected Services and Major Retail Centers publications of Bureau of Census for the S.M.S.A. involved.
2. Delineate the trade area involved.
3. Make a preliminary selection of the needed establishments based on your "Basic Business Data Tables," and recommended adjustments.
4. After making the necessary adjustments to the preliminary selection, including the consideration of compatibility of the businesses, select the most profitable group of establishments as to rent-producing ability.
5. Be sure you have provided ample parking space.

8

How to Estimate
Market Value

MARKET APPROACH

The premise of the market approach is: The value of a property does not exceed the value of an acceptable substitute. The value to the typical buyer is the basis of comparison. It is related to the law of supply and demand. This is one of, if not the most important principle in the valuation of real estate. It is the basis of this approach which is another standard approach used to estimate value. The market approach is also known as the comparative approach and comparative market data approach.

The basic procedure in estimating the value by the market approach is that of comparing the subject appraised property with comparable properties that have been sold recently and with those that are currently for sale. Great weight is given to the supply and demand of comparable properties, and to any trends that may have been occurring in the market that would influence the possible value of the property being appraised. The appraised property is compared as to all the major factors involved, and its comparative value is estimated based upon comparable properties. After several properties have been compared with the appraised, the typical indicated value is accepted as the market value of the property. This must be tempered with the supply and demand situation at the time of the appraisal, realizing that the appraised value is a matter of opinion.

It should be remembered that the market approach is only one approach to the appraisal of real estate. It might seem that if the purpose of an appraisal is to estimate the market value of the property, the value indicated by the market approach should be used; however, this is not necessarily true, as the comparisons indicate what someone paid and not all the sellers and buyers are fully informed as to the value of property. The market approach is based on a comparison of past sales, with current asking prices of properties and trends. However, an interpretation of this data might not necessarily indicate what the final opinion should be unless it is compared to the other methods used in estimating value, for other considerations are involved which should be considered. A form of market data is also used in the economic and the physical approaches: The physical approach is based on current prices of materials and labor; in the economic approach the rental income is a market estimate as is also the operating expense and some forms of the capitalization rate. Accordingly, all appropriate methods should be used to formulate the value estimate.

COLLECTION OF COMPARABLE MARKET DATA

First, it should be emphasized that a great deal of time can be used in the collection of market data. When appraising a property, the uninitiated may have some problem in limiting the area of research. Naturally, if you cover an area larger than that required to appraise the property, you will have expended more time and expense than necessary. Normally, in residential properties one would not search an area greater than the subdivision involved if it concerns properties of a similar price range. This area would not be exceeded except when insufficient comparables were found. Normally, three or four comparable sales are considered sufficient for residential properties and five or more as appropriate for commercial properties. This, of course, will vary depending upon the actual circumstances involved. It may be necessary to search competing areas, depending upon the type of property and market activity.

The actual collection, analysis and interpretation of market data can become one of the most detailed and complex operations involved in the appraisal process. Data as to sales that have occurred in the area involved may concern the last year or several years, as required under the circumstances. A few or a great quantity of sales may be involved. The motivation of the seller and buyer may be difficult to determine exactly in some instances. The length of time that properties were on the market may vary considerably and may be of great significance. Income tax considerations of the principals involved may be important. The financing terms involved in the property sold may be of great importance. The actual comparison of the property sold to that being appraised can be broken down into major components of significance or into minute items.

In the market approach we must also consider comparable properties that are for sale. In some instances, properties that have been offered for sale but have been withdrawn from the market will be of some significance in estimating the market value. This information may be somewhat difficult to obtain.

The following are also important items of consideration. Data as to owner occupancy versus rental occupancy can be of importance, depending on the motivation of the typical buyer involved. The possibility of the typical buyer deciding to construct a new building may be of considerable importance. This, of course, would be limited by vacant land available for such use, and/or to the feasibility of removing any present improvements if no vacant land is available. Would it be more economically feasible for such parties to actually build their own property in the neighborhood, rather than to buy or rent? Are there any adverse influences in the neighborhood, such as smoke fumes or noises, which could become a hazard or a nuisance?

In comparing the subject appraised to past sales, properties for sale, or past offerings, adjustment must be made for any differences from the subject appraised property. If at all possible, the properties compared must have similar highest and best uses. They should be similar properties in size and design, and have similar forms of depreciation and adverse influences, if any.

The foregoing is an indication of how detailed comparisons may become. It is generally advisable to use standard blank forms in the collection and comparison of market data, and I include copies of forms that have been helpful to me in this area. In the following sections the uses of these forms are described in the discussion of the somewhat detailed procedures involved in the comparison of market data. Of course, each appraiser may want to design his own forms. The important thing is that he use a reliable and standard method to reduce the time and expense involved and to assure the proper end result.

Exhibit 8—1. Market Approach Form.

MARKET APPROACH:

Area and time period of research for sales of comparable properties:

Data as to comparable sales found:

Data as to comparable properties for sale:

Supply and demand as to comparable properties:

Trends and Comments:

INDICATED VALUE BY THE MARKET APPROACH: $_____

Please refer to Exhibit 8-1, "Market Approach," below which is a work-sheet that may or may not be included in the appraisal report. It is very important to consider the supply and demand of comparable properties and any trends that may be occurring in the market that would influence the possible value of the property to be appraised. Otherwise, only past history would be reflected. As concerns the *Area and time period of research for sales of comparable properties* mentioned on the form, normally only those that have sold within about the last year are used. If you can't find sufficient comparables that have sold that recently, you will have to use the most recent that you can find. You may secure information concerning sales that have occurred from the county records, abstract or title companies, or tax assessors. You may secure further information from real estate dealers and owners. You should ascertain that a bona fide sale has occurred before using the data. Normally, it is best to secure sales that have occurred in the same neighborhood as the subject appraised. If you can't find them in the same neighborhood, it will be necessary for you to go into competing areas. This is necessary quite frequently in appraising commercial and industrial properties. In any event, in using the form in Exhibit 8-1, record the area and the time period of research involved for the comparable properties based on when the comparative sales occurred.

Before completing the form, it will be necessary to compare the data as indicated below.

COMPARISON OF MARKET DATA FOR 1- AND 2-FAMILY DWELLINGS

We are now concerned with the *Data as to comparable sales found.* Please refer to Exhibit 8-2, "*Market Data Comparison (Residential Properties)*." We must have certain information, as noted on the form, concerning the comparable properties in order to make a comparison. Note the items listed in the left-hand column of the form in Exhibit 8-2. The form is self-explanatory. Enter the sales price and date sold in the column headed *Data*. The market may have changed since the sale. As to the *Motivation of Sale,* we are concerned with whether it was a normal sale or whether it was a forced sale, etc. (This information is not always available.) When a property must be sold immediately, it is usually sold for less than market value. Also, investors don't pay quite as much for properties as a potential occupant-owner might pay. If we are dealing with properties that are typically owner-occupied, we should be concerned

Exhibit 8-2.　　**MARKET DATA COMPARISON** *
(Residential Properties)

SALE NO.								
STREET ADDRESS								
	DATA	ADJUSTMENT	DATA	ADJUSTMENT	DATA	ADJUSTMENT	DATA	ADJUSTMENT
SALES PRICE								
DATE OF SALE								
MOTIVATION OF SALE								
LOT SIZE AND APPEAL OF LOCATION								
GARAGE(S)								
LIVING AREA OF DWELLING								
ARCHITECTURAL APPEAL: QUALITY, APPEARANCE UTILITY								
EXTRAS								
AGE & CONDITION								
MISCELLANEOUS								
COMPARATIVE SALES PRICE								

FORM NO. 6-D, WINSTEAD APPRAISAL SERVICE, HOUSTON

* Winstead, *Appraisal Practice Course I*, Houston, Texas: Winstead Appraisal Service, © 1961, page 93.

with properties having similar ownership. Next, we need to know the *Lot Size and Appeal of Location.* These are very important factors. As to the *Garage(s),* we must consider the size of the garage, whether detached or attached. Next is the *Living Area of Dwelling.* The square foot or cubic foot area of the dwelling is listed. If unknown you will need to secure a good estimate. Next we need to know the *Architectural Appeal* of the property, such as the *Quality,* the *Appearance* and the *Utility* of it. Naturally, if we are dealing with a brick house, we should compare it with another brick house. If possible, compare it with a property that is comparable in quality, appearance and utility. If there is any material difference, we will have to make an adjustment for it. Next we are concerned with *Extras,* such as air conditioning, central heating, built-in range and oven, and so on. Any significant item not the same as the property appraised should be considered. We must consider the *Age and Condition* of the property, and then, under *Miscellaneous,* any other item that might pertain to the comparable marketability of the property.

If at all possible, this form or a similar form should be used, but in any event, a comparison must be made . . . this is very important. The market approach is normally the best approach that can be used for residential properties, particularly for the older properties.

Assuming that you have completed the information concerning three or four comparable sales, designate an index or item number to each sale. In the last column, or in a column on another page, enter the information concerning the appraised property so that you can readily compare it with the comparable sales. Complete the entry of all the information as appropriate. Then compare each item with that item of the appraised property and adjust on the basis of how you think the typical buyer would. Starting with the *Date of Sale,* if the property being compared was sold, say, a year ago, it might be that the values have gone up some since then, and it might be worth more now. If the property sold has increased in value $250, enter a plus $250 under adjustment. Now consider the *Motivation of Sale.* Of course, most sales are bona fide transfers involving actual sales of the property, but if this is not apparent you must ascertain it. If it was a forced sale, and you think the party bought it for, say, $500 less than it should have sold for, you would add a plus $500 to adjust it to a sale representing the typical market price. If possible, you should only compare sales involving similar motivations. If there would be a much larger adjustment for motivation, I would not use the comparable. Ordinarily any multiple of adjustment would not be for less than $100.

The next item to consider is the *Lot Size and Appeal of Location*. If there is any material difference in the size of the lot (site), make a plus or minus adjustment for the estimated difference in value concerned, and do the same thing as to the appeal of location, bearing in mind the attitude of the typical purchaser of the property concerned. Remember that you are trying to adjust the sale so that you will arrive at the comparative price of the appraised property. If an item of the sold property is worth more than the appraised, deduct that amount, and if it is worth less add the difference to the sales price of the comparable sale. Next is *Garage(s)*. Compare as to size and construction and then make the appropriate up or down adjustments. Next is the *Living Area of Dwelling*. Ordinarily, you would adjust for the difference in the estimated cost of the two dwellings involved. Next is *Architectural Appeal: Quality, Appearance, Utility*. This is largely a matter of observation and you will have to adjust the property up or down as compared to the appraised property, based on your estimate of market reaction. The next line involves *Extras*. Consider any extras which are different from those possessed by the appraised property. Next is *Age and Condition* of the property. Adjust for the difference in the physical deterioration of the two properties. If there is a difference in age and condition that is apparent, adjust the comparable up or down as appropriate.

Under *Miscellaneous*, try to cover all items that were not considered heretofore. If there is any economic or functional obsolescence involved in the comparable that is not involved in the appraised property, make the necessary adjustment in the comparable here if not deducted elsewhere. Ordinarily, for this purpose, you should not attempt to compare properties with different economic or functional obsolescence. Check over the properties for any other items not mentioned and make the necessary adjustment. After all the adjustments have been made, total up the column, adjusting for plus and minus factors, and the net amount will be the *Comparative Sales Price* based on that comparable.

After following this procedure for each other comparable used, check each one again carefully; as a general rule, you will have to make some additional adjustments.

SELECTION OF THE MARKET VALUE INDICATED

After you have reviewed the data and made appropriate readjustments, you may average out the indicated comparative sales prices of the properties compared, or you may assume the typical price indicated by the compared properties as the indicated comparative value. It is generally considered proper to use the typical price indicated. Of course, there is not much choice where only three comparables are used, as the two closest related prices should be indicative of the value. If several comparable properties are used, say 5, 6 or 7, you will perhaps have enough to indicate an upper limit of value and a lower limit of value. Then, by the process of elimination, you arrive at what you feel is the indicated value. A good method to select the indicated value when more properties are compared is to select the most common values indicated, take that group and select the bracket indicated, and then make the final selection from the bracket.

Refer now to *Supply and demand as to comparable properties* in Exhibit 8-1 and consider the volume sold in the past year and the amount for sale now. Provide your estimate of the present situation. Under *Trends and comments,* indicate any general trends found that concern a decrease or increase in value of the neighborhood properties, and provide your estimate of the effects. Consider all of the information as developed on the form (Exhibit 8-1), and make a final estimate of the comparative market value indicated and enter the amount on the form. Usually, the value indicated by the market approach will be that as indicated on the form in Exhibit 8-2, but some of the data on the form in Exhibit 8-1 may indicate an adjustment to be in order.

A form similar to that in Exhibit 6-4 is very useful in recording sales information.

METHOD OF ESTIMATING MARKET VALUE OF APARTMENTS AND COMMERCIAL PROPERTIES

Comparison method

You may compare apartment, commercial and even some industrial properties on a form similar to Exhibit 8-2 providing you have closely comparable properties. (Otherwise you should use the "Gross Rent Multiple Method" discussed in the next paragraph.) The following is a suggested list of items to consider, which you may adjust as appropriate:

Sales Price	Location
Date of Sale	Site
Motivation of Sale	Overall Price of Property
Age, Condition and Depreciation	per S.F. of Building
Size and Utility	Income and Expense
Quality	Miscellaneous
Appearance	

Gross annual rent multiple

In order to use this method with any reliability, the appraiser must have considerable data as to the multiples of many similar properties. In constructing such data, the gross annual rent multiple is computed by dividing the sales price by the gross annual income of the property. When such multiples are available on sufficient comparable properties to estimate the typical multiple, it can be used as an indication of the comparative market value. The indicated value is computed as follows:

Gross annual income of property	$20,000
Indicated gross annual rent multiple	6
	$120,000

This method should only be used when complete market data is unavailable, and then only when based on reliable information.

DISCUSSION

There is a close relationship between the market, physical, and economic approaches. In the physical approach, in estimating the replacement or reproduction cost of the property, the cost or prices used are based on the current market prices of the items concerned, including the labor costs.[1] The economic approach is based on the rental income and expense of the property at the time.[2] The better your understanding of the underlying forces affecting market value, the better your ability to appraise a property and to correlate all three approaches used to estimate the value.

Cover the full sweep of the market, the past as applied to the present, and trends indicating the future in so far as possible. No one, of course, can estimate the future to any high degree of accuracy. However, one can look at the past as it affects today, consider the thinking of the current day as to the current value and expected changes, and arrive at a value that is reasonable at the time it is made. No one can do more except by fortuitous circumstance. Certainly, one cannot become merely a recorder of past history and base his estimates of value entirely on the past, for if the market was thus formed, it would never change. If the market indicates anything, it indicates change. It is never exactly static.

---

[1] Unless a different appraisal date is involved.

SUMMARY

1. The premise of the market approach is: The value of a property does not exceed the value of an acceptable substitute.
2. For comparison, three or four nearby comparable sales are used for the typical residential appraisal and five or more for the typical commercial appraisal, depending on the current market activity.
3. The market data must be thoroughly analyzed and weighed as to its comparability.
4. The supply and demand situation is an extremely important factor and must be considered.
5. Motivation of the sale is very important.
6. Consider the indicated trends as they affect the market value of properties.

How to Appraise
Rent Producing
Properties

ECONOMIC APPROACH

The three appraisal approaches—physical (cost), market, and economic (income)—also apply to the appraisal of income properties; however, the economic approach has added significance for such properties, as investors do not ordinarily pay more than the value indicated by it.

In this approach the income is the yardstick of value. The premise of the economic approach is: the current value of a property is the present worth of the right to collect the future net benefits from the property. This approach tends to set the lower limit of value. The potential future net earnings of the real estate are the basis of the value estimated by this approach. The net earnings (or benefits) involved are based on the following:

> Gross benefits expectable:
>   Gross contract and economic rent for the real estate from
>   all sources for all spaces as if 100 per cent occupied
> Less expenses expectable:
>   (1) Vacancy and collection losses
>   (2) All other real estate expenses

Economic rent is used here as that rent reasonably expected if the property were offered on the market for a reasonable length of time. Capitalization is the name of the procedure used for this type of valuation. It involves the conversion of the future anticipated income into present value.

The methods discussed below are the principal forms of capitalization now in use.

ANNUITY CAPITALIZATION

This is a process of computing the sum of the present values of future payments of an annuity whereby each payment is discounted for loss of interest return for the time interval to date due. The efficacy of the process is indicated by the fact that the present worth of an annuity will be the same as the principal amount of a loan when the periodic payments, term, and rate of interest involved are the same.

This form of capitalization is concerned with income from real estate that constitutes an annuity type of income, that is, a series of specified rent payments made at equal stated intervals for a prescribed period of time in accordance with a contract. If the property has a lease by a financially responsible individual or organization, the future net income stream based on the lease is discounted to find the present worth by the use of annuity tables as discussed under the appraisal of lease interests. If the lease is of short duration, say less than four years, and the difference in contract rent and economic rent is not significant, it would ordinarily not be treated as an annuity.

There are several different types of annuities from real estate. See the chapter on appraisal of lease interests for a detailed discussion. The Inwood Tables of "Present Worth of One Per Annum" are most commonly used to discount level annuity payments. An annuity income that increases or decreases at a fixed rate and is payable at equal stated intervals for a definite period of time is an unusual type for which special increasing and decreasing annuity tables are used to estimate the worth. A series of periodic payments which are to run indefinitely are classed as a *perpetuity* type of annuity, but compound interest tables are not required for estimating its present worth. Most real estate appraisers do not ordinarily think of a perpetuity as an annuity. Accordingly, capitalization by the perpetuity process is discussed below. Annuity capitalization involving annuities for prescribed terms ending at a specific time is discussed in detail in the chapter pertaining to the appraisal of lease interests.

PERPETUITY CAPITALIZATION

This is the most basic form of capitalization. It is used in the valuation of land when its income may be assumed to continue indefinitely.[1] The procedure involved is merely to divide the annual net income of the land by the interest return generally required by investors, viz:

Annual net income from land $6,000
Capitalization:
$6,000/.06 = $100,000, the land value.

This is true if .06 is the correct rate because then $6,000 is .06 of the total value. Dividing by the rate produces the 100 per cent amount. This is proven as follows: .06 × $100,000 amounts to $6,000. This amounts to the same as saying the present value of a perpetuity of 1 per annum = 1/i. In this case "i" represents the applicable interest rate. Therefore, if, for instance, you desire to establish a scholarship of $6,000 per year and you can secure 6 per cent per year on the investment, you must keep $100,000 so invested.

DIRECT CAPITALIZATION

The procedure used by this method is similar in form to that for perpetuity capitalization except that it may also be used to capitalize the annual net income not only from the land but from the building also. This is permissible because the capitalization rate used is an over-all rate that represents the relationship between a property and the annual net income to the property. The overall rate to be used should be the typical rate indicated by several comparable properties that have been sold recently. An over-all rate is computed by dividing the net annual income of a comparable property by its sales price. This is repeated for each property of the comparable group from which the typical rate is selected.

Example:

$$\text{Over-all rate} = \frac{\text{Annual net income } \$8,250}{\text{Sales price of property } \$100,000} = .0825 \text{ (or 8.25\%)}$$

Assuming that the .0825 is the typical over-all rate indicated by the group of comparables and $8,250 is the annual net income of the property being appraised, the following procedure is used to estimate the capitalized value:

$$\$8,250/.0825 = \$100,000.$$

---

[1] The land in this case is not considered to depreciate.

This procedure can be used for capitalizing the annual net income of land or that for both land and building. The overall capitalization rate is a fixed relationship between the value of the property and its net annual income. Accordingly it is just a divisor considered to properly indicate the value under the conditions assumed.

MORTGAGE-EQUITY CAPITALIZATION METHOD

This method involves the capitalization of the annual net income to the equity after debt service but before any allowance for recapture of investment. A new mortgage loan of $75,000 is assumed below. The capitalization rate of 9% used is the assumed return on the equity investment required by typical investors. The amount of the new mortgage loan is added to the equity valuation to produce the total value of the property.

Example:

Annual net income before recapture	$ 9,000
Less annnal debt service (Principal and interest)	
$608.58 per month × 12 (16 yr. loan at 6%)	7,303
Annual net income to equity	$ 1,697
Equity valuation:	
$1,697/.09	$18,856
New mortgage loan	75,000
Total indicated valuation	$93,856
Say,	$94,000

Ordinarily this procedure should only be used when a new loan can be secured on the property, otherwise use another method, such as Ellwood's, discussed below. If it can be refinanced, you may capitalize as above and apportion the value according to the actual loan balance. If there is a burdensome mortgage loan on the property and it can't be refinanced with an equitable one, the effect of this on the market value of the property should be considered in the other approaches.

ELLWOOD'S CAPITALIZATION METHOD

This is another form of mortgage-equity capitalization. It was presented in *Ellwood Tables for Real Estate Appraising and Financing* in 1959, and in a revised edition in 1967. It is a very important method.

The book provides special tables of base rates for two-thirds and three-fourths mortgage loans and formulas to compute the rates for other mortgage ratios, etcetera. The tables or formulas can be used to construct capitalization rates to appraise properties involving problems similar to the following:

Assumptions:

A property has $40,000 of net annual income (before depreciation or debt service). The investor is purchasing the property with a 75 per cent loan (loan 75%, equity 25%) at 6 per cent interest per annum with full amortization by level installments in 20 years. The investor wants a 12 per cent yield on the 25 per cent equity, and he believes he can sell the property for 9 per cent less than his cost after ownership of the property for ten years. If the instructions provided in the *Ellwood Tables* are followed, a capitalization rate can be constructed that will provide for these assumptions, and a capitalization of the net income with the rate will indicate the present value of the property based on the assumptions. It is necessary to have the *Ellwood Tables* to construct the rates with ease and speed even though you may be familiar with the business mathematics involved.

STRAIGHT-LINE RECAPTURE CAPITALIZATION [2]

If a property is improved with a building and rented (not leased) on a periodic basis for an indefinite period, or on a short-term lease basis for a specific level amount per period not constituting an annuity, the straight-line recapture capitalization method is commonly used.[3] This type of capitalization assumes that the building will have a more or less definite economic life when a new building will be required if it is desired to continue the operation. Accordingly, straight-line recapture capitalization requires that a return be made at each period of rent collection to provide for the complete recapture of the capital invested in the building improvements by the end of their forecasted economic life. The rental income estimate should be based on that currently attainable. When formulating the capitalization rate for this type of capi-

---

[2] Also known as straight capitalization—straight line depreciation method.

[3] Actually this form of capitalization gradually reduces the amount of income assumed each year, which is normally about as well as anyone can forecast the market. The rate of reduction may be computed as follows:

Interest rate × recapture rate/interest rate + recapture rate.

talization, it is customary to base it on the market rate applicable to the property. Frequently it is constructed by adding the pro rata amount of the interest rate that would be charged for a mortgage loan on the property to the pro rata amount of the return required for such equity investments. To this is added the rate required each year to recapture the investment by the end of the economic life of the improvements. For instance, if a building is assumed to last 40 years, a 2½ per cent return would be required each year to provide for recapture of the capital in the improvements.[4] The total rate is termed the building capitalization rate and, as you can see, it is made up by adding the indicated interest rate to the return required to recapture the present value of the improvements. The land receives only an interest return because the land can be used over and over again after the present building is gone. The following illustrates one form of this type of capitalization:

Net Annual Income to Property	$ 10,000	
Less Return on Land		
$25,000 @ 6%	$ 1,500	
	$ 8,500	
Capitalization: $8,500/9%[5] =	$ 94,444	
Land Value	25,000	
	$119,444	

RESIDUAL TECHNIQUES AS USED IN STRAIGHT-LINE CAPITALIZATION

There are three basic techniques, which are known as the residual techniques of capitalization. They are the building, the land, and the property residual techniques. They are used particularly with the straight-line method. However, they may be adjusted to most other methods.

Building residual technique

Please refer to Exhibit 9-1. The entries in this example involve a hypothetical appraisal and should not be used with any other. You will note a vacancy and collection loss was deducted from the estimated gross

---

[4] Sometimes the "recapture rate" is termed "future depreciation rate."
[5] This is made up of the interest rate of 6% and recapture rate of 3%.

EXAMPLE OF BUILDING RESIDUAL TECHNIQUE
(To be used when the land value is known best)

Assumption: Rental rate: $1,250 per month. The landlord is to maintain the property inside and out. No utilities are to be paid by the landlord. The building is rented unfurnished. Terms of rent: on month to month basis.

FORECASTED ANNUAL INCOME AND EXPENSES

Estimated Gross Income $15,000
Vacancy and Collection Losses (5%)   750
Effective Gross Income $14,250

(The total of expenses, as noted below, is assumed for purpose of this illustration. Normally, the expenses should be listed in detail.)

Total Expenses . . . . $ 4,250
Net Income to Property $10,000
Less Income Attributable to Land, $20,000 at 6%   1,200
Income Attributable to Building for Interest and Recapture . . . . . $ 8,800

$8,800 Is a 10%* Annual Return On $88,000
Land Value   20,000
ESTIMATED VALUE BY THE ECONOMIC APPROACH $108,000

* Capitalization rate:
  Assumed interest rate 6%
  Recapture of capital (return of building's value) 4%
    (4% is the return required to return the value of the building by the end of the estimated remaining economic
    life of 25 years)
  Building capitalization rate 10%

Exhibit 9-1.

EXAMPLE OF LAND RESIDUAL TECHNIQUE
(To be used when the building value is known best)

Assumptions: All data up to and including the net income is the same as the previous example.

Net Income to Property..	$10,000
Less Income Attributable to Buildings $88,000 at 10%*............	8,800
Income Attributable to Land...................................	$ 1,200

$1,200 is a 6%** Return On	$20,000
Buildings	88,000
ESTIMATED VALUE BY THE ECONOMIC APPROACH	$108,000

---

* Building capitalization rate of 6% interest + 4% for recapture = 10%.

** Only the interest rate applies to land, because it will be there after the building is gone and may be used again.

Exhibit 9-2.

income, and this resulted in a net of $14,250 for the effective gross annual income. The total expenses involved with the property were assumed to be $4,250. The expenses were not itemized in order to facilitate the example. Deducting the $4,250 from the effective gross income leaves a net income to the property of $10,000. Since the object of this technique is to determine the building value when the land value is known, it is necessary to deduct the interest return on the land. In this case the land is worth $20,000 and the proper interest is assumed to be 6 per cent for this type of property. Accordingly, 6 per cent of

$20,000 or $1,200 indicates the income attributable to the land. Deducting $1,200 from the $10,000 net income to property leaves the income attributable to the buildings in the amount of $8,800. The capitalization rate is assumed to be 10 per cent which is made up of 6 per cent for the interest rate and 4 per cent for recapture of the value of the buildings. The estimated remaining economic life of the improvements is considered to be 25 years. The property is then capitalized by dividing $8,800 (income attributable to the improvement), by .10, which indicates a value of $88,000, making the total indicated value by the economic approach, $108,000.

Land residual technique

See Exhibit 9-2. In the example we are involved with the same property and the same income and expenses. Therefore, starting with the net income to the property of $10,000, deduct the return for both interest and recapture of the value for the building. As you will note, the same capitalization rate is used for this as in the first example. Ten per cent (.06 + .04) of the building value of $88,000 amounts to $8,800. Deducting this from $10,000 (the net income to the property) leaves an income attributable to the land in the amount of $1,200. This is the interest return for the land. Since the land itself is not considered to depreciate, for this purpose the return to the land is divided only by the interest rate, which is 6 per cent in this case. Dividing $1,200 by .06 indicates a value of $20,000. Adding the value of the improvements of $88,000 to the land value indicates an estimated value of $108,000 by the economic approach, the same as we found in the first example.

Property residual technique

Refer to Exhibit 9-3. You will note that we are still involved with the same property. Therefore, starting with the net income to the property of $10,000 it is necessary that we deduct the return required to recapture the value of the buildings (but not interest thereon) by the end of its economic life. Since the building is valued at $88,000 we deduct 4 per cent of that, or $3,520. This leaves a net interest income attributable to buildings and land in the amount of $6,480. To capitalize this, we divide it only by the interest rate, since we have already deducted the return to recapture the value of the buildings. Therefore, $6,480 divided by 6 per cent (.06) interest, amounts to $108,000, the estimated value by the economic approach.

EXAMPLE OF PROPERTY RESIDUAL TECHNIQUE
(To be used when neither the value of the building nor
land is known very well, but that of the building is
known best.)

Assumptions: All data to and including the net income is the same as the previous
example.

Net Income to Property.......................................$ 10,000
Less Income Required for Recapture of Building
     Investment $88,000   at 4%....................................... 3,520
Income Attributable to Building and Land as Interest Return...............$ 6,480

$6,480 is 6% Annual Return On........................$108,000
ESTIMATED VALUE BY THE ECONOMIC APPROACH $108,000

Comments: Capitalization: In this case, only the assumed interest rate is divided into the net income, as the annual 4% required
      for the recapture of the building value was deducted previously.

Exhibit 9-3.

Next, see Exhibit 9-4, which is an example of another property residual method. You will note we first capitalize the net income of the whole
property by using the capitalization rate of 10 per cent used in the
previous examples. When we capitalized the income to the land and
buildings simultaneously, we assumed that the economic life of both
land and buildings would be 25 years. Since urban land ordinarily does
not wear out as in the case of buildings, we must add the estimated present value of the future ownership of the land 25 years from now. This
is termed the land reversion. The table for "Present Worth of One Dollar"

is used for computing the value of the reversion. Refer to this table in the Appendix. The estimated land value is multiplied by the reversionary factor to arrive at the present worth of the land reversion 25 years hence. Adding the present worth of the land reversion to the capitalized annual net income completes the estimate.

EXAMPLE OF THE PROPERTY RESIDUAL TECHNIQUE
(To be used when neither the value of the
land or improvements is known well, but when
the land value is known better.)

Assumptions: All data to and including the net income is the same as the previous example.

Net Income to Property... $ 10,000

$10,000 Is a 10% Annual Return On $100,000
Land Reversion, $35,000 X .2330*.................................   8,155
ESTIMATED VALUE BY THE ECONOMIC APPROACH $108,155

Round to $108,200

Comments: Building capitalization rate: 10% for the total property as in the previous examples involving the total rate. The land reversion is based on recovering the land at the end of the estimated remaining economic life of the improvements, which is 25 years. Since suburban land values have historically increased in value, it could well be the land will be worth $35,000 25 years from now. Use your judgment as to what the land will be worth in the future and discount it for its present value. The interest rate used should be adjusted according to how you think the market will treat it. The reversion factor used is from the table, "Present Worth of One Dollar."

* 6% interest rate factor of Present Worth of $1.00 deferred 25 years.

Exhibit 9-4.

REVISION OF THE OPERATING EXPENSE STATEMENT FOR FORECAST OF THE ANNUAL INCOME AND EXPENSE

Exhibit 9-5 contains, among other things, an illustration of an operating statement prepared for use in the economic approach. The form of the operating statement will vary for different types of properties, particularly for office buildings, motels, hotels, hospitals and nursing homes. The exhibit also illustrates the building residual technique of the straight-line capitalization method. Refer to this exhibit in connection with the following discussion.

It is recommended that you secure an operating statement covering the income and expenses for at least the last year's operation of the property that you are appraising. If you can secure statements for the past three years it would be better, as it would provide a better background for revising the operating statement to use for the forecast of annual income and expenses. It is generally necessary to revise the statements due to the fact that the appraiser is interested in the typical annual income and expenses, while the owner's records are normally for accounting purposes and the income and expense is entered in the books as they occur. Thus, the owner may include the full cost of a new roof in one year rather than treating it as a reserve and charging a pro rata part for the year.

National statistical data are available as to income and expense for apartments, office buildings, and shopping centers. *The Apartment Building Experience Exchange Report* published annually by the Institute of Real Estate Management, 36 South Wabash Avenue, Chicago, Illinois, is a very helpful publication. The *Office Building Exchange Report* published by the National Association of Building Owners and Managers, 134 South La Salle Street, Chicago, Illinois, is also very useful for the appraisal of office buildings. A very useful publication for shopping centers is *The Dollars and Cents of Shopping Centers* (a study of receipts and expenses), published by Urban Land Institute, 1200 18th Street, N.W., Washington, D.C.

Income estimate

After reviewing the owner's statement as well as investigating the rental market for this type of property, you should be in a position to estimate the volume of the gross income for the property. Check to see if the rental rates are too high or too low. If a lease is not involved you should adjust your income estimate to reflect the rate the property could be rented for.

Since the current value of a property is the present worth of the right to collect the future net benefits from the property, the net income estimate of the property must be based on that reasonably expectable in the future, not necessarily the present net income. This, of course, pertains to all items involved which affect the net income to the property. The more refined the techniques of the appraiser become in estimating the various factors of the economic approach, of course, the more realistic the value estimate can be. The maximum rental for the property cannot be higher than the tenants can afford to pay nor less than required to pay out the property. Of course, no one can be expected to be able to actually predict what the income or expenses will be years hence; nevertheless, the appraiser must make a forecast based upon a reasonable expectation after considering the current situation and the trends. The stability of the business and income of the tenants is of great significance. If a temporary situation exists whereby there is an exceptionally high rental income, the prospective duration must be considered. You may capitalize any excessive amount of actual income separately at a high capitalization rate and add it to the capitalized value computed for the reasonable amount. Each such situation must be handled on the basis of its own merits.

Vacancy and collection allowance

If you are not familiar with the vacancy and collection losses typical for such property in the area, it will be necessary for you to discuss with owners or dealers as to their experience, and use the typical percentage indicated. Normally, it may vary from about 3 to 10 per cent or more, for commercial properties depending on the local situation, etc.

Operating and maintenance

You should be concerned with the expense necessary to operate and maintain the property, but with none here that involves capital expenditures such as a completely new roof. Include the typical management expense for a property, even though it may be owner operated, otherwise the proper net income for capitalization would not be indicated. The management fee may vary from about 3 to 10 per cent or more, depending upon the locality and the property. The local real estate board is a good source for this information. Any wages involved not included in the management charge should be charged under Payroll Expense. Advertising, legal, auditing and other professional fees, telephone, office expenses and office supplies not included in the management contract may be carried as Other Administrative Costs. For utilities, enter only the expense assumed by the owner. Owners of similar properties or utility companies are good sources for this. List the forecasted average annual expense estimated for the items involved.

Under Painting and Decorating (Interior) list the typical average annual expense. Include exterior painting in General Maintenance and Repair (interior and exterior) as it is for such items not included elsewhere. The typical annual expense should be listed. Supplies, services and miscellaneous are for any other operating and maintenance expenses not properly chargeable elsewhere.

Reserve for replacements

Under this heading are listed the necessary periodic replacements. As an example, if a new roof is required every 15 years, list $\frac{1}{15}$ of that for the annual expense. This applies to any capital item requiring full periodic replacement. Equipment that is built-in or so affixed to the building as to constitute an item of real estate and which requires periodic replacement should be similarly treated unless it is treated as an operating or maintenance expense. Whether easily removable items of equipment are considered as real estate depends on the customs and regulations of the area.

Fixed expenses

List the regular real estate taxes. Find out what they are, or should be if it is a proposed project. Find out what the building insurance expense is, or what it should be if proposed. Perhaps the owner will carry a three or five year insurance policy to save some money, so use the pro rata cost of insurance for the annual charge. This should be for all classes of insurance coverage pertinent to the real estate. Sometimes property owners do not carry sufficient insurance, and if this is the case find out what the cost should be for the proper amount.

CAPITALIZATION PROCEDURE TO USE

Use the capitalization method you feel is most applicable to your appraisal problem. In selecting a technique of the straight-line recapture method, if you have more confidence in the building value, which

Exhibit 9-5.

ILLUSTRATION OF THE CAPITALIZATION OF THE INCOME FROM A GARDEN APARTMENT PROJECT

(This is provided as an illustration only of the computations which may be involved in this approach for a garden apartment project. The estimates pertain to no particular property, and are merely illustrative of form. It is assumed the building has 40 years of remaining economic life and that the correct interest rate is 6 1/2% for land and buildings.)

FORECASTED ANNUAL INCOME AND EXPENSES
(Owner pays utilities)

Estimated Gross Income		$	330,595
Less Vacancy and Collection Losses (10%)			33,060
Effective Annual Gross Income		$	297,535
Operating and Maintenance Expenses			
Management	$16,529		
Payroll Expenses	15,868		
Utilities	31,737		
Other Administrative Costs	5,289		
Painting and Decorating (Interior)	4,958		
General Maintenance and Repair (Int. and ext.)	9,917		
Supplies	1,652		
Services	3,637		
Miscellaneous	1,653		
Reserve for Replacements			
Roofing $24,000 /15	1,600		
Heating and AC System $145,000 /15	9,667		
Miscellaneous $80,000 /15	5,333		
Fixed Expenses			
Insurance	5,287		
Real Estate Taxes	40,000		
Total Expenses		$	153,127
Net Income to Property		$	144,408
Less Income Attributable to Land			
$350,000 at .065			22,750
Income Attributable to Buildings		$	121,658
$121,658 /.09 (9% return on $121,658)		$	1,351,756
Land Value			350,000
ESTIMATED VALUE BY THE ECONOMIC APPROACH		$	1,701,756

Rounded to $ 1,702,000.

perhaps is based on the physical approach, use the land residual technique. If you have more confidence in the land value, which may have been estimated through the market approach, use the building residual technique. If you feel unsure about either, use a property residual technique. After you have completed the capitalization and arrived at the estimated value by the economic approach, explain how you estimated the capitalization rate under "Comments" and any other data you think should be explained.

SHORT-CUT METHOD FOR LOW TO MEDIUM PRICED ONE- AND TWO-FAMILY DWELLINGS

This is not an actual method of capitalization, but an abbreviated method used for one- and two-family dwellings. The method concerns the monthly gross rent multiple of comparable properties in the neighborhood. If used properly, it is a fair indication of value for such properties. To use it, you must be familiar with the sales prices and the rental rates of the properties concerned.

Monthly gross rent multiple method

Assuming that you have a list of a number of comparable properties that have sold within the last year or two and you know their gross monthly rental rates, divide the sales price of each one by its gross monthly rental, and the quotient is the gross monthly rent multiple. After finding the rent multiple for a number of such neighborhood dwellings that are comparable to the subject property, estimate that typical of the group considered. After estimating the typical rental rate that should apply to the subject appraised, multiply it by the typical gross rent multiple found to find the indicated income value. This offers a check against the physical and market approaches. The indicated income value will not be correct unless you use the typical comparable gross rent multiple and rental rate for the neighborhood. If this procedure is used, the value indicated by the method will generally set the lower limit of the value of the property appraised. The following indicates how the computations may be shown in a report:

Gross monthly rental rate:	$ 100
Gross monthly rent multiple:	115
Indicated economic value:	$11,500

TECHNIQUES IN ESTIMATING BUILDING CAPITALIZATION AND INTEREST RATES

Definitions of certain terms

Interest Rate: The fixed percentage rate of loan principal that is to be paid each period as rental for borrowed money. The rate is generally expressed as a certain percentage per year.

Capitalization Rate: There are several different types of this rate, but those the student should know at this time are described below.

Gross Capitalization Rate: It is a fixed percentage relationship between the value of a property and its gross annual income. About the only time it is used is when converting a gross rent multiple into an over-all capitalization rate as described in this chapter under "Over-all Rate Technique."

Over-all Capitalization Rate: It is a fixed percentage that represents the relationship between the capitalized value of a property and the annual net income to the property. For instance, to divide the annual net income by the sales price of a property indicates its over-all capitalization rate, thus: \$8,000/\$100,000 = 8 per cent. It doesn't directly consider the amount of recapture necessary for depreciable buildings or the ratio of the land to buildings, but you can compute the rates assumed by it under specific conditions. The over-all rate computed as above should only be used in the direct capitalization method unless it is adjusted as discussed later.

Building Capitalization Rate: It is a percentage which is the sum of the interest rate and the recapture rate which represents the relationship between the building(s) [6] and the net income attributable to the building(s). The recapture rate pertains to the rate necessary to return or recapture the value of the building(s) within the remaining economic life of the building(s).

Premise: The higher the quality of a property and its income, the lower the interest and/or capitalization rates.

It goes without saying that the capitalization rate is very important. In the straight line capitalization method a change in the interest rate component for both building and land makes the following changes:

---

[6] Building(s) as used in this context refers to the building(s) plus other construction improvements on the site.

A 1 per cent decrease in the interest rate of the building residual technique increases the value approximately 9 per cent, and a 1 per cent increase decreases it approximately 8 per cent.

In the land residual technique a 1 per cent decrease increases it approximately 17 per cent, and a 1 per cent increase decreases it approximately 12 per cent. The interest rate required by typical investors or indicated by comparable properties is generally considered the proper rate, assuming the properties are rented at market rates, vacancies are typical, and management is good. The recapture rate must be based on the estimated remaining economic life of the buildings of the property appraised unless the investor requires an earlier return. In capitalizing income pertaining only to land, the applicable market interest rate is used, plus an adjustment for any extra hazards. The building capitalization rate is not to be used in the direct capitalization method unless it is converted to an over-all rate as explained later.

TECHNIQUES IN SELECTING CAPITALIZATION RATES

Over-all rate technique

The rate computed by this method should be based on the over-all capitalization rates of several different comparable properties. They must be closely comparable properties, including their remaining economic life. To compute the over-all rate you merely divide the net income of a property by its sales price. This should be done for at least three or four comparable sales, and then the typical is selected for use in the appraisal. As an example, the rate is expressed in one rate as: $10,000 (annual net income)/$100,000 (sales price) = .10 (10%). The rate as expressed must only be used in direct capitalization, for instance: net return to property $10,000/.10 = $100,000 property value.

You may also compute the over-all rate from the gross annual rent multiple:

Assume a gross annual rent multiple of 6.875

Compute the gross capitalization rate: 1./6.875   .14545

Less the per cent that the total annual expenses,
    vacancy and collection loss are of the gross
    income (say 45% for example): 45% × .14545   .06545

Over-all capitalization rate   .08 or 8%

Before the over-all capitalization rate may be used in other than the direct capitalization method it must be divided proportionally into its applicable components of recapture rate for the building(s) and the interest rate return on both the building(s) and land as follows and re-assembled. Multiply the recapture rate by the percentage of the building(s) value of the total property and deduct that from the over-all rate to find the interest rate, then add the full recapture rate to the interest rate to secure the building capitalization rate. For instance . . .

> Assume an over-all rate of 8%; buildings and other improvements being worth 25% of the total; remaining economic life of 33 years.[7] Then proceed as follows:

Over-all rate	.0800
Less proportionate of recapture rate: .25 × .03	.0075
Interest rate on land and building	.0725
Add full recapture rate	.03
Building Capitalization Rate	.1025 or 10¼%

You should use the above procedures on several comparable properties for proper justification.

Residual rate technique (for interest and building capitalization rates)

The procedures used in Exhibits 9-6 and 9-7 illustrate two related techniques and are generally self-explanatory. You must use the procedure on several comparables to secure the indicated rates. The main difference between the two is that in Exhibit 9-6 the interest rate for the land is estimated first and separately: and it may not necessarily agree with the interest rate computed in Exhibit 9-7. Either is considered an approved technique if sufficient comparables are used for the rate selection; however, there has been argument for years as to whether the interest rate on the land may properly be different than that on the building. Suffice to say there are good arguments for both sides. Since the land owner and building owner are frequently different men, and since ground lease interest rates are frequently lower than interest rates on buildings, it would seem that a different interest rate for land may be proper. This

---

[7] 1.00/33 yrs. = .03030, but it is generally rounded to .03.

Exhibit 9-6.

CAPITALIZATION RESIDUAL PROCEDURE
For Computation of the Building Capitalization Rate

Present value, or reported sales price of property: $100,000

Present value of building(s) only: $50,000

Going interest rate on comparable land notes: 6 1/2%

Annual net income to property...(land and buildings)................ $8,000

Less return to land:

$$\frac{\$50,000}{\text{(Land value)}} \quad X \quad \frac{6\ 1/2\%}{\text{(Going land rate)}} \quad = \qquad \underline{3,250}$$

Annual net return to building(s)................................. $4,750

Indicated capitalization rate

$$\frac{\$4,750}{\substack{\text{(Net income return to}\\ \text{building}}} \quad \text{divided by} \quad \frac{\$50,000}{\text{(Current building)}} \quad = \qquad \underline{.095}\ (9\ 1/2\%)$$

Less recapture rate:
  100%/33 years (remaining economic life of building(s)   =   .030 (rounded)

INDICATED INTEREST RATE FOR THE BUILDING   .065 (6 1/2%)

Indicated Interest Rate for Land: (See going land rate above)

_____

Comments: If you do not know the going rates on land notes in the neighborhood, it will be necessary for you to use the procedure described under that title which follows in another paragraph. This method should be used when the land value is known best. It is a companion procedure of that in Exhibit 9-7. This procedure indicates a different interest rate may properly apply to land and the building, as these rates will not necessarily agree by this procedure.

Exhibit 9-7.

INTEREST RESIDUAL PROCEDURE
FOR COMPUTATION OF THE BUILDING CAPITALIZATION RATE
AND PROPERTY INTEREST RATE

Present value, or reported sales price of property: $100,000

Annual net income to property.................................$8,000

Less return for physical value of improvements:*

    Current value of improvements: $50,000

    Estimated remaining economic life: 33 years.

    Recapture rate: 100%/33yrs. = .03 (rounded)

$50,000	X	.03	$1,500
(Current value of improvements)		(Recapture rate)	

Annual net income for interest on land and improvements............ $6,500

INDICATED INTEREST RATE FOR LAND AND BUILDING:

$6,500	divided by	$100,000	=	.065 (6 1/2%)
(Net income for interest on land and improvements)		(Sale price or assumed value of property)		

Indicated Interest Rate for Land and Building (s): .065 (6 1/2%)

Indicated Recapture Rate: .030

Indicated Building Capitalization Rate: .095 (9 1/2%)

Comments: This method should be used when the building value is known best. It is a companion procedure of the land residual value technique.

* All buildings and other improvements on the land.

is especially proper considering there is typically less risk in the land investment than in the building on it, assuming the building is the highest and best use. In using either residual procedure you should be sure to use enough comparables to secure an indication of a good typical or average rate. You may find it helpful to maintain a current file on rates computed in this manner for quick use with new appraisals.

It is interesting to note that the over-all capitalization rate for the hypothetical property in Exhibits 9-6 and 9-7 is 8 per cent while the building capitalization rate is 9½ per cent. The over-all rate is indicated by dividing the net income by the sales price: $8,000/$100,000 = .08 or 8 per cent. Since different types of capitalization rates can be produced from the same property you must know how the capitalization rate was computed before you can use it properly. The difference in the rates is explained by the fact that land (for building purposes) is not ordinarily considered to depreciate, though the building does. If we wish to use the building capitalization rate in direct capitalization we must reduce it to the percentage applicable, as follows:

You will note the improvements in Exhibit 9-7 are 50 per cent of the total value, the appropriate recapture rate is 3 per cent and the interest rate is 6½ per cent, making a total rate of 9½ per cent, therefore:

$$\frac{1}{2} \times .03 + .065 = .015 + .065 = .08 \text{ or } 8\% \text{ (over-all capitalization rate)}$$

Band of investment theory in selecting the interest rate

This technique involves the following: First, determine the typical loan value ratio used by lenders on similar properties and the interest rate charged for the loans on those properties. Secondly, ascertain the rate of return on equities required by investors from similar properties. For illustration, assume that the typical mortgage represents 60 per cent of the value of the property and 6 per cent is the going interest rate. Assuming that the equity is 40 per cent and that the rate of return demanded by equity investors for this type of property is 10 per cent, we would compute the rate as follows:

Computation of Interest Rate

.60 of .06 = .036
.40 of .10 = .040
Total   .076 (7.6%)

If a second mortgage is involved, the method will involve three calculations instead of two shown above. You may cite the comparable properties to develop the rate in order to substantiate the interest rate used. After having estimated the interest rate, add the necessary recapture rate for the return of the value of buildings within their economic life. If you estimate that the buildings have a remaining economic life of 25 years, you must add .04 to the .076 above, making the capitalization rate of .116 (11.6 per cent). The recapture rate is that indicated by the building itself. It is the rate necessary to return the value of the improvements within their remaining economic life. If the remaining economic life of the improvements is estimated to be 33⅓ years, the rate for the return of the value of the improvements would be 3 per cent and that would be added to the interest rate. The band of investment method is one of the best methods of selecting the interest rate in formulating the building capitalization rate. It is quite popular and has considerable merit.

Ellwood's method

L. W. Ellwood in his *Ellwood Tables for Real Estate Appraising and Finance* has developed a method which appears to be very practical for computing over-all capitalization rates to meet specific investment assumptions. It is more or less an improved band of investment method. You should refer to his tables for construction of the rate, as otherwise it is somewhat technical and involved.

Going interest rate method

(This method may be used to estimate the land interest rate as well as for the building.) This is one of the quickest methods to use, and it does have merit. It requires an intimate knowledge of the current interest rates charged for comparable real estate mortgage loans or good information from active lenders in the neighborhood to determine the going rates. When the indicated interest rate is selected, it is adjusted for any additional risk or return required. If a building is involved, the required recapture rate is added to complete the building capitalization rate.

Example:

Going real estate loan rate	6%
Extra return and/or risk applicable	½%
Estimated proper interest rate	6½%
Recapture rate 100%/40 yrs.	2½%
Assumed capitalization rate	9%

To be most indicative, the estimated interest rate should be based on recent mortgage loans made in the neighborhood of the appraised or, if no recent ones have been made there, those made in the nearest comparable neighborhoods may be used. Only those made on comparable properties should be employed. Only those loans that involve a comparable term in years and repayment schedule should be considered. Mortgage loans having government or other types of mortgage insurance should not be compared unless the appraised would have the same type loan available to it.

The rates presently available in the market should receive the greatest weight if the current conditions do not involve a temporary shortage or over-abundance of mortgage money. The mortgage market will fluctuate; but unless a tremendous market disturbance is involved, the changes should not be violent.

An adjustment factor should be made for any long-term risk or market factor that should receive special consideration. The recapture rate must be computed on the basis of the rate required to return the current value of the building within the estimated remaining economic life of the building. As a general rule, the capitalization rate estimated by this method, if properly formulated, will approximate the rate indicated by the methods previously discussed.

Summation method

This is an old-type method used to estimate the interest rate by adding to what is termed a safe, or riskless rate, other rates for the various risks involved with real estate mortgage loans. The safe rate is usually based on the yield rate from long-term government securities. The following is a somewhat typical example of this method:

Safe rate (riskless rate)	3%
Rate for non-liquidity of investment	1%
Rate for burden of management	1%
Rate for general risk factors	1%
Total interest rate	6%

Sometimes it appears that this method is really used to substantiate in the appraiser's mind that which he considers the going interest rate on mortgages. While it would seem to have some validity for that purpose, the more modern methods appear to be based more on known factors. Of course, if this method is used for the building capitalization rate, you must also add the required recapture rate for the improvements to provide for recapture of the investment within the remaining economic life involved.

POINTERS

✔ The "over-all rate technique" is a good method but time consuming, unless you maintain a file for the purpose. You must base the rate on closely comparable property sales.

✔ The "residual rate techniques" are good methods, but time consuming, unless you maintain a file for the purpose. The residual techniques are especially good for justification purposes.

✔ The "band of investment method" is a rapid method if you already have information as to the rates on comparable mortgages and equities, otherwise it will involve considerable research.

✔ Ellwood's method is realistic, practical and is relatively rapid if you have his book, *Ellwood Tables for Real Estate Appraising & Financing*. A second and revised edition was published in 1967 by The American Institute of Real Estate Appraisers.

✔ The "going interest rate" method is the most rapid method to use if you are intimately familiar with the rates charged for comparable loans on comparable properties in the neighborhood. Otherwise, it will require some research. Be sure to add for any extra hazards.

✔ I wouldn't use the outmoded "summation method." It is a rather specious method involving too much personal judgement in lieu of market indicators.

✔ Of course the capitalization rate must be compatible to the capitalization method used.

SUMMARY

1. The premise of the economic approach is: The current value of a property is the worth of the right to collect the future net benefits of the property. This approach tends to set the lower limit of value. Normally investors do not pay more than it indicates.
2. Capitalization is the method used to estimate the value by this approach. It involves the conversion of the future anticipated income into present value.

3. There are five main types of capitalization: (1) Annuity, (2) Perpetuity, (3) Direct Capitalization, (4) Mortgage-Equity, (5) Straight-Line Recapture.

4. There are three residual techniques. They are the building, the land, and the property residual techniques.

5. The economic approach is the most important approach for income property.

6. The higher the quality of a property and its income, the lower the capitalization and/or interest rate, or vice versa.

7. Capitalization Rate Techniques
    a. Over-all Rate Technique
    b. Residual Rate Technique
    c. Band of Investment Theory
    d. Ellwood's Method: This is a method in which a capitalization rate is constructed to represent specific investment assumptions as set forth in *Ellwood Tables for Real Estate Appraising and Financing*. It is employed in direct capitalization.
    e. Going Interest Rate Method
    f. Summation Method

10

Correlation

The premise of the correlation is: the procedures, techniques, and computations of the approaches used to estimate the preliminary values are applicable, accurate, interrelated, and provide a sound basis on which to form a conclusion of value. Correlation as used in the appraisal process is the procedure used to form the final conclusion of value. This is one of the most important steps in the appraisal process, particularly when a complex appraisal is involved. The process assists in the discovery of errors that might not otherwise be discovered before the appraisal is submitted to the client. It helps to form a reasonable and supported final opinion of value. Even though the actual steps of the correlation may not be set forth in an appraisal report, the appraiser is obligated to use the procedure in forming the final opinion of value.

REVIEW AND BRACKETING OF THE INDICATED VALUES

First, check to see if you have listed and properly considered the interests appraised, as well as the purpose and the planned use of the appraisal in accordance with the authorization of the client. Then check to see if you have really appraised it on that basis. Appraisals are sometimes required "as of" some past date; if this is the case be sure it is indicated in the appraisal. Check to see if the property is identified correctly as to location and that the dimensions and area of the land and building improvements are correctly shown. Of course, these basic elements must

145

be known before commencing the appraisal; otherwise, the complete report may be of no value. Next, check to see if you have included the applicable appraisal processes.

It is wise to review the city, neighborhood, and site data used. Is the city data pertinent? Has the neighborhood been analyzed properly? Have you painted a proper picture of the neighborhood so that the reader may visualize it? Is it pictured in its true respect to such an extent that the trends are readily apparent? Has the site analysis been completed so that all the necessary information is supplied? Are the necessary photographs enclosed to properly show the property? Have all the building improvements been sufficiently described so that the client will be informed as to quality of construction and design involved, as well as the age and condition? Are the building improvements adequate for the use contemplated? Have you estimated the remaining economic life of the improvements? Is the estimate justified by the physical and functional utility of the building, and by the economic situation, age, and character of the neighborhood?

If the physical approach was used is its data properly related to that contained in the other approaches used? Have you or can you justify the estimated land value? Did you use comparable land sales to estimate the land value? If comparable sales are unavailable did you use the land residual technique to justify the estimate? Could you discuss the reasons the subject appraised is worth more or less than the comparable sales used? Are the cost estimates justified? It is a good idea to check the cost data used against that from other sources. In this connection, especially, it is helpful to have two of the nationally recognized cost manuals. They can be adjusted for local use and are very helpful. Many times a good check of the physical approach is to compare the costs used with that of other similar properties appraised. You can make a quick over-all check by the cubic- or square-foot costs involved. As applicable, recheck the estimates made of physical deterioration and functional and economic obsolescence. Quite frequently these factors are a source of error, for they are largely a matter of opinion. Is the physical deterioration estimate based on actual observation of the property or is it just based on age-life? Does actual market reaction justify the functional and economic obsolescence estimated?

If the economic approach was used is its data properly related to that contained in the other approaches? There are many elements to check in this approach. All of the estimates from that for gross income through the indicated economic value may be rechecked. Definitely, the arithmetic should be checked. Have you, or can you justify the rental income estimate? Is it based on actual comparable rentals? Is the allowance for vacancies and collection losses justifiable? Are all of the expense estimates based on actual comparable operating statistics? Have you used the proper method of capitalization? Have you justified the capitalization rate?

If the market approach was used is its data properly related to that contained in the other approaches? Have you compared the appraised with the comparable sales by a standardized method so that all points of comparison have been considered in a uniform manner? Have you, or could you, explain the reasons the subject appraised is more or less valuable than the individual comparables? One of the best ways to check the market approach is by using the gross rent multiple method, if the multiples are based on good comparables. It goes without saying that this method could be worse than useless if not based on good comparable market data. If based on the proper data it can be very helpful. The gross annual multiple is not limited to a whole number and may be 5.4, and so on.

FORMULATION OF THE FINAL OPINION OF VALUE

The economic approach indicates the lower limit of value and the physical approach the upper limit of value. If you feel that the bracket of value indicated by the approaches is correct, select the final value from within it. This is the normal procedure. If the selection is not obvious, state the reasons for the final selection. *In any event, the final opinion of value should be yours. Let it be your opinion only, but one that is substantiated by your appraisal.* On the opinion of value you will rise or fall.

In most appraisals the estimated value is rounded to the nearest multiple similar to the following:

Value Range	Multiple
$ 50,000	$ 50
$ 100,000	$ 100
$ 250,000	$ 250
$ 500,000	$ 500
$1,000,000	$1,000
And so on . . .	

The reasoning and presentation of the appraisal should not only properly support the final opinion of value, but should do so in a manner that will be clear and understandable to the client. In order to do this, of course, you must understand his point of view, and informed as to his knowledge of the appraisal process.

The following is an appraisal check list that may be helpful.

CHECK LIST

Identification

Is the legal description and street or other address correct?
Are all the building improvements on the subject site?

Purpose of the Appraisal

Was the designated or appropriate type of value appraised?
Are the designated property rights to be appraised the basis of the appraisal?
Is the planned use of appraisal known?
Is the type and date of value shown?

Assumptions and Contingencies

Are any special assumptions and contingencies involved?
If so, the client's attention should be directed to them.

Physical, Social and Economic Data

Has the location been analyzed correctly?
Does the zoning or restrictions permit the use of the proposed or present use of the site?

Description of Site

Are the dimensions and area of the site shown?
Can the improvements be properly operated on the site?
Is there proper ingress and egress to the property provided by dedicated streets or street easements?
Are all the necessary utilities available to the site?
What is the highest and best use of the land?

Description of the Improvements

Has the property been properly described as to its size, use, functional detail, age and condition?

Physical Approach

Is the data used properly related to that used in the other approaches?

Has the land value been justified?

Can the reproduction or replacement cost, new, of improvements be justified?

Is the amount of depreciation reasonable for the age, condition, and utility of the structure and the location?

Economic Approach

Is the data used properly related to that in the other approaches?

Has the proper capitalization method been used?

Is the estimated gross annual income based on actual or reasonably comparable properties or reliable statistical data?

Is the site and/or improvements rented from month to month or leased for a long term, and have the actual lease or rental rates, terms and conditions been considered?

Have you provided for a reserve for replacements? If not, can you justify the omission?

Is the net income reasonable?

Is the assumed remaining economic life of the property reasonable in consideration of the age and/or type of structure and the character of the neighborhood?

Has the capitalization rate been justified, or is it justifiable?

If applicable, have you provided for the recapture of the building improvements within their economic life?

Market Approach

Is the data used properly related to that in the other approaches?

Have the most recent comparable offerings and sales been secured?

Has a comparison actually been made with the comparable offerings and/or sales?

What is the supply and demand status?

Could an equal property be sold for more?

Could an equal property be purchased for less?

What about the possibility of new competitive construction?

Could an equal property be constructed for less money, after adjusting for depreciation?

Are there any observable trends in the neighborhood that should be considered?

Correlation of the Estimated Values

Are the estimates made in the approaches used mutually supported by related data?

Have all arithmetic computations been rechecked?

Have the values of each approach been compared and adjusted appropriately?

Has a bracket of value been established?

Is the reasonableness and plausibility of the final opinion of value substantiated by the report?

SUMMARY

1. Correlation as used in the appraisal process is the procedure used to form the final conclusion of value.
2. Differences in the preliminary value estimates may be decreased during the review and comparison.
3. As a general rule, a value within the bracket of the high and low indicators will be selected. Should you select a final value otherwise, you should substantiate the action. In any event the final value estimate should be substantiated by your report.

11

Appraisal of
Lease Interests

(Annuity Capitalization)

INTRODUCTION

Definitions and basic information

Lease: A legal contract (normally written) between the owner of a property and a tenant whereby the owner agrees to rent the property to the tenant for a specified term of time and rental, usually payable at specific periodic intervals.

Reversion (as used here): The value of the rights of a property that revert back to the owner at the end of the leased term.

Lessor: The owner of a property who has contracted to lease the property to a tenant.

Lessee: The tenant of a property who has contracted to lease the property from the lessor.

Annuity: A periodic payment (at regular intervals) customarily due in level amounts, or in increasing or decreasing amounts of money at a prescribed rate, for a definite period of time,[1] on the basis of a valid legal contract made by a financially responsible person or organization. An-

---

[1] That is, starting and ending at a specific time.

nuities are classified into two types: (1) *Ordinary annuities* are those involving a series of payments where each periodic payment is made at the end of the period. (2) *Special annuities* are: (a) *an annuity due* involves a series of payments, with each payment to be made at the beginning of the period involved, (b) *a deferred annuity* is an ordinary annuity whose series of payments are deferred for a prescribed time, (c) *increasing and decreasing annuities* are usually ordinary annuities in which the periodic payments increase or decrease at a uniform straight-line rate, payment to be paid at the end of each period.

Discounting process: A process whereby future income is discounted for the loss of interest from the current or discount time to time of collection of the money involved. Accordingly, this produces the present worth of the future income. It is the basic process used to estimate the current value of lease income constituting an annuity. The exactness of the discounting computations is indicated by the following: What is the present worth of $10,000 payable annually for five years, discounted at 6% per annum? Table I, "Present Worth of $1.00 per Annum" indicates that the factor or multiple for this is 4.212.

$$4.212 \times \$10,000 \text{ amounts to } \$42,120.$$

What is the annual payment required to pay a loan of $42,120 payable in five equal annual installments including interest at 6% per annum? Since the present worth of $1.00 per annum factor is a reciprocal of the factor for the periodic payment necessary to pay off a loan of $1.00 we may readily answer the question as follows:

Amount of loan		$42,120
Payment factor 1./4.212 or	.2374169
Annual payment		$10,000

When you don't have the loan payment tables, it is helpful to know that you can convert the present worth of $1 per period factors to the loan payment factors. These tables are compound interest functions and are very useful. There are six standard tables for compound interest and annuity computations: (1) Amount of 1, (2) Amount of 1 per period, (3) Sinking Fund, (4) Present Worth of 1, (5) Present Worth of 1 per Period, (6) Periodic Payment Worth 1 Today or Periodic Payment to Amortize 1. You can solve most any problem in financial mathematics with them. The compound interest and annuity tables required for this chapter are listed in the Appendix. They refer to 1 as $1. If you are not knowledgeable as to such tables and their uses you may refer to any good text on business or financial mathematics. *The Mathematics of Accounting:* 4th Edition, by Curtis, Cooper and McCallion, Prentice-Hall, Inc., 1961, is one of the best. *Financial Compound Interest and Annuity Tables:* 3rd ed., 1964, Financial Publishing Co. is one of the most complete books of such tables and contains some excellent instructions on their use. *The Mathematics of Accounting* explains in detail how such tables are constructed and used.

Income from leased property ordinarily involves income for a definite term of months or years. When the income is in the form of an annuity, it is necessary to compute its value through the discounting process by the use of annuity tables. In the valuation of lease interests, ordinarily the appraiser is involved only with one lessor and one lessee. If the property is subleased, and the valuation of the subleasehold is required, the problem is somewhat more complicated.

The value of the lessor's (landlord's) interest is the present value of the contract rents plus the present value of the reversion of the land and improvements, if any, at the end of the term of the lease. Naturally, the lease being considered must be a valid contract with a responsible tenant for a stated lease rate and term.[2] The Inwood Table of *Present Worth of One Dollar Per Annum* is generally used for the valuation of contract rents in level annual amounts.[3] The reversion table, *Present Worth of One Dollar* is used for computing the present value of the reversionary rights of the owner at the end of the lease when the use rights of the property revert back to the owner.[4]

The lessee's (tenant's) interest is the "economic rental value" of the property less the value of the lessor's interest in the property. The economic rental value is the capitalized value of the annual current net rental value of the property, considering it is available for rental or lease on the open market.

In the valuation of all interests (the freehold) great credence is given

---

[2] The lease rental must be a level or an increasing or decreasing amount at a definite rental rate at least for each period involved in the lease.

[3] Use the "Present Worth of Increasing and Decreasing Annuities" tables for leases that have income that increase or decrease according to the compound interest tables. This type of lease income is unusual.

[4] The necessary compound interest tables are included in the Appendix.

the market approach. It should be noted that the valuation of all the interests to leased property may be greater than the property would have if it were not leased. This is due to the fact that when leased property is worth more than when not leased, another element of value has been added; namely, the intangible value of the lease above the tangible value of the land and improvements. This is about the only time the situation exists where the value is above the tangible value, except in a case of valuable established "good will" in some commercial properties, or "possession value" of a residence when there is a great scarcity of existing properties and construction is greatly behind demand. The latter situation is rare, of course, but it did exist for some time during and shortly after World War II.

The computations involved in the valuations of leased fees and leaseholds are described below. (The illustrations are for form only, and do not necessarily indicate the proper interest rate)

VALUATION OF A LEASED FEE (LESSOR'S INTEREST); PROPERTY RESIDUAL TECHNIQUE

Refer to Exhibit 11-1. The illustration involves the appraisal of a leased fee. Referring to the information for *Lessee, Rate and Terms,* you will note the rental is payable in advance and that this fact and the other data is listed appropriately under *Schedule of Income.* Since the rental is payable in advance, one year was deducted from the first term of four years, and for schedule purposes this was indicated on line (A) and (B) in Column 2. The other two terms of the lease are also listed on lines (C) and (D) in Column 2. Six per cent (6%) interest was assumed as the proper interest rate for the credit rating of the lessee and listed in Column 3. In Column 4, the *Discount Factor Years* are computed as illustrated, viz., B years (4 yrs. − 1 yr.) [5] are 3; B + C years (3 years + 10 years) are 13; B + C + D years (3 + 10 + 46 years) are 59. The discount factors used in Column 5 are from the table, "Present Worth of One Dollar Per Annum," [6] and are based on the Discount Factor Years in Column 4.

---

[5] One year was deducted for the lease being paid one year in advance. If it had not been, the years indicated on line (B) would be 4 years and none on line (A) Column 2, and the discount factor years in Column 4 and Column 5 would be different.

[6] The table will be found in the Appendix.

Exhibit 11-1. VALUATION OF THE LEASED FEE

(one rental rate, or graduated rents)

Date of Estimate:
Location of the Property:
Lessor: John Jones Interests (Owner)
Lessee, Rate and Terms: Justrite, Inc., 60 year lease payable annually in advance, first 4 years @ $10,000.; next 10 years @ $11,000.; 46 years @ $12,000.†
Discount Table Used: Present Worth of $1. per annum, (Compound Interest Table)

SCHEDULE OF INCOME

1 Annual Net Income	2 Term of Years	3 Interest Rate Used	4 Discount Factor Years	5 Discount Factor	
(A) Advance Payment, if any: $10,000.	*	XXXXXXXXX	XXXXXXXXXXXX	XXXXXXX	If only one lease rate, complete line "B", AND "A" if applica-
		XXXXXXXXX	XXXXXXXXXXXX	XXXXXXX	ble. If a
	1	XXXXXXXXX	XXXXXXXXXXXX	XXXXXXX	graduated rental
(B) $10,000.	** 3	6%	(B Years) 3	2.673	rate, complete all lines as applicable.
(C) $11,000.	10	6%	(B+C Years) 13	8.853	
(D) $12,000.	46	6%	(B+C+D Years) 69	16.131	

COMPUTATIONS:

(A): Advance payment, if any .... $ __10,000.__

(B):
B Years factor __2.673__ x __$10,000.__ (B income) .... $ __26,730.__

(C):
B + C Years factor   8.853
Minus B   "   "   2.673
Deferred factor   6.180   x __$11,000.__ (C income) .... $ __67,980.__

(D):
B + C + D Years factor __16.131__
Minus B + C   "   "   8.853
Deferred factor   7.278   x __$12,000.__ (D income) .... $ __87,336.__
(If further graduated rentals are involved, continue the process and add)

Computed Value of the Income Stream: .... $192,046.
Value of the Reversion, if any:
   Assumed future value of the land: (60 yrs. hence) ... $ __75,000.__
   Present value of the improvements: $ __120,000.__
   Depreciated value of improvements at reversion: ..... $ __6,000.__
   Reversion factor for A+B+C+D years*** __.0303__ X $ __81,000.__ = ... $ __2,454.__

ESTIMATED VALUE OF THE LEASED FEE $194,500.

(All three approaches should be considered in the valuation of lease interests.)
Comments:
The estimated remaining economic life of the warehouse is 60 years. It is estimated the building will have about $6,000. in salvage value at the end of its economic life.

---

* On line "A" indicate "1" here for a one year advance payment.
** Deduct 1 year if paid in advance 1 year.
***Present Worth of $1., (Compound Interest Valuation Premise) at __6%__ interest, deferred __60__ years.

  †(Lessee to pay taxes, insurance and complete maintenance of the property)

Winstead, *Appraisal Practice Course I*, Houston, Texas: Winstead Appraisal Service, © 1961, page 96.

Under Part (A) of *COMPUTATIONS*, the advance payment is entered in the far column. Under Part (B) the B years factor and Annual Net Income is entered, the multiplication is performed and the product entered on far right. Under Part (C), the B + C years factor, and the B years factor are entered, the subtraction completed and the balance entered as the deferred factor. The deferred factor is then multiplied by the C Annual Net Income and the product entered on the far right.

A similar procedure is followed for Part D. The far column is then totaled to find the *Computed Value of the Income Stream.* If further graduated rentals were involved, the process would have been continued and included as part of the income stream.

The assumed value of the land 60 years hence was entered on the first line under *Value of Reversion,* and that for improvements on the next line. Since the remaining economic life of the improvements coincides with the end of the lease, the improvements will have only salvage value at that time. The reversion value of the land and improvements at the end of 60 years (A + B + C + D years) was computed and added to the value of the income stream for the total estimated value for the leased fee.

Of course, you are not required to use a form similar to the illustration. Another procedure for computation of the leased fee is to discount each graduated term of the lease as you come to it (by use of the table, *Present Worth of One Dollar per Annum*) and compute the present value of the deferred and discounted graduated lease term by use of the table Present Worth of $1. This procedure is illustrated in Exhibit 11-2.

VALUATION OF A LEASEHOLD (LESSEE'S INTEREST)

See Exhibit 11-3. The illustration involves a leasehold appraisal. The lease is graduated, but not payable in advance. If it had involved an advance payment, "1" would have been deducted from *Term of Years* on line (A) in Column 4. You will note "Rental Value" is entered in Column 1 under "Present Net" as the property is not subleased.[7] The rental value (the present market rate if the property were not presently leased) for each term is entered on the appropriate lines on the schedule. *The Leased Rental Rate* is entered in Column 2, and the resultant *Net Rental Gain* in Column 3. The term of years for each term is entered in Column 4. In this case there are two years remaining in the *1st term.*

---

[7] If the property was subleased, the sublease rate would be entered in lieu of the rental value.

ESTIMATED VALUE OF THE LEASED FEE
(Use the Compound Interest Table, "Present Worth of $1.00 per Annum")

Advance payment, 1 year		$ 10,000
1st term 3 year balance, 6%		
2.673 x $10,000		26,730
2nd term 10 years, 6% deferred 3 years		
13 year factor	8.853	
Less the three year factor	2.673	
	6.180 x $11,000	67,980
3rd term, 46 years, 6% deferred 13 yrs.		
59 year factor	16.131	
Less the 13 year factor	8.853	
	7.278 x $12,000	87,336
Computed value of the income stream		$192,046
Value of the reversion		
Assumed future value of the land*	$75,000	
Depreciated value of improvements at reversion	6,000	
(Present Worth at 6%, deferred 60 years) .0303** x	$81,000	
		2,454
Estimated value of the leased fee		$194,500

---

* 60 years hence.
** Use the table, Present Worth of $1.00, which is in the Appendix.

Exhibit 11-2.

Exhibit 11–3. Form for Valuation of Leasehold or Subleasehold.

VALUATION OF LEASEHOLD

(One rental rate or graduated rates)

Date of estimate:
Location of the property:

Lessee, ~~sublessee~~, rate and terms: Profitwise Co. Rate & Terms: 2 Years remaining at $7,200. per year; 5 years @ $7,800; 30 years @ $8,000.
Estimated remaining economic life: 37 years. Lessor pays taxes on land. Lessee owns building and pays all expences incident to it.

SCHEDULE OF NET RENTAL GAINS: (The net rental gain is that after all rents, insurance, taxes, operating expenses, interest on capital investment in improvements and a reserve to return the present value of the improvements owned at the end of the lease term, are deducted.)

PRESENT NET RENTAL VALUE: $8,400. per yr. net (cont'd under Comments)

1 Present Net * Rental Value	2 Net Leased Rental Rate	3 Net rental Gain	4 Term of Years	5 Interest Rate	6 Discount Years	7 Discount Factor ***
(A) None			**	XXXXXXXX XXXXXXXX	XXXXXXXX XXXXXXXX	XXXXXXXX XXXXXXXX
(B) 1st Term $8,400.	$7,200.	$1,200.	**	7%	(B Years) 2	1.808
(C) 2nd Term $8,400.	$7,800.	600.	5	7%	(B+C Years) 7	5.389
(D) 3rd Term $8,400.	$8,000.	400.	30	7%	(B+C+D Years) 37	13.117

COMPUTATIONS:

(A) Advance payment rental gain, if any .... $ None

(B) B years factor _1.808_ x _$1,200._ (rental gain) .... $ 2,170.

(C):
B+C Years factor 5.389
Minus B years factor 1.808
Deferred factor........ 3.581 x _$600._ (rental gain) .... $ 2,149.

(D):
B+C+D years factor 13.117
Minus B+C years factor .. 5.389
Deferred factor .... 7.728 x _$400._ (rental gain) .... $ 3,091.

(If further graduated rentals are involved, continue the process and add)

PRESENT WORTH OF RENTAL GAINS $ 7,410.
Present value of improvements owned by Lessee $ 40,000.
Adjustment for improvements, if any, at end of the leased term $ -0-
TOTAL ESTIMATED VALUE OF (LESSEE'S), ~~(SUBLESSEE'S)~~ INTERESTS $ 47,410.
(All three approaches should be considered in the valuation of lease interests.)

Say ($ 47,400.)

Comments:
It is considered the property could be sub-rented for $8,400. net per year with sub-lessee paying all taxes, insurance and for complete maintenance of the property.

---

* (Present net rental value, or sub-lessee's net lease rate; indicate which)

** (If payments are paid in advance by both parties, enter 1 under Term of Years on line "A", and deduct one from the first lease term and enter the balance of that term on line "B" in the same column.)

***(Present Worth of $1.00 per Annum, Compound Interest Tables

FORM NO. 16-B WINSTEAD APPRAISAL SERVICE, HOUSTON, TEXAS   © 1961

Seven per cent (7%) is the estimated proper interest rate considered to apply to the lease, and this is entered in column 5. The balance of the columns are completed as applicable. In Column 6 is entered the total years for the Discount Years involved. B Years is 2; B + C Years is 2 plus 5, or 7; and B + C + D is 2 plus 5 plus 30, or 37. Referring to Column 7, the discount factors were found by referring to the table, *Present Worth of One Dollar per Annum* for 2, 7 and 37 years respectively at 7 per cent interest, and these factors were entered in the column as appropriate.

Under *Computations,* Part A is not completed as no advance payment is involved. For Part B, the B Years factor, 1.808, is entered as is the *Net Rental Gain* of $1,200. The multiplication is done and the product is entered in the far column. Under Part C, the B + C Years factor is entered, then the B Years factor is subtracted from it. The resulting sum is the "Deferred Factor" of 3.581 and it is multiplied times the *Net Rental Gain* of $600 for the *2nd Term,* and the product is entered in the far column. A similar procedure is followed for Part D. If further graduated rentals are involved, just continue the process and add in. Add the total for *Present Worth of Rental Gains.* The *Present Value of the Improvements Owned By Lessee* in this case is $40,000. The estimated remaining economic life of the improvements owned by the lessee is 37 years, which coincides with the end of the lease term, so there was no *Adjustment for Improvements.* The total of the column is the *Total Estimated Value of Lessee's Interests.*

Of course, if the lease had been for only one term, only that pertaining to one term would have been completed. This calculation may be listed without using a blank form as discussed for the leased fee.

Many appraisers prefer to value leaseholds by use of the table *Present Worth of One Dollar per Annum* in conjunction with the table *Present Worth of One Dollar,* the latter table being used for the deferred period as noted in Exhibit 11-4, on page 160 (7 per cent interest rate is also used in this example).

VALUATION OF A SUBLEASEHOLD

The valuation of the sublessee's interest (the subleasehold) is similar to that for the lessee's interest. Accordingly, you may use a method similar to that shown in Exhibit 11-3 or 11-4.

First 2 years net annual income:

$8,400 - $7,200 = $1,200

$1,200 X 1.808* $ 2,170

Next 5 year net annual income, deferred 2 years:

$8,400 - $7,800 = $600

$600 X 4.10* = $2,460

Deferred 2 years   .8734**   2,149

Next 30 year annual net income deferred 7 years:

$8,400 - $8,000 = $400

$400 X 12.409* = $4,964

Deferred 7 years   .6227**   3,091

Present Worth of rental gains $ 7,410

Present value of Improvements owned by Lessee   40,000

Total estimated value of Lessee's Interests $47,410

                                              Rounded to $47,400

---

* Present Worth of $1.00 Per Annum factor for the period mentioned above.
** Present Worth of $1.00 factor.

Exhibit 11-4. Valuation of Leasehold (Alternate Procedure).

VALUATION OF ONE UNKNOWN INTEREST BY DEDUCTION

Since the total market value is normally the full value of all interests in a property, if only one interest is unknown it may be found by deducting all the others from the total value. The valuation of a sandwich lease may be found in this manner. A sandwich lease is the leasehold (lessee's interest) when there is a subleasehold (sublessee's interest).

ANNUITY CAPITALIZATION RESIDUAL TECHNIQUES

The following are techniques involving the Inwood Table, *Present Worth of One Dollar Per Annum* which may be used to estimate the value of all interests (the freehold) of leased real estate, as well as for land or buildings.

You will note the process in Exhibit 11-5 is the same as for the straight-line method except the net to the building is multiplied by a factor to produce the capitalized value of the building. Note, though, the building value is $24,490 more by this method. Quite a difference, considering

---

EXAMPLE OF BUILDING RESIDUAL (INWOOD)

Computed Value of The Income Stream	$10,000
Less Interest on Land	
$20,000 at 6%	1,200
Income Attributable to the Building	
For Interest and Recapture	$ 8,800
(Factor for 25 years at 6% is 12.783 per Inwood Table)	
Building capitalization	
12.783 x $8,800	$112,490
Land Value	20,000
Estimated Property Value	$132,490

Exhibit 11–5. Annuity Capitalization (Example of Building Residual).

that indicated by the straight-line method was $88,000. The total value of the property in the straight-line method was $108,000, as shown in the chapter titled "Economic Approach."

You will note that Exhibit 11-6 involves the same process as in the

---

EXAMPLE OF THE LAND RESIDUAL (INWOOD)

Computed Value of the Income Stream	$10,000
Annual amount to amortize to building value at 6% in the estimated 25 years of remaining economic life of the building:	
$112,490 / 12.783	8,800
Net Income to Land	$ 1,200
Land Capitalization $1,200 / .06	$ 20,000
Building Value (Found in building residual)	112,490
Estimated Property Value	$132,490

Exhibit 11–6.   Annuity Capitalization (Example of Land Residual).

---

technique for the straight-line method except the building value is divided by the factor to compute the amount of the annual deduction to amortize the building value. The factor is used as a divisor in this case because the present worth of one per annum factors are the reverse of the factors for amortization schedules for direct reduction loans, *viz.* 1./12.783 is .078229 which is the amount required per dollar for a 25-year loan at 6 per cent payable annually on a direct reduction basis. Multiply the building value by .078229 and you will get the same product, rounded to the nearest dollar.

POINTERS

✔ Many appraisers evaluate lessor's and lessee's interests so seldom that they must review the procedure each time. It is really not complicated but it can be tricky.

✔ Be sure the income to appraise actually constitutes an annuity for all practical purposes; otherwise, the estimated rental income available on the market should be capitalized by another method of capitalization.

✔ The value of all the interests in a leased property should be the same as the market value of the whole property, unless one or more of the lease interests are leased at a rate higher than the current market rate. The latter involves the "two property concept" described earlier in this chapter.

✔ In selecting interest rates for use in the techniques mentioned in this chapter, you should select them on a market rate basis. The rate should be for the type of lessee involved. All other things being equal, an AAA national firm would be discounted at the market rate for that class firm, which, of course, would be at a much lower rate than for a class B local firm. The Dun and Bradstreet ratings of the firms should be considered.

SUMMARY

1. The value of a lessor's interest is the present value of the contract rent plus the present value of the reversion of the land and improvements, if any, at the end of the term of the lease.
2. The lessee's interest is the economic rental value [8] of the property less the value of the lessor's interest in the property.
3. A sublessee's interest may be valued similarly to that for a lessee's interest by using the procedure shown in Exhibit 11-3.
4. The value of all interests in a property that is leased should ordinarily be the market value as indicated by using all three standard approaches. If one or more of the interests is leased at a higher rate than could be obtained on the current market, special consideration must be given to ascertain if it should be valued higher than what it would indicate on the open market.
5. Annuity capitalization should only be used when lease interests are involved.

---

[8] or market value, as applicable.

12

Equity Valuation, Yield, and Leverage

These items are of great importance, particularly to the income property investor, and hence to the appraiser. Along with the hazards of the investment, they are the prime factors of consideration. The amount of net profit return available on the equity cost, and the leverage potential are of much allure to the investor. The informed investor compares the potential profit against the hazards of the investment in order to make his investment decision. The more he is informed as to the yield rate and leverage expectable, the better the judgement he can make.

DEFINITIONS

Yield and rate (as used herein):

Yield is the amount of net profit return on the equity cost. The current yield rate represents the ratio of the current net annual profit (after debt service) to the equity cost. This includes both the net cash return and the equity increase due to loan payments.

Leverage (as used herein):

Leverage is the net annual profit increase due to the loan interest rate being lower than the yield rate and/or a value increase in the property

165

as a result of inflation and so forth, while the loan payments and terms remain fixed.

EQUITY VALUATION

In order to appraise the equity in a property, the whole property should be appraised first. The applicable appraisal procedures should be used. When the value of the whole property has been appraised, the value of the equity is the difference between the outstanding indebtedness and the appraised value of the whole property.

If you are concerned only with the available cash price for the equity, the market approach will of course be of primary importance. It will be necessary to consider any expenses that will be entailed in converting the equity into cash. Of course the expenses may include necessary repairs, refinance charges, and so on. In any event the whole property should be appraised on the basis of its highest and best use, and on the basis of the best financing available in order to estimate the benefit of any probable leverage.

YIELD AND RATE

To solve a wide range of yield problems I suggest the following:

(1) A full range of amortization schedules showing loan payments to principal and interest and the balance at the end of the period. In the Appendix of this book you will find a table for monthly amortization rates for whole year terms from 5–30 years at interest rates from 4½–7%. The Financial Publishing Company, 82 Brookline Ave., Boston, Mass. publishes books for most amortization schedules used.

(2) Compound interest and annuity tables for the problems encountered. (When you become proficient in the use of these tables you won't require a separate book on amortization rates and loan balances as you can compute the information from the tables.) Certain commonly used compound interest and annuity tables will be found in the Appendix hereto. *Ellwood Tables for Real Estate Appraising and Financing*, 2nd Edition 1967, published by American Institute of Real Estate Appraisers, Chicago, Ill. is a good source for such tables. The Financial Publishing Co. mentioned in 1, above, publishes *Financial Compound Interest and Annuity Tables* which is perhaps the most complete book of such tables.

(3) If you are not familiar with the interplay of income tax, depreciation and amortization as it affects real estate, the Institute for Business Planning, 2 West 13th St., New York City has some publications cover-

ing such matters. They have a very comprehensive loose-leaf service titled *Real Estate Investment Planning* which covers the subject quite thoroughly.

The following is a basic procedure for estimating the equity yield, and rate. It also indicates the potential leverage as a result of the yield rate being higher than the fixed interest rate on the loan.

> **Assumptions.** There is a good investment property for sale at $104,000 and your client wants to know the probable yield and rate, assuming that he buys it for $100,000.
>
> Age of building: 10 years.
>
> Estimated remaining economic life of the building: 33 years.
>
> Allocation of cost: 50% to land and 50% to building and improvements.
>
> Indebtedness: It has a new $65,000 loan, payable annually in 20 years with 5½% interest. Payment is $5,439.16 per year of which $1,864.16 of the first payment applies to reduce the principal balance of the loan.
>
> Annual net income to the property before loan payment: $9,000.

Computation

		Over-all Cap. rate:
Current annual net income on $100,000 price	$9,000.00 [1]	(9%)
Less annual payment (of principal and interest) on $65,000 loan	5,439.16	Return Rates:
Net cash income to $35,000 equity price	$3,560.84 [1]	(10.1738%)
First year reduction of loan principal (equity increase)	1,864.16 [1]	(5.3262%)
Yield and rate on $35,000 equity price	$5,425.00 [1]	(15.5000%)

Proof by capitalization: (Using the yield rate as the capitalization rate)

$5,425/15.5% amounts to	$ 35,000.00
Amount of loan involved	65,000.00
Value of Property Indicated by Its Yield	$100,000.00

---

[1] The smaller sum is divided by the larger amount involved to compute the per cent. The rates apply to the first year.

LEVERAGE

When the yield rate is higher than the interest rate on the loan the difference is a type of "leverage." Another type of leverage inherent in real estate results from the fact that real estate loans are fixed obligations for a prescribed amount of money and time as well as interest rate. An increase may occur as a result of the location, management, a general price rise, and so on. If the market value of the property goes up the owner gains by any net difference. This can become a quite sizeable amount of appreciation. The price rise after World War II is a good example of a general price rise that affected most real estate. Of course prices can go down and do, but over the years the general price level has gradually gone up with occasional set-backs that seriously lowered prices for a period. Assuming a favorable location, investors who are prepared to weather a long storm usually come out quite satisfactorily. Of course, not all properties reap the full benefit of a general price rise.

The following is an example of leverage as it affects the equity return:

	Before	After	Percent Increase
Annual Net Income	$50,000	$60,000	20%
Loan Payment	30,000	30,000	None
Equity Return	$20,000	$30,000	50%

The following is an example of leverage as it affects the equity value:

	Before	After	Percent Increase
Property Value	$625,000	$750,000	20%
Loan	375,000	375,000	None
Equity Value	$250,000	$375,000	50%

When the above occurs you may anticipate increased competition. The rule that "exorbitant profits breed ruinous competition" has been amply demonstrated over the years.

SUMMARY

1. When appraising the whole property for valuation of the equity,

the appraisal should be based on the best available financing, and highest and best use of the property.

2. Yield is the amount of net profit above the equity cost. The current yield rate is computed by adding the current net cash equity return (after debt service) to the current equity increase due to loan amortization and then dividing the sum by the equity cost.

3. When the yield rate is higher than the loan interest rate, the difference is a form of leverage.

4. Another type of leverage results from the fact that real estate loans are fixed obligations for a prescribed amount of money, as well as interest rate. When the market rises the owner gains the difference, which can amount to a sizable leverage.

13

Condemnation
Appraisals

CONDEMNATION OF REAL ESTATE FOR EMINENT DOMAIN

When governmental bodies and certain public utilities require land for their use, they are authorized under the authority of eminent domain to institute condemnation action after taking certain prescribed steps. The condemning authority normally has appraisals made of the market value of the property to be taken and, in addition to that, of any damages or enhancement to any remainder of the property left that is not taken for the public use. Then the authority offers what it considers just compensation for the property to be taken and for the estimated net damages, if any, to the remainder involved. As a general rule, it is wise for the owner, also, to have an appraisal made before accepting an offer, since appraisals made for the condemning authority are made from their point of view and may not coincide with the owner's interests. If the offer is not accepted there are provisions for a hearing before special commissioners or some other body, and then by actual court process, if required. Appraisals and testimony of the appraisers are generally used at each step of the process, particularly by governmental bodies and public utilities, and it is wise for the owner to do likewise.

VALUATION PROCEDURE

The valuation procedures used vary somewhat from state to state. Just compensation is generally the basic purpose of condemnation appraisals. The following is a more or less basic procedure, but you should secure information from your attorney as to the proper procedure to use in the jurisdiction involved.

Value of the whole property (before the taking) [1]

First, an appraisal of the whole property is made in accordance with the procedures heretofore discussed for the usual type of appraisal. As a general rule, the market value is appraised, but this may differ in some states. If the whole property is being taken, this is all there is to the process; otherwise proceed as noted below.

Value of the land and improvements to be taken (before the taking)

That part of the land and its improvements to be acquired for public use are generally termed the "part to be taken" or "severed land." This is the part the condemning authority should pay for in full without considering enhancements or damages to the remainder. The land is being taken from the owner. The taking includes all permanent improvements thereon. The value is to be "before the taking." You must have exact information as to the boundaries of the taking and the remainder. The condemning authority should supply all the necessary maps and field notes for this purpose, as well as any other pertinent information in their files. This will not only save the appraiser considerable time, but will provide better appraisals. Where the taking is extensive, aerial photographs are very helpful and should be provided by the condemning authority.

Value of the remainder (before the taking)

The "remainder" is the balance of the property after the part to be taken is deducted from the whole property involved, and its value here is estimated by deducting the value of the taking from the value of the whole property before the taking.

Value of the remainder after the taking, but excluding community enhancements and damages

In making the appraisal of the remainder, you must consider the end results of the severance of the part taken from the whole property, *con-*

---

[1] "Whole property" means all of the land involved which is under one ownership and control. Its value is to be that before the contemplated public improvements, if any, are started.

sidering the proposed public improvements being in-place on the part taken. Consider the value of the remainder on the basis of its utility or inutility as a separate property. Its marketability may be seriously impaired, but then again, its value may be enhanced. The following are a few of such special damages generally encountered:

SEVERANCE DAMAGES TO THE REMAINDER

Severance damages are damages to the remainder of the property not taken and generally involve one or more of the following items:

(1) Reduction in the marketability of land and/or improvements due to a loss in utility due to a change in the size or shape, or of imbalance.

(2) A lowering of the highest and best use of the remainder.

(3) Loss of ingress and egress to roads and other transportation facilities.

(4) Repairs, remodeling, and so on, which may be required before the remainder is usable as a separate property.

(5) Consideration should be given to the possibility that it may be years before the proposed public improvements are actually constructed. The development or improvement of the property involved may be brought to a standstill during this time, resulting in a considerable loss to the owner.

Items of severance damage not to be considered:

The following are usually considered non-compensable:

(1) Damages that affect all property in the community.

(2) Future loss of profits.

(3) Expense of moving removable fixtures and personal property.[2]

(4) Loss of business due to inability to secure a suitable replacement site.[2]

(5) Loss of good will.

(6) Increased insurance requirements.

(7) Loss from forced sale of personal property.

Secure full information as to those applicable in your state, should you make a condemnation appraisal. Personally, I don't think items 3, 4, 5, 6 and 7 are properly non-compensable, if the damages are the result of the taking.

---

[2] It is understood that some states are now providing an allowance for this and that others are considering a change in this respect.

SPECIAL BENEFITS

When considering the marketability of the remainder after the taking, consider any special benefits that may offset the severance damages.

The benefits considered here must be direct, real, and immediately pending, and they cannot be a matter of speculation or based on an occurrence that may or may not occur sometime in the future. In most jurisdictions special benefits are not includible except insofar as they offset severance damages. These benefits may be estimated by one or more of the three appraisal approaches, but market value is normally the value desired. Enhancements enjoyed by the community as a whole are not includible.

NET DAMAGES

After the "value of the remainder, after the taking," has been estimated, deduct it from the "value of the remainder before the taking." The balance is the net amount of the special damages or special benefits, as the case may be. After this computation has been made, list out and explain the basis of the severance damages and special enhancements, if any. A review should be made to exclude any non-compensable damages or non-includible enhancements. Be sure to make a complete list and explanation for the inclusion or non-inclusion of all items. This is necessary so that the client will have full information as to your reasoning and so you will have the information available for court testimony.

POINTERS

✔ When a partial taking is involved the condemning authority should provide its appraiser and the owner with the necessary maps, details, and information as to the planned use of the property, construction schedule, and so forth. It might be as much as ten years or more before the proposed freeway, or other improvements, are completed. The construction schedule may not be known, and even if it is, it can be changed. This can work a serious hardship and loss on the owner, particularly if the land is ripe for development. If a roadway is to be elevated or sunken, the remainder might also be taken for all practical purposes. The traffic may be diverted, or access to the roadway may be denied to the remainder.

Exhibit 13-1.

ILLUSTRATION OF PARTIAL TAKING COMPUTATIONS

A Partial Taking With Severance Damage to Remainder

Value of the whole property (before taking)	$100,000
Value of land and improvements to be taken (before taking) . . .	35,000
Value of remainder (before taking)	$ 65,000
Value of remainder (after taking)*	60,000
Net Severance damages to the remainder**	$ 5,000

Recommended compensation for the taking and damages
        ($35,000 + $5,000) $40,000

A Partial Taking With Special Benefits to Remainder

Value of the whole property (before taking)	$100,000
Value of land and improvements to be taken (before taking)	35,000
Value of remainder (before taking)	$ 65,000
Value of remainder (after taking)*	70,000
Net special benefits, or enhancement to the remainder **	$ 5,000
Recommended compensation for "taking"	$ 35,000

It is important that all severance damages and special benefits be described in full so that the data will be available for the client as well as for preparation of any court testimony involved.

---

 * Excluding community enhancements or damages
** Since this is net, there could be special benefits and damages that offset each other.

Exhibit 13-2.

CONDEMNATION APPRAISAL REPORT FOR HIGHWAY RIGHT-OF-WAY

(ILLUSTRATION)

I. VALUATION OF THE WHOLE PROPERTY

1. Identification:

    Street address:
    Legal description:
    Owner and address:
    Occupancy and Use: Owner occupied as a dwelling.

2. Purpose of the Appraisal:

    The purpose of this appraisal report is to estimate the Market Value of the fee simple title (excepting oil, gas and sulphur) of the real estate as of September 7, 19X7.

    Market Value may be defined as follows: Market Value is the price which the property would bring when it is offered for sale for a reasonable time by one who desires, but is not obliged to sell, and is bought by one who is not compelled to buy it, taking into consideration all of the uses to which it is reasonably adaptable and for which it either is or in all reasonable probability will become available within the reasonable future.

3. Floor and Plot Plans: Photographs:

    A combined floor and plot plan are attached, as well as three photographic views of the property. The drawings indicate the portion of the land and buildings to be taken.

4. Description of the Neighborhood:

    This is an aging, moderate priced residential neighborhood, consisting principally of single family houses in the price range of $7,000 to $12,500, about 30 to 45 years of age. The properties are about 60 percent owner-occupied and maintenance is fair. The trend of the neighborhood values are down as a result of functional obsolescence of the properties due to outmoded design and arrangement. The location is close to most schools and churches. It is about three miles north of the central business district. It is zoned to one family use with a minimum lot size of 5,000 sq. ft.

5. Description of the Site:

    Size: 50' x 100'.
    Area: 5,000 sq. ft.
    Physical description: Generally level with slope and drainage to the rear of
        the site.

    Streets and Utilities: Asphalt surface street; no curb or gutter. Has concrete side-
                walk. All public utilities are connected.
    Highest and best use of the land: The present use.

6. Description of the Improvements:

Main structure: A one story, wood frame structure with wood siding; brick pier foundation; asphalt shingle roof; shiplap and paper interior walls; pine finish flooring; linoleum bath and

Exhibit 13-2 (continued).

kitchen floors. Construction and grade of materials is of medium quality. There is a living room, dining room, two bedrooms, a kitchen and one bathroom. There is a front and rear open porch. The plumbing fixtures are old style, medium grade. Heating is by gas jets only. Venetian blinds are on all windows.

Other structures: There is a wood frame two-car garage with a large bedroom above; no plumbing; outside stairway; shiplap and paper interior walls; pine finish floors in bedroom; garage floor is concrete slab; asphalt shingle roof; cheap concrete beam foundation; economy type construction and materials.

Other items: The landscaping is good; there are numerous shrubs, a good lawn and several large shade trees. There is a concrete ribbon driveway to garage and a concrete entry walk to the house.

Age and condition: The main building is about 35 years old and in fair condition generally. The garage and room are about 30 years old and in fair condition.

Required repairs: The exterior walls will require painting in about one year.

7. Cost Approach:

Estimated reproduction cost, new:

Main structure:	1,172 sq. ft. at $7.43	$ 8,708
Other structures:	629 sq. ft. at $2.61	1,642
All other improvements:	*	1,113
Total estimated reproduction cost:		$11,463

Estimated depreciation:

Physical deterioration	$3,571	
Functional obsolescence	1,500	
Economic obsolescence	None	
Total estimated depreciation		$ 5,071
Estimated depreciated value of the improvements		$ 6,392
Estimated land value		2,000
Estimated value by the cost approach:		$ 8,392
	Rounded to	$ 8,400

Remarks as to depreciation: The physical deterioration is based on the age-life and observed condition method with no overall factor used. The functional obsolescence is based on the market reaction to properties of similar out-moded design and arrangement.

8. Income Approach

Since this is a one-family property only the gross monthly rent multiple method is used.

Estimated gross monthly rental rate obtainable:	$75.00
Indicated rent-multiple:	x 110
Estimated income value:	$8,250

---

* This includes, among other items, open porches, outside stairways, stoops, landscaping, etc.

Exhibit 13-2 (continued).

9. Market Approach:

Supply and demand of comparable properties: There is a good supply of comparable
properties for sale. The demand is good, but it is considered that the supply is greater
than the demand by evidence of the quantity of properties for sale and the nearby large
neighborhoods of similar homes.

Trends: The value for this class of property is generally decreasing as compared to
newer homes for sale.

Comparative value: Based upon a comparison of the appraised with recent sales of comparable properties as described in Exhibit No. 1 enclosed,** I estimate the value of the
appraised to be as noted below.

Estimated value by the market approach: $8,400

10. Correlation:

        Indicated values:

        Cost approach $8,400

        Income approach $8,250

        Market approach $8,400

        Since two of the values coincide and the third is close, the value indicated by
the cost and market approaches is considered most indicative.

11. Final Value Estimate of the Whole Property: $8,400

    II.   RECOMMENDED AWARD FOR PART TAKEN AND DAMAGES TO REMAINDER

Legal description of part taken: (Not provided for this illustration.)

Dimensions and area of site taken: The west 40' x 100' (4,000 sq. ft.) portion of the land
which contains all of the main buildings and essentially all other improvements. The land
is being taken for right of way of the _____Freeway.

** Not enclosed for this illustration.

Exhibit 13-2 (continued).

Computation of the Recommended Award

Value of the whole property (before the taking) $8,400

Value of the land and improvements to be taken (before the taking)..... 8,000

Value of the remainder (before the taking) 400

Value of the remainder (after the taking)........................... 250

Net severance damages to the remainder 150

RECOMMENDED COMPENSATION FOR THE TAKING

(Taking $8,000 + damages of $150...................... $8,150)

Comments:

All of the buildings and other improvements are taken and only a 10' x 100' rectangular strip of land remains, and it is improved with grass only. The narrow width fronts on the street. The land is zoned to single family residential use with a minimum lot size of 5,000 square feet. The remainder is only usable by the adjoining land owner and can only be sold for about $250.

CERTIFICATION

I certify that I have no present or prospective interest in the property and that my appraisal is not contingent upon the appraised value or award.

Respectfully submitted,

_____

Appraiser

✔ Unless a partial taking has a higher and better use separately, it should be included in the appraisal of the whole property involved. The reason for this is that the part taken plus any damages to the remainder does not exceed the value of the whole property involved. Next, you should value the part to be taken separately and then estimate the damages or enhancements to the remainder. The owner is due the market value for the property being taken from him and no speculative enhancement to the remainder should off-set this.

✔ If the part to be taken has a highest and best use which does not require the use of the remainder, then the part to be taken may be appraised completely as a separate tract of land. The right to do this is very important and not always fully understood. I think the right to consider the part to be taken as separate or severed land is indicated by the following: If the owner should sell either the part to be taken or the remainder before the taking, there would in fact be a separate ownership. How else could the tract then be valued, but as a separate property? This right of the owner to sell proves the point. The owner would certainly have the right to do this until the land is taken. If this right is observed it will help to prevent an unjust award for a taking. The condemning authority can obtain valuable commercial land for the price of lower value acreage if it can influence the court into interpreting the taking as a matter of merely decreasing the depth of a tract, or by assuming some other unwarranted interpretation.

✔ Ordinarily, whether appraising the whole property, the part taken, or the damages to the remainder, market value should be the basis, but all three approaches should be used where possible.

✔ An appraisal of the remainder before the taking and then after the taking, considering the conditions that will probably exist after the taking, should indicate the damages, if any, to the remainder. Damages are quite difficult to assess and the "before and after" procedure is the best method to use for estimating damages.

COURT APPEARANCES

When you make condemnation appraisals you are obligated, if the client is willing to pay your fee, to testify in court as an expert witness for the client. When you do appear in court as an expert witness, you should observe the following:

Be thoroughly prepared. Bring your appraisal up to date. Review it thoroughly and make a brief of it for ready reference when on the stand. Don't take any written or printed material to the stand, such as personal notes, that you do not want the opposing attorney to see. Never let anyone influence you to testify to anything that is not your honest opinion. Naturally, you should not be in court for any purpose other than to present your honest opinion. If you adhere to this you won't have to worry. After all, an appraisal is nothing but the opinion of the appraiser. Be sure the facts that you based your opinion on are correct.

The opposing attorney will try to cross you up in every way he can in order to win the case. He may do everything he can to cause you to lose your temper or become flustered. Relax, give your honest answer, and he will probably be the one who becomes flustered. Don't try to beat him at his own game. You are only a witness on the case—let him be the lawyer. He must put on a show for his client. Remember, the judge is in charge and will ordinarily stop the attorney who goes too far. Your attorney should offer the required objections as necessary for your assistance.

Don't wear flashy clothes in court unless that is your usual manner of dress. Whatever you do, don't allow anyone to put you in the position of appearing to be a person who would testify untruthfully. If you are honest and give your opinion in a straightforward way, the jury and judge will have a favorable impression.

Ordinarily, when you answer a question on the stand, look at the questioner. Otherwise, the jury may think you are avoiding his gaze and may doubt your word. Your attorney may instruct you to look at the jury when you answer questions—but do what you feel is natural under the circumstances. There will be times when your answer will be of such a nature that the jury should be "included," for instance, when you are explaining something. If the opposing attorney requests that you address the jury directly, do so. Do not avoid their gaze.

A word of caution: Never testify to anything unless you have personally confirmed the facts. Don't do this even if your attorney presents you with the information. Perhaps someone he has the utmost confidence in gave it to him—but his reliable source might have received it secondhand also. Don't rely on hearsay in court. Rely on matters you have personally confirmed—and your own opinion of the facts. Attorneys are advocates of their clients, but an appraiser is permitted only to be the advocate of the truth because his position is that of a witness.

SUMMARY

1. Government bodies and certain public utilities are authorized under the authority of eminent domain to institute condemnation action to acquire certain properties when required for use in the public interest. Certain procedures, including appraisals, are recommended so that the owners will not be deprived of property without just compensation for the property taken and for the net damages done to the remainder, if any.
2. Any enhancement to the remainder considered must be direct, real, and immediately pending and not a matter of speculation or based on a future occurrence that is problematic.
3. Damages and benefits enjoyed by the community as a whole are not to be considered even though they affect the remainder of the property taken.
4. The current market value as of the date of the taking is normally the basis of just compensation.
5. Owners of property to be taken should have appraisals made to assure that they receive the proper award, for the condemning authority may differ in its ideas as to what just compensation is.
6. Before making condemnation appraisals, become familiar with the laws and regulations applicable in the state or other jurisdiction involved.

14

Reporting
Techniques

Frequently the principal problem in an appraisal is not the actual technical aspects of the appraisal process, but the presentation of the conclusions in the report in such a manner that the reasoning is clear and obviously correct. What may seem most apparent to you may not be so to the client. The difference in the meaning and usage of words complicates this further. To be acceptable, the findings and conclusions must be expressed in a manner understandable to the client. If the client is not familiar with the appraisal process, you must explain the methods involved.

Time is one of the first essentials for a good appraisal report and quite frequently it is the main problem. More often than not, the client needs the report immediately. Time is of the essence, and he will press you to complete it with great haste. Then again, the client may not want to pay a fee commensurate with the complexity of the problem involved. This may tend to cause you to unintentionally limit the amount of time available for the report. Regardless of the time or payment allowed, you must be justified in your final conclusions, and they must be presented in a manner which is understandable. You should not accept an assignment which does not allow sufficient time and payment. It is better to forego the business than to do a job unworthy of a good reputation.

The more experienced you become in the preparation of appraisal reports, especially narrative reports, the more time you will devote to the planning of the report and the presentation of the conclusions. In this connection, it is helpful to be familiar with the client's viewpoint as to the importance of the various factors involved so that suitable emphasis can be made. The appraisal report must be formed with the purpose and the use of the report clearly in mind. It must be formed to present the reasonings and conclusions involved favorably.

The standard short form type of report offers many problems in this respect. In most cases, it does not provide sufficient space for elaboration or embellishment of the main factors. Most forms appear to be designed to cover only the bare essentials, present the alternative value estimates, and point up the final conclusion. Forms designed for national use do not always fulfill local requirements. Short standard forms generally go through a gradual process of change, but most of them retain the basic design whereby the final conclusion is supposed to be obvious if the questions posed are answered. Regardless of the brevity of the standardized short form report, it is designed for efficiency and fulfills a great need. Most people immediately concerned with a review of such reports are educated and experienced enough to make the forms quite usable and efficient.

In presenting data in the narrative report, do not overemphasize minute details. Guard against letting the purpose and use of the appraisal become secondary to the details of the appraisal.

The approaches are really preliminary estimates. By treating them as such, one need not feel as bound by procedure, and one's reasoning may become more flexible. This may help the appraiser to be more realistic and thorough in the very important job of correlation and formulation of the final conclusion of value. The final conclusion must be reasonable and properly supported by the details of the appraisal report. If your final opinion of value is not one that the client readily recognizes as being proper, it will be absolutely essential that all the necessary facts supporting the value are apparent in the report; otherwise, you may find that you are minus a client.

In the narrative report, always include a summary of the main findings and conclusions at the front of the report for the use of the busy client. Here, too, is a good place to spend more time and thought as to the information he may need. In any event, you must not allow a set form or procedure to prevent a proper appreciation and understanding of the conclusions.

PREPARING THE NARRATIVE REPORT

At first you may have some difficulty in writing the narrative report, particularly if you didn't enjoy writing essays and themes in school, but after some actual experience you will find it is not as difficult as you imagined. Actually, the narrative report is more or less the narrative of the items set forth in the standard short form type of report. The same basic data and methods are involved, but the narrative is more flexible and it allows for a substantiation of the reasoning used in the formulation of the conclusion of value. Exhibit 14-1 is a suggested outline for the report and sequence of preparation. The sequence is indicated by numerals in the first column.

Exhibit 14-1.

SUGGESTED SEQUENCE OF PREPARATION AND OUTLINE OF REPORT

Sequence of
Preparation INTRODUCTION AND IDENTIFICATION

(12) Title Page (If not indicated on the outside of the binder)

(12) Table of Contents

(12) Letter of Transmittal
(Including identification of property appraised, purpose of appraisal, date of value, and definition of value if appropriate.)

(11) Summary of the Appraisal

(10) Method of Valuation

LOCATION ANALYSIS (Physical, Social and Economic Data)

(4) City and/or Area Data

(3) Neighborhood (Including Land Use, Zoning and/or Restrictions)

(2) Site Appraised

Dimensions, Size and Shape

Physical Description

Streets and Utilities

Land Use Zoning and Restrictions

Highest and Best Use of Land

Exhibit 14-1 (continued).

(1)

DESCRIPTION OF BUILDINGS AND LAND IMPROVEMENTS* APPRAISED

Type of Building (s), Units and Use

Structural Outline

Electrical Outline

Mechanical Outline

Miscellaneous

Functional Analysis

Age and Condition

Present Use and Highest and Best Use

Drawings (Include copies of those appropriate)

Sequence of
Preparation

PRELIMINARY ESTIMATES OF VALUE

(5)

Physical Approach

Estimate of Reproduction or Replacement Cost New

of the Building and Land Improvements

Justification of the Cost Factors (if applicable)

Amount of Depreciation

(Describe any physical deterioration and functional

or economic obsolescence.)

Justify the Depreciation Estimate

Summation of Reproduction or Replacement Cost, Less

Depreciation

(7)

Economic Approach

Current Recent Income and Expenses Data

Present Tenant, Lease or Rental Rate and Terms

Comparable Rental Rates

Forecasted Future Gross Income, Vacancy and Collection

Loss, Expenses and Reserve for Replacements

(Justification as applicable)

---

* Or proposed construction.

Exhibit 14-1 (continued).

Net Income Forecast

Forecasted Remaining Economic Life of the Buildings

Capitalization Rate, and Justification

Capitalization and Indicated Value by this Approach

(6)   Market Approach

Comparison with Comparable Offerings and Sales

Supply of and Demand of Comparable Properties

Availability of Competing Sites for New Construction

Trends (as they appear to affect the appraised property)

Estimated Market Value of the Property (and, if applicable,

of the land separately)

Sequence of
Preparation

(8)   CORRELATION OF THE ESTIMATES VALUES

(9)   FINAL OPINION OF VALUE

ENCLOSURES

(The enclosures should be prepared as soon as possible.

Prepare as many as you can before the actual comparisons, etc.)

Photographs (You may want to place the photographs at the

front of the report.)

City or Area Map (Location of the appraised indicated

thereon, as applicable)

Location Map (Indicate location of appraised and comparable sales)

Plot Plan, Floor Plan Drawings, and other Drawings of the

Improvements (as applicable)

List of Standard Contingent and Limiting Conditions

Qualifications of the Appraiser

Other Data, as required

PREPARATION OF THE REPORT

Title page

Prepare a title page (this may be placed on the front of the report binder) of the report in a form similar to the following:

APPRAISAL REPORT

Western Hills Apartment Project

_____City, _____State

Your Name, Title

_____City, _____State

Table of contents

This should be prepared by listing the main headings and other important data by page number. The enclosures may be listed by page number or enclosure number.

Letter of transmittal

The letter of transmittal of the report to the client should contain the following basic information, if not provided elsewhere:

(1) Property appraised
(2) Purpose and use of the appraisal, date of value, and rights appraised
(3) Definition of value (if applicable)

(4) Number of copies of report enclosed, with information as to the number of pages

(5) Any special assumptions and contingencies not included elsewhere or those that need a special notice

(6) Opinion of value

(7) Certificate.

The property should be identified as to the type of property appraised, street address, and legal description. The purpose and use of the appraisal should be as of the date requested by the client. If appropriate, give a definition of the value appraised. If it is necessary to make any unusual assumptions and contingencies, these should be listed in the letter of transmittal so that they will be readily apparent and place the client on notice. The standard list of assumptions and contingencies customarily included in the appraisal should be on a separate page of the report. You may include a certificate above your signature similar to the following: "I certify that I have no present or prospective interest in the property appraised," or otherwise as applicable and appropriate.

Summary of the appraisal

If the report is voluminous, provide a brief summary of the report in front of the report under this heading. This is very important, particularly if the client doesn't have the time to read the report in detail. It should be on a separate page. The summary may be quite helpful to the appraiser if it should become necessary for him to serve as an expert witness in court in connection with the property. In any event, all of the most important data will be readily available for the reader of the report. Information included is similar to Exhibit 14-2.

The summary should be as brief and as concise as possible, but provide the basic essentials.

Method of valuation

Briefly describe and explain the procedures used in the appraisal. State what approaches were used, and if one is omitted, state why. If the client is not familiar with the appraisal process, briefly explain it to him.

City data or area data

If the report is being prepared for an out-of-town client, or if it is possible that the report will be forwarded to an out-of-town client, include very basic data as to the city or area involved.

Exhibit 14-2. SUMMARY OF IMPORTANT DATA AND CONCLUSION

Proposed Project:

Apartments   Utility and washateria:
Living area: Land area:
Carports: Open parking spaces
Other:

Tabulation of Apartments and Forecasted Rental Schedule

Services Provided:

Type	Units	Area	Mo. Rate	Total Per Month

Subtotal .... $_____

Total Forecasted Annual Income from Apartments............... $_____

Total Forecasted Annual Other Income......................... $_____

Total Forecasted Annual Gross Income......................... $_____

Preliminary Value Estimates:

    Indicated value by the market approach: $_____

    Indicated value by the physical approach:

    Estimated construction cost $_____

    Land Value $_____

    Total............................... $_____

    Rounded to.......................... $_____

   Indicated value by the economic approach: $_____

    Capitalization rate: _____

    Assumed economic life of improve-
    ments; _____years.

CONCLUSION AS TO TOTAL VALUE (As of completion date if applicable) $_____

Neighborhood and site analysis

The neighborhood and site should be analyzed as recommended. The information should be briefly described in narrative form.

Description of the building and/or proposed construction and land improvements

You should briefly describe any existing buildings and/or proposed construction and land improvements. The data should be listed in a very brief form under the indicated title and you should not attempt to provide much narrative. Otherwise, the report may become too voluminous. List the basic information under the main divisions concerned.

Physical approach

Prepare this approach as appropriate to the problem.

Market approach

This approach should be prepared as appropriate. Normally, the comparison charts, if any, are not actually included in the appraisal report but are retained in the appraiser's file for reference.

Economic approach

Complete the approach as appropriate to the problem.

Correlation and final estimate of value

Correlation should be completed as necessary to select the proper opinion of value.

Enclosures

This includes photographs, exhibits, and other illustrations used in connection with the appraisal, but not included in the main part of the report. Be sure to enclose the floor plan drawings if an existing property is involved. If the appraisal concerns proposed construction, it is quite helpful to have the blueprints reproduced to letter size and included in the report. This not only assists the client and all reviewers considerably, but is of great importance to the appraiser in that the drawings of the proposed construction are physically included within the appraisal report. Ordinarily, it is not necessary to have the complete blueprint drawings reproduced, but the plot plan, the floor plan(s), and a typical elevation should be included. Usually a location and neighborhood map are included. You may use a part of a legal map or part of a street map of the proper size, and reproduce it for enclosure in the report so that the location data may be shown. It is quite helpful to use the city planning map as it directs everyone's attention to the proposed street or freeway changes in relation to the appraised property. Whichever map is used, it should be large enough to include the location of the comparable sales involved as well as the location of the appraised property.

It is a good policy to include a standard list of contingent and limiting conditions similar to those shown in Exhibit 14-3. Ordinarily, in a narrative report a separate page is listed showing the qualifications of the appraiser. It is a matter of good form and a savings to have the standard list of contingent and limiting conditions and the qualifications of the appraiser printed in volume. You may have your typed page reproduced by the offset printing process.

Form of the report

Of course, it is necessary that the narrative report be in typewritten form. The neater the type, the better. It is very unusual for any type of appraisal report to be submitted in handwritten form except certain types of short form reports prepared for F.H.A. or intra-company use. Be sure to prepare a carbon copy or photo copy of the report for your file.

The narrative report should be typed double-spaced with about $1\frac{1}{4}$ inch at the left margin and one inch at the right margin (more space is needed on left for binding.) The typing should be started within $1\frac{1}{4}$ inch to $1\frac{1}{2}$ inch from the top of the page, and about $1\frac{1}{4}$ inch margin should be left at the bottom of the page. However, this will vary depending upon the report binder that you may use. It is good business to secure a good quality binder; and if you are doing sufficient business, you should have a supply printed for your individual use. It goes without saying that a good grade of typing paper should be used. It is wise to have at least four copies of the report prepared when it is typed. Retain at least one carbon copy and any extra copies of the report for yourself. Quite frequently the client will need several copies and he may request additional copies later.

Before having the report typed, it is a good idea to check over it very carefully to correct the grammar and spelling. If you are not fully quali-

CONTINGENT AND LIMITING CONDITIONS OF THIS APPRAISAL

This report involves a professional, confidential relationship between the appraiser and the client. All rights of publication or advertising through any type of media are reserved by the appraiser, and neither all nor any part of the report may be so divulged without the specific written authorization of the appraiser, particularly as to valuation conclusions.

This appraisal is contingent upon fully responsible ownership and competent management and upon the principals having adequate working capital and reserve funds available to properly conclude any transaction and/or construction involved and for the successful operation or marketing of the property. If an income-type property is involved, the estimated value is contingent upon the rental income and occupancy forecasted.

Unless noted otherwise, the fee simple interest in the property is appraised. The legal description provided for the appraisal is assumed to be correct. The title to the property is assumed to be good and marketable and free and clear of any liens, unless noted otherwise. The appraisal is contingent upon the appraised project not involving a violation of any law, zoning regulation, or restriction.

Any drawings, etc. submitted with the report are provided to assist the reader in visualizing the property. No responsibility as to any legal, auditing, engineering, or survey matters is assumed, as they are not within the scope of this appraisal. The data provided by others is considered to be reliable, but of course no warranty may be made.

The distribution of the valuation in the report between the land and any improvements involved applies only under the existing use, or in accordance with the stated assumptions. When such values are indicated separately, neither should be used in conjunction with any other appraisal.

The appraiser is not required to appear or testify in court by reason of this appraisal, unless arrangements are made otherwise. No liability is assumed as a result of the appraisal. The appraised value is the opinion of the appraiser and involves an interpretation of data and beliefs into an estimate based on the observed situation at the time.

Due to the variable nature of building cost estimates, if any new construction is included in this appraisal the valuation is subject to the following: If the total of all direct and indirect costs of the new construction, including the expense to secure the necessary occupancy plus the appraised value of the land and any remaining existing improvements, is materially lower than the total of the appraised value, the said appraised value is reduced accordingly. (The total cost contemplated above includes all costs of labor and materials, contractor's overhead and profit, architect's and appraiser's fees, other professional services, financing costs, brokerage commissions, taxes, insurance, administrative expense, closing costs, interest during construction, a reasonable estimate of the expense that may be incurred from the completion of construction to time of normal occupancy, and any other expense necessary for the project.) It shall be the responsibility of the client to inform the appraiser and any investors involved of the facts if any material change is involved.

Exhibit 14-3.

fied in this respect, it is advisable that you get someone who is to review it. If you can depend upon your secretary or typist to properly spell the words and assist in the correction of the grammar you have a jewel indeed! It is also advisable to recheck all of your arithmetic computations before and after the report has been typed. Nothing will degrade a report more than poor arithmetic, inadvertent errors, or poor grammar, spelling, and typing. It is very important that your reports be prepared in a thoroughly professional manner, even if you have to send them out for preparation.

OTHER APPRAISAL REPORTING TECHNIQUES

Letter of opinion

Appraisers are often called upon to give an opinion of value without submitting a formal report. Clients requesting this may be trying to reduce the expense of a formal appraisal, or they may be trying to save time and need the information quickly. When such reports are necessary and permissible, you may issue a letter of opinion, but first make a preliminary appraisal and qualify your opinion in the letter as a preliminary appraisal subject to your making a final appraisal of the property. You must have a copy of the preliminary appraisal in your file for substantiation, and it should be a complete basic type of appraisal, even if in pencil form. There is a good possibility you will need it; therefore, be sure to have it ready.

The letter of opinion is a written letter providing for the following basic information:

> (1) Identification of the property, including its dimensions, size, location, type of value, and property rights appraised.
> (2) Assumptions and contingent and limiting conditions of the opinion. Qualify your opinion as being the result of a preliminary appraisal, subject to a final detailed appraisal.
> (3) The age and condition of the property, and estimated remaining economic life of the building.
> (4) The date the estimated value is to apply.
> (5) The stated opinion of value.
> (6) Any other information supplied is left to the discretion of the appraiser or the requirements of the client.

Certificate type of report and standard short form report

The certificate type of report is a printed short form report with a certificate above the appraiser's signature. It is an abbreviated form of the standard short form report. Ordinarily the certificate or short form type forms are not used if the value is over $100,000, or a complex appraisal is involved. The certificate used is generally similar to the following:

> *I certify that I have no personal interest, present or prospective, in the above described property, and that my employment in making this valuation is not contingent upon the amount of the valuation.*

If the form doesn't provide for all the basic data of an appraisal, you should add it.

The standard short form report consists of a printed form which usually provides for the bare essentials of an appraisal but is more detailed than the certificate type of report. The forms usually provide for a listing of the values estimated by the three basic approaches. As a general rule there is a certificate at the end of the report similar to the one used for the certificate type report.

POINTERS

✔ Before proceeding with an appraisal assignment, be sure you understand the problem and the viewpoint of the client—otherwise you may be wasting your time.

✔ If you take an assignment to prepare a letter of opinion or certificate type of report, don't reduce your fee drastically. In some cases, these opinions of value may be about as valuable to the client as a narrative report, particularly if your appraisals are generally accepted. In any case you must make a preliminary appraisal of the property in pencil form, so about all that is saved is the dictation, typing, the paper, in some cases the cost of exhibits, and the binding expense.

✔ Set your fee as required to cover the time, expense, and *responsibility* involved.

✔ Be sure to retain a file copy of all reports prepared.

✔ You may appraise a property even though you own a part of it or have an interest in it, but you must divulge your interest prominently in the report—preferably by amending the certificate. Of course, this must be acceptable to your client.

SUMMARY

1. Present the conclusions so that the reasoning is clear and obviously correct. If the client is not familiar with the appraisal process, you must explain the basic methods involved.
2. The time and fee allowed by the client may not be sufficient; nevertheless, if you accept the job you must be justified in the conclusions, and they must be presented in an understandable manner.
3. Experience will teach you to require an adequate fee and allowance of time. It will also teach you to devote more time to the planning of the appraisal and to the understanding of the client's viewpoint.
4. Most short form type of appraisal forms are designed to cover only the bare essentials, present the alternative value estimates, and point up the final conclusion. Ordinarily this type of report is not used when the value is over $100,000 or a complex problem is involved.
5. The narrative report is more or less the narrative of the items set forth in the standard form report. Usually the same basic data is involved, but more substantiation is provided. It may be arranged to solve the problem involved in a more demonstrative fashion.
6. Whatever form is used, great care should be taken to have the report prepared in a professional and expert form of presentation.
7. You may prepare a letter of opinion when the client must meet a deadline, or when he must secure a preliminary commitment for a loan. However, since you must make a preliminary appraisal for your file and indicate in the letter that it is subject to a final detailed appraisal, there isn't a great amount of time saved.

15

Work Systems
and Office Files

If there is any choice involved, give serious consideration to the type of work you accept. As a general rule, you will find that by specializing in one type of appraisal, say condemnation appraising for the state highway department or primarily residential appraising for the Veterans' Administration, you can turn out a greater quantity of work due to the routine established. However, there is considerable risk involved in specializing in assignments from one particular organization in that you have all your eggs in one basket, and if there is a personality conflict with an official of the organization, you may find that you are suddenly out of business in so far as that organization is concerned. By doing business with many different clients, you are better prepared to weather the changes and have a broader background and perspective.

EFFICIENCY IN THE PROCESSING OF APPRAISAL BUSINESS

It goes without saying that the more qualified you are, the more efficiently the business can be handled. Of course, unless you are handling the most remunerative appraisal business that you can secure, your income will never be as high as it should be. No one needs a business that provides such a low income that he does not receive a living wage for his labors after paying all the expenses involved. Unless you maintain adequate records, you may not know which type of business is producing a fair return. The appraisal of single family dwellings, if done properly, takes much more time and expense than is generally appreciated. The fees for residential appraisals are generally too low for first class professional work. This is particularly true for existing properties.

There is much more involved in the appraisal of real estate than just the labor itself. It has been found that the actual expense of most appraisers doing business on a professional basis will range from about 40 to 55 per cent of the gross income produced each year, depending upon the quantity and quality of the business received. Until the appraiser has done enough work to determine what his appraisal expense is, he must rely on his colleagues for this information. In any event, he must refrain from lowering fees in order to secure business. This is the sure way to ruin, not only for himself but for the profession generally. The profession cannot retain qualified personnel unless adequate fees are received. It is wise to find out what the customary fees are in the community, and if they are not high enough, the appraiser should use his influence to see that they are raised so that qualified appraisers can stay in business.

The expense involved in appraisal work is generally quite a shock to appraisers who have been employed by a governmental agency or large corporation where they are not in close contact with the costs of the various supplies and services used by them in the performance of their appraisal work. An independent appraiser working out of his own home, without an outside office, will find that his expenses may amount to as much as 40 per cent of his gross annual income, depending upon the nature of the business.

EXPENSES INVOLVED IN APPRAISING

Charge for owner-appraiser's time
Office rent or return on space
Taxes
Insurance
Professional dues
Telephone(s)
Listings in directories, etc.
Subscriptions (technical and allied)
Cost manuals
Licenses

Map and atlas services, or lease rental thereof
Return on investment
Salaries
Social security, etc.
Sales data expense
Reproduction of drawings, blueprints, etc.
Utilities, fuel, and janitor service where not
    included in rent
Income and other taxes
Postage
Field supplies
Answering service
Delivery service
Auto expenses
Repairs to auto
Equipment maintenance
Books and special publications
Films
Film processing
Aerial photos
Printing
General Office Supplies:

>   Letterheads, bond paper, second sheets,
>   onion sheets, billheads, accounting rec-
>   ords, carbon paper, tablets, scratch paper,
>   report binders, letter and report files,
>   staples, paper clips, rubber bands, type-
>   writer ribbons, typewriter and pencil
>   erasers, pencils, rubber stamps and pads,
>   envelopes, stencils, stencil correction fluid,
>   mimeograph ink, photo films, microfilms
>   (presently unusual except in larger of-
>   fices), copier fluid (if used), copier nega-
>   tives and copier paper, etc. (if used).

*Reserve for Other Replacement and
    Retirement*

Provisions for personal retirement
Office equipment
Field equipment
Automobile(s)
Other

If you have been in business for several years, you will be in a much
better position to estimate your expenses. You should estimate the cost

of processing the various types of appraisals that you do, based on your records. Then you are in an excellent position to determine the type of business you should seek. The indicated type will probably change every few years. In any event, you should estimate as closely as possible the minimum fee that you should charge. Be sure to include a fair allowance for your time and the responsibility involved with the appraisal. You should remember that the appraiser has a great responsibility to his colleagues, client, and the community, and if his appraisal is worth anything, it is worth a good fee. If competent appraisers could secure the fees that their appraisals are worth to the client, they would generally receive much more.

PROCESSING APPRAISALS

The better the organization and procedures that you have for your office and field work, the more efficient your appraisal work will be. It is generally wise to have a separate file for all incoming appraisal requests, even if it is just a desk file. As each appraisal request is received, a binder should be prepared for it, and all papers concerning it should be kept in that one file, except perhaps your contract for the appraisal work which may be kept in a central file for contracts. The individual file binders for appraisals should be properly identified as to the client and the appraisal. If the appraisal is to contain a large number of papers, legal size expandable type binders should be used. I recommend that you maintain a current work file for appraisals in process and subdivide it similarly to the following, providing a file separator for the main headings:

> Inspections (site, buildings and neighborhood)
> Reinspections
> Computations, etc.
>> Physical Approach
>> Economic Approach
>> Market Approach
> Review and Check of Arithmetic
> Correlation and Conclusion
> Typing Process
> Proofreading
> Billing
> To Permanent Files

If the appraisal organization employs many appraisers, similar files should be maintained for each section of appraisers with a central status card file maintained in the headquarters for ready information as to location and status.

When a field inspection is to be made by the appraiser, he should make all the other pending inspections for that area, if possible, to save time and expense. If enough qualified personnel are available, assignments should be made on the basis of specialization. After the appraiser makes the field inspection, he may have an assistant handle as much of the office work as possible. The appraiser should work closely with the assistant, outlining the various procedures involved and the various formulas to be used. Normally, the appraiser will personally handle the narrative and analysis pertaining to the site, property, and neighborhood, and then outline to his assistant the procedures to use in the detailed calculations involved. He supervises the work as necessary and the assistant makes the routine computations. The appraiser reviews the computations and prescribes the adjustments to be made. The process is repeated until the appraiser is in a position to select the final opinion of value.

The more qualified the personnel, the more efficient the process becomes. As all appraisers know, most of the time the client will want the appraisal as quickly as possible; and, of course, he wants the best work possible. The more these requirements are fulfilled, the better the appraiser's business will be, all else being favorable.

OFFICE RECORDS

An appraisal office should maintain the following files as appropriate:

Accounting Records

These may be only as required for income tax, but if a large business is involved a complete set of books should be maintained. Good blank form single-entry accounting procedure books in loose-leaf are available for most professions and small businesses.

Appraisals

These should be filed alphabetically by the name of the client or by the type of appraisal, or numerically, and cross-indexed. File closely related correspondence and records with the appraisal.

General File

This, of course, is a file for all miscellaneous correspond-

ence and records. If correspondence pertaining to each
appraisal is filed with the appraisal, this file should be
somewhat limited.

Cost Data Files

Sales Data Files

Subdivision and Land Date Files

Microfilm Files

Generally only the larger organizations will have microfilm reader-machines and files.

The usual appraisal office will have a small library of pertinent technical
and trade publications in the form of periodicals, books, and manuals.

OFFICE EQUIPMENT

Of course, you will need suitable office furniture, but your most important item of equipment is a modern calculator. If you are going to
have any volume of business, obtain one or more as your business ex-
pands. Other than the necessary training you couldn't make a better investment. You can buy good used machines quite reasonably. You will
need a good typewriter. You should have a modern electric carbon im-
print typewriter if you have appraisals involving narrative reports. Have
your reports prepared by an expert typist. This is most important. A
good copying machine is very useful in reproducing maps, documents,
reports, etc.; however, for high quality reproductions it is generally best
to have this done at a professional shop. This is necessary when having
blueprints reproduced in letter size for inclusion in the appraisal report.
Professional work of this type is essential.

It is helpful to have a mimeograph machine to prepare forms for your
personal use, as well as to reproduce an appraisal report in quantity when
required. If you have reasonably priced offset printing available it is
better than mimeographing for reports. As a general rule, not more than
five copies of an appraisal report will be required. The copies may be reproduced from the original by the use of a good photo copy machine.
Xerox and Copease machines make very satisfactory copies from either
original or carbon copies.

At the start you will need at least one metal filing cabinet. It should
be of legal size and four files high. An electric recorder suitable for dictat-
ing and transcribing is very helpful in the office. A portable recorder is
especially good for taking notes for neighborhood descriptions in high

speed areas, and for inspecting large buildings. If the tape is interchangeable with the office machine as to size and speed so much the better. Your secretary can transcribe from the other while you are in the field.

You will need 12-inch architectural and engineers' rulers. The architects' rule should provide for the ratio of from $\frac{1}{16}$ to 3, and the engineers' from $\frac{1}{10}$ to $\frac{1}{60}$. Good quality rulers of synthetic material are best for the purpose.

There are several mechanical systems on the market for data recording and retrieval which can be of considerable assistance to the appraiser, but they are too expensive for most individual appraisers. The computer services may offer the most valuable assistance to appraisers since they can not only record and retrieve data with great speed, but they can perform comparison and other computations required. Of course, the appraiser must supply the judgment factors. However, the cost for these services is prohibitive for most individual appraisers.

FIELD EQUIPMENT

Essential items

1. Automobile.
2. Measuring tapes. These should be of 50–75 ft. lengths for residential use and 100 ft. for commercial use.
3. Camera. A Polaroid Land camera (large size) is very helpful. Sometimes it may be difficult to get film developed as quickly as desired, and the Polaroid provides you with pictures you can take back to your office for immediate reference. This is very helpful and important. A 35 mm. or other camera from which a rectangular picture of suitable size and quality can be developed at a reasonable price is very helpful when several prints of each photo or enlargements are required. For special photos, a camera having interchangeable wide-angle and telescopic lenses is helpful. A good picture is really worth a thousand words in an appraisal report. We should use professional photographers more, but the time and expense, as usual, are limiting factors.
4. Clip-board. I think the best type is that which has a fold-over top and a place to hold extra graph paper and so forth. Regular letter size is the handiest.
5. Flashlight. An ordinary two-battery size is sufficient. Just keep it handy when needed for looking into basements, attics, and so on.
6. Portable case to store and transport the above items.

Very helpful items, but not essential

1. Recorder. (For my personal use I classify this as essential).
2. Measuring wheels. It is very helpful to have a measuring wheel that registers the distance automatically. The Rola-tape Company, Santa Monica, California, makes one that registers up to 100 feet and then rings a bell and starts over. It has a 7.5-inch diameter wheel and an expandable handle. It indicates divisions of a foot and inches. This company makes a larger model specifically for land use. The first mentioned wheel is useful for approximate land distances and can be used to measure buildings quite satisfactorily for appraisal use if you have a smooth and hard surface to roll it on. Its limitation is that it only registers to 100 feet. Roto-Rule, 2100 Oakton Street, Park Ridge, Illinois, makes a 3.75-inch measuring wheel with a meter that registers up to 999'11" which is a very good device to use where you have a smooth, hard surface. Its limitation is the small wheel and that you must reverse the wheel back to "0" when you want to start another measurement; however, it is arranged so that this can be done in about five seconds. It is a good all-around measuring device and has an expandable handle. Another small measuring wheel is made by Pix Products Company, Cedar Rapids, Iowa, which does not record the total of the distance but makes a click at each foot so you count them. It has a 3.75-inch wheel that is divided into inches and a marker which indicates the inch measurement where the wheel stops. This wheel is very useful for residences and is especially good for interior room measurements. It has a handle that can be disassembled. It is the lowest priced.
3. Planimeter. This is almost a magical device based on higher mathematics. If a site plat is drawn accurately to scale, you merely follow the perimeter of the site drawing and it automatically computes the square inch area of the paper area. You then convert that area to the scale involved.

APPRAISAL FEES

The fees for appraisals for the Federal Housing Administration and the Veterans' Administration and most state, county, and city departments employing independent appraisers, are usually the same for all appraisers and are based on a minimum competence and other considerations. Most other fees are a matter of negotiation. The best way to formulate the fee to charge is to estimate the processing time and the expense required. Generally, you will find there is a more or less stand-

Exhibit 15-1.
LETTER AUTHORIZATION OF SERVICES.

Dear Sir:

This is to request that you appraise the property described as follows:

This appraisal report is to be addressed to:

The purpose of the appraisal is to:

Prepare the report in _____ copies and distribute as follows:

For the services to be rendered I, we, or either of us, the undersigned, promise to pay you as follows:

I/we also agree to pay you 10% per annum on any past due principal and interest. All amounts shall be paid at your office. The fee is not contingent upon the appraised value or on anything else unless specifically mentioned herein. In the event of default, this will serve as a lien on any property that I/we own. I/we agree to pay all collection charges if this is placed in the hands of a recognized collection agency. If legal proceedings are instituted for the collection of any amount unpaid of this agreement I/we agree to pay in addition thereto, all court costs and such sum as the court may adjudge reasonable as attorney's fees in such suit.

Unless arrangements are made otherwise, the appraisal fee is payable when the report is completed. Should work on the appraisal be suspended or cancelled, I/we agree to pay you immediately for the proportionate amount of work and expense involved, and any past due sums shall bear interest at the rate of 10% per annum.

Should any material change(s) be made as to the basis of the appraisal, the property, or any plans and specifications involved, necessitating a revision of any work in progress or completed, the fee shall be adjusted on the basis of the time and expense involved.

You may telephone (me)(us) at _____

(My)(Our) office address is _____

Yours very truly,

_____

_____

ard hourly rate in the city for professional appraisals. This should be adjusted, considering the complexity and responsibility of the appraisal and the demand for your services. Be sure to include an allowance for all expenses involved. If you have kept adequate records, you can form a good estimate of the expense. If you are new, it may take you longer than an experienced appraiser to perform the work, and you could hardly charge the same fee unless you are employed by a governmental agency. Then again, if you are new, you might not go into the appraisal as thoroughly as you should, and might take less time than necessary to do the job properly. Low fees won't draw good appraisal business. Charge enough to pay all expenses and leave enough to support yourself and your family properly and to provide a reserve for the future. Don't forget to charge for the responsibility involved.

AUTHORIZATION OF SERVICES

Require a written authorization for all appraisals involving a substantial fee. I have used the authorization letter illustrated in Exhibit 15-1 for some time and have found it very satisfactory. If there is any question as to the client's reliability require at least one-half of the fee in advance and the balance placed in escrow to be paid to you upon completion of the report, or require full payment in advance. Don't take an unsecured note from anyone who is questionable. If you accept a note, I would suggest that you require adequate collateral to guarantee performance, otherwise you may only have a paper souvenir for your services. In instances where a large fee and a large amount of time and expense are involved and the client owns the property I think it wise to have your attorney prepare a mechanic's lien contract and note and have the signatures duly notarized and the instrument recorded as required in your state. All of the contingencies listed in Exhibit 15-1 should be included in the contract. If the client doesn't own the property you should substitute a regular contract and a secured note in place of the mechanic's lien. Be sure that provisions are made for the client to pay the collection, legal, and court expenses in event of default. The notes should provide for the maximum interest rate on all delinquent amounts. Charge more for deferred payments, since you will need a reserve for collection losses and expenses.

SUMMARY

1. It is generally wise to do appraisals for at least several different clients rather than one.
2. Expenses may vary between 40–55 per cent, or more of the gross annual amount of appraisal business handled, depending on the type and quantity of the business.
3. The better organization and procedures that you have for your office and field work, the more efficient your appraisal work will be. Computer services may be of great assistance, but too expensive at present for most appraisers.
4. Adequate office records should be maintained.
5. Secure suitable office and field equipment.
6. Require a written authorization for all appraisals involving a substantial fee. If there is any doubt as to payment, require at least one-half cash down and the balance placed in escrow for payment on completion of the report.

SELECTED TABLES FOR LOAN PAYMENTS AND YIELD ON MORTGAGES PURCHASED AT DISCOUNT

from
Casey, *Real Estate Desk Book*

New York, N.Y.: Institute for Business Planning, Inc.
© 1961, pages T22-T26

Self-Liquidating Mortgage Payments - Monthly Interest

This table is especially useful in connection with mortgages on residences. These usually call for monthly payments. The following table shows the constant monthly payment required to liquidate a mortgage loan of $1,000 running for any number of whole years between 5 and 30 years inclusive and at any of the following interest rates: 4 1/2%, 5%, 5 1/4%, 5 1/2%, 5 3/4%, 6%, 6 1/2%, and 7%.

Years of Loan	4 1/2%	5%	5 1/4%	5 1/2%	5 3/4%	6%	6 1/2%	7%
5	$18.65	$18.88	$18.99	$19.11	$19.22	$19.34	$19.57	$19.80
6	15.88	16.11	16.23	16.34	16.46	16.58	16.81	17.05
7	13.91	14.14	14.26	14.38	14.49	14.61	14.85	15.09
8	12.43	12.66	12.78	12.90	13.03	13.15	13.39	13.63
9	11.28	11.52	11.64	11.76	11.89	12.01	12.26	12.51
10	10.37	10.61	10.73	10.86	10.98	11.11	11.36	11.61
11	9.62	9.87	9.99	10.12	10.25	10.37	10.63	10.88
12	9.01	9.25	9.38	9.51	9.63	9.76	10.02	10.28
13	8.48	8.74	8.86	8.99	9.12	9.25	9.52	9.78
14	8.04	8.29	8.42	8.55	8.68	8.82	9.09	9.35
15	7.65	7.91	8.04	8.18	8.31	8.44	8.72	8.99
16	7.32	7.58	7.71	7.85	7.98	8.12	8.40	8.67
17	7.03	7.29	7.43	7.56	7.70	7.84	8.12	8.40
18	6.77	7.04	7.17	7.31	7.45	7.59	7.87	8.16
19	6.54	6.81	6.95	7.08	7.22	7.37	7.65	7.94
20	6.33	6.60	6.74	6.88	7.03	7.17	7.46	7.75
21	6.15	6.42	6.56	6.70	6.85	6.99	7.29	7.59
22	5.98	6.26	6.40	6.54	6.69	6.84	7.13	7.43
23	5.83	6.11	6.25	6.40	6.54	6.69	7.00	7.31
24	5.69	5.97	6.12	6.27	6.41	6.56	6.87	7.18
25	5.56	5.85	6.00	6.15	6.30	6.45	6.76	7.07
26	5.45	5.74	5.89	6.04	6.19	6.34	6.65	6.96
27	5.34	5.64	5.78	5.94	6.09	6.24	6.56	6.88
28	5.24	5.54	5.69	5.84	6.00	6.16	6.48	6.80
29	5.15	5.45	5.61	5.76	5.92	6.08	6.40	6.72
30	5.07	5.37	5.53	5.68	5.84	6.00	6.33	6.66

SELECTED TABLES FOR LOAN PAYMENTS AND YIELD ON MORTGAGES PURCHASED AT DISCOUNT.

Constant Payments on Mortgages With "Balloons"

The following table reflects the practice of determining a combined interest and amortization rate to be paid over the term of the mortgage. Very often, the full principal will not have been liquidated by the end of the term. The term "balloon" refers to the balance due on the mortgage at the end of the term.

This table is designed to be used as a quick guide in determining what percentage of a mortgage will be paid off at the end of 5, 10 and 15 years. This is very useful in planning the purchase of property, since it tells you how much of the mortgage will be paid off at the time you may be considering selling or refinancing. This table also shows what term will be required to amortize the mortgage in full. When using this table, you determine the annual payments as a percentage of the original mortgage. For instance, quarterly payments of $4,250 on a $200,000 mortgage add up to constant payments of 8½% per year. If your interest rate is 6%, it will take 20 years and 9 months to liquidate the mortgage in full. At the end of 5 years, the mortgage will be reduced by $28,900 (14.45%); in 10 years, by $67,820 (33.91%); and in 15 years, by $120,260 (60.13%).

Approximate Percentage of Principal Paid

Constant Payment	Int. Rate	5 Yrs.	10 Yrs.	15 Yrs.	Fully Paid in Yrs.	Mo.
5%	4%	5.50	12.22	20.41	40	6
5½%	4%	8.25	18.33	30.62	32	9
	4-1/4%	6.92	15.47	26.04	35	3
	4-1/2%	5.57	12.54	21.25	38	3
6%	4%	11.01	24.44	40.83	27	9
	4-1/4%	9.69	21.66	36.45	29	3
	4-1/2%	8.35	18.81	31.88	31	0
	4-3/4%	7.00	15.88	27.12	33	3
	5%	5.64	12.87	22.14	36	3
6½%	4%	13.76	30.55	51.04	24	3
	4-1/4%	12.46	27.85	46.87	25	3
	4-1/2%	11.14	25.08	42.51	26	6
	4-3/4%	9.81	22.23	37.96	28	0
	5%	8.46	19.30	33.21	29	9
	5-1/4%	7.09	16.30	28.25	31	9
	5-1/2%	5.71	13.21	23.07	34	6
7%	4%	16.51	36.66	61.25	21	6
	4-1/4%	15.23	34.04	57.29	22	3
	4-1/2%	13.93	31.35	53.14	23	3
	4-3/4%	12.61	28.58	48.81	24	3
	5%	11.28	25.74	44.28	25	3
	5-1/4%	9.93	22.82	39.55	26	9
	5-1/2%	8.56	19.82	34.61	28	3
	5-3/4%	7.18	16.73	29.44	30	3
	6%	5.78	13.56	24.05	32	9

211

SELECTED TABLES FOR LOAN PAYMENTS AND YIELD ON MORTGAGES PURCHASED AT DISCOUNT.

			Approximate Percentage of Principal Paid (Continued)			
Constant Payment	Int. Rate	5 Yrs.	10 Yrs.	15 Yrs.	Fully Paid In Yrs.	Mo.
7½%	4%	19.26	42.77	71.46	19	3
	4-1/4%	18.00	40.23	67.70	20	0
	4-1/2%	16.71	37.62	63.77	20	6
	4-3/4%	15.41	34.94	59.66	21	3
	5%	14.10	32.18	55.35	22	3
	5-1/4%	12.77	29.34	50.85	23	3
	5-1/2%	11.42	26.42	46.19	24	3
	5-3/4%	10.05	23.43	41.22	25	6
	6%	8.67	20.35	36.08	27	3
8%	4%	22.01	48.88	81.67	17	6
	4-1/4%	20.76	46.42	78.12	18	0
	4-1/2%	19.50	43.89	74.40	18	6
	4-3/4%	18.22	41.29	70.51	19	3
	5%	16.92	38.61	66.43	19	9
	5-1/4%	15.60	35.86	62.15	20	6
	5-1/2%	14.27	33.03	57.68	21	6
	5-3/4%	12.92	30.12	53.00	22	3
	6%	11.56	27.13	48.10	23	6
8½%	4%	24.77	54.99	91.87	16	0
	4-1/4%	23.53	52.61	88.53	16	6
	4-1/2%	22.28	50.16	85.03	17	0
	4-3/4%	21.02	47.64	81.35	17	6
	5%	19.74	45.05	77.50	18	0
	5-1/4%	18.44	42.38	73.46	18	6
	5-1/2%	17.13	39.62	69.22	19	3
	5-3/4%	15.80	36.82	64.78	20	0
	6%	14.45	33.91	60.13	20	9
9%	4%	27.52	61.10		15	0
	4-1/4%	26.30	58.80	98.95	15	3
	4-1/2%	25.07	56.43	95.66	15	6
	4-3/4%	23.82	53.99	92.20	16	0
	5%	22.56	51.49	88.57	16	6
	5-1/4%	21.28	48.90	84.76	17	0
	5-1/2%	19.98	46.25	80.76	17	6
	5-3/4%	18.67	43.51	76.56	18	0
	6%	17.34	40.70	72.16	18	6
9½%	4%	30.27	67.21		13	9
	4-1/4%	29.07	64.99		14	3
	4-1/2%	27.86	62.70		14	6
	4-3/4%	26.63	60.35		14	9
	5%	25.38	57.92	99.64	15	3
	5-1/4%	24.12	55.42	96.06	15	6
	5-1/2%	22.84	52.85	92.30	16	0
	5-3/4%	21.54	50.21	88.34	16	6
	6%	20.23	47.48	84.18	17	0

212

SELECTED TABLES FOR LOAN PAYMENTS AND YIELD ON MORTGAGES PURCHASED AT DISCOUNT.

Constant Payment	Int. Rate	5 Yrs.	10 Yrs.	15 Yrs.	Fully Paid in Yrs.	Mo.
10%	4%	33.02	73.33		13	0
	4-1/4%	31.84	71.18		13	3
	4-1/2%	30.67	68.79		13	6
	4-3/4%	29.43	66.70		13	9
	5%	28.20	64.36		14	0
	5-1/4%	26.95	61.94		14	6
	5-1/2%	25.69	59.46		14	9
	5-3/4%	24.42	56.90		15	0
	6%	23.12	54.26	96.21	15	6
10 ½%	4%	35.78	79.44		12	3
	4-1/4%	34.61	77.37		12	6
	4-1/2%	33.43	75.25		12	9
	4-3/4%	32.23	73.05		13	0
	5%	31.02	70.80		13	3
	5-1/4%	29.79	68.47		13	6
	5-1/2%	28.55	66.07		13	9
	5-3/4%	27.29	63.60		14	0
	6%	26.01	61.05		14	3
11%	4%	38.53	85.55		11	6
	4-1/4%	37.38	83.56		11	9
	4-1/2%	36.22	81.52		12	0
	4-3/4%	35.04	79.41		12	0
	5%	33.84	77.23		12	3
	5-1/4%	32.63	74.99		12	6
	5-1/2%	31.40	72.67		12	9
	5-3/4%	30.16	70.29		13	0
	6%	28.90	67.83		13	3
11½%	4%	41.28	91.66		10	9
	4-1/4%	40.15	89.75		11	0
	4-1/2%	39.00	87.79		11	3
	4-3/4%	37.84	85.76		11	6
	5%	36.66	83.67		11	6
	5-1/4%	35.47	81.51		11	9
	5-1/2%	34.26	79.28		12	0
	5-3/4%	33.03	76.98		12	3
	6%	31.79	74.61		12	6
12%	4%	44.03	97.77		10	3
	4-1/4%	42.92	95.98		10	6
	4-1/2%	41.79	94.06		10	9
	4-3/4%	40.64	92.11		10	9
	5%	39.48	90.10		11	0
	5-1/4%	38.30	88.03		11	3
	5-1/2%	37.11	85.89		11	3
	5-3/4%	35.90	83.68		11	6
	6%	34.68	81.40		11	9

Yield on Mortgages Purchased at a Discount

In the following table there is shown the yield to the investor on a mortgage purchased at a discount. Yields are given for mortgages calling for interest rates of 5%, 5 1/2%, and 6% which were purchased at discounts running from 1/2% to 6% and which have 10, 15, 20, 25, 30 or 40 years to run.

	Years to Run on Mortgage					
	10	15	20	25	30	40
			Yield			
% Disc.	%	%	%	%	%	%
	(Mortgage Interest Rate: 5%)					
1/2	5.11	5.08	5.06	5.05	5.04	5.04
1	5.22	5.15	5.12	5.1	5.09	5.07
1 1/2	5.33	5.23	5.18	5.15	5.13	5.11
2	5.44	5.31	5.24	5.2	5.18	5.15
2 1/2	5.55	5.39	5.30	5.26	5.22	5.19
3	5.67	5.47	5.37	5.31	5.27	5.22
3 1/2	5.78	5.55	5.43	5.36	5.32	5.26
4	5.89	5.63	5.49	5.41	5.36	5.3
4 1/2	6.01	5.71	5.56	5.47	5.41	5.34
5	6.12	5.79	5.62	5.52	5.46	5.38
5 1/2	6.24	5.87	5.68	5.58	5.5	5.42
6	6.36	5.95	5.75	5.63	5.55	5.46
	(Mortgage Interest Rate: 5 1/2%)					
1/2	5.61	5.58	5.56	5.55	5.55	5.54
1	5.72	5.65	5.62	5.6	5.59	5.58
1 1/2	5.83	5.73	5.68	5.66	5.64	5.62
2	5.94	5.81	5.75	5.71	5.68	5.65
2 1/2	6.06	5.89	5.81	5.76	5.73	5.69
3	6.17	5.97	5.87	5.82	5.78	5.73
3 1/2	6.29	6.05	5.94	5.87	5.83	5.77
4	6.4	6.13	6.	5.92	5.87	5.81
4 1/2	6.52	6.22	6.07	5.98	5.92	5.85
5	6.64	6.3	6.13	6.03	5.97	5.89
5 1/2	6.75	6.38	6.20	6.09	6.02	5.94
6	6.87	6.47	6.26	6.15	6.07	5.98
	(Mortgage Interest Rate: 6%)					
1/2	6.11	6.08	6.06	6.05	6.05	6.04
1	6.22	6.16	6.13	6.11	6.09	6.08
1 1/2	6.34	6.24	6.19	6.16	6.14	6.12
2	6.45	6.32	6.25	6.21	6.19	6.16
2 1/2	6.56	6.4	6.32	6.27	6.24	6.2
3	6.68	6.48	6.38	6.32	6.29	6.24
3 1/2	6.79	6.56	6.45	6.38	6.34	6.28
4	6.91	6.64	6.51	6.44	6.38	6.33
4 1/2	7.03	6.73	6.58	6.49	6.44	6.37
5	7.15	6.81	6.64	6.55	6.49	6.41
5 1/2	7.27	6.9	6.71	6.6	6.54	6.45
6	7.39	6.98	6.78	6.66	6.59	6.5

SELECTED COMPOUND INTEREST AND ANNUITY TABLES

from
U.S. Corps of Engineers, *Real Property Appraiser's Handbook*
Washington, D.C.: U.S. Government Printing Office, pages 118-130

TABLE I

Present Worth of $1 per Annum
(Inwood Coefficient)
For Computing Lessor's Interest, or Lessee's Profit

Speculative interest rates

Years	4%	4½%	5%	5½%	6%	6½%	7%	7½%	8%	9%	10%	11%	12%	13%	14%	15%
1	0.961	0.957	0.952	0.948	0.943	0.939	0.935	0.930	0.926	0.917	0.909	0.901	0.893	0.885	0.877	0.870
2	1.886	1.873	1.859	1.846	1.833	1.821	1.808	1.796	1.783	1.759	1.736	1.713	1.690	1.668	1.647	1.626
3	2.775	2.749	2.723	2.698	2.673	2.648	2.624	2.600	2.577	2.531	2.487	2.444	2.402	2.361	2.322	2.283
4	3.630	3.587	3.546	3.505	3.465	3.426	3.387	3.349	3.312	3.240	3.170	3.102	3.037	2.974	2.914	2.855
5	4.452	4.390	4.329	4.270	4.212	4.156	4.100	4.046	3.993	3.890	3.791	3.696	3.605	3.517	3.433	3.352
6	5.242	5.158	5.076	4.996	4.917	4.841	4.766	4.694	4.623	4.486	4.355	4.231	4.564	3.998	3.889	3.785
7	6.002	5.893	5.786	5.683	5.582	5.485	5.389	5.297	5.206	5.033	4.868	4.712	4.564	4.423	4.288	4.160
8	6.733	6.596	6.463	6.334	6.210	6.089	5.971	5.857	5.747	5.535	5.335	5.146	4.968	4.799	4.639	4.487
9	7.435	7.269	7.108	6.952	6.802	6.656	6.515	6.379	6.247	5.995	5.759	5.537	5.328	5.132	4.946	4.772
10	8.111	7.913	7.722	7.538	7.360	7.189	7.024	6.864	6.710	6.418	6.145	5.889	5.650	5.426	5.216	5.019
11	8.760	8.529	8.306	8.093	7.887	7.689	7.499	7.315	7.139	6.805	6.495	6.206	5.938	5.687	5.453	5.234
12	9.385	9.118	8.863	8.618	8.384	8.159	7.943	7.735	7.536	7.161	6.814	6.492	6.194	5.918	5.660	5.421
13	9.986	9.683	9.394	9.117	8.853	8.600	8.358	8.126	7.904	7.487	7.103	6.750	6.424	6.122	5.842	5.583
14	10.563	10.223	9.899	9.590	9.295	9.014	8.745	8.489	8.244	7.786	7.367	6.982	6.628	6.302	6.002	5.724
15	11.118	10.739	10.380	10.038	9.712	9.403	9.108	8.827	8.559	8.061	7.606	7.191	6.811	6.462	6.142	5.847
16	11.652	11.234	10.838	10.462	10.106	9.768	9.447	9.142	8.851	8.313	8.022	7.379	6.974	6.604	6.265	5.954
17	12.166	11.707	11.274	10.865	10.477	10.110	9.763	9.434	9.122	8.544	8.201	7.549	7.120	6.729	6.373	6.047
18	12.659	12.160	11.690	11.246	10.828	10.432	10.059	9.706	9.372	8.756	8.365	7.702	7.250	6.840	6.467	6.128
19	13.134	12.593	12.085	11.608	11.158	10.735	10.336	9.959	9.604	8.950	8.514	7.839	7.366	6.938	6.550	6.198
20	13.590	13.008	12.462	11.950	11.470	11.019	10.594	10.194	9.818	9.128	8.649	7.963	7.469	7.025	6.623	6.259
21	14.029	13.405	12.821	12.275	11.764	11.285	10.835	10.413	10.017	9.292	8.772	8.075	7.562	7.102	6.687	6.312
22	14.451	13.784	13.163	12.583	12.042	11.535	11.061	10.617	10.201	9.442	8.883	8.176	7.645	7.170	6.743	6.359
23	14.857	14.148	13.489	12.875	12.303	11.770	11.272	10.807	10.371	9.580	8.985	8.266	7.718	7.230	6.792	6.399
24	15.247	14.495	13.799	13.152	12.550	11.991	11.469	10.983	10.529	9.707	9.077	8.348	7.784	7.283	6.835	6.434
25	15.622	14.828	14.094	13.414	12.783	12.198	11.654	11.147	10.675	9.823	9.161	8.422	7.843	7.330	6.873	6.464
26	15.983	15.147	14.375	13.662	13.003	12.392	11.826	11.299	10.810	9.929	9.237	8.488	7.896	7.372	6.906	6.491
27	16.330	15.451	14.643	13.898	13.210	12.575	11.987	11.441	10.935	10.026	9.307	8.548	7.943	7.409	6.935	6.513
28	16.663	15.743	14.898	14.121	13.406	12.746	12.137	11.573	11.051	10.116	9.307	8.602	7.984	7.441	6.961	6.534

TABLE I (continued).

	1	2	3	4	5	6	7	8	9	10	11	12	13	14	15	16	
30	6.566	7.003	7.496	8.055	8.694	9.427	10.274	11.258	11.810	12.409	13.059	13.765	14.534	15.372	16.289	17.292	30
31	6.579	7.020	7.518	8.085	8.733	9.479	10.343	11.350	11.917	12.532	13.201	13.929	14.724	15.593	16.544	17.588	31
32	6.590	7.035	7.538	8.112	8.769	9.526	10.406	11.435	12.015	12.647	13.334	14.084	14.904	15.803	16.789	17.874	32
33	6.600	7.048	7.556	8.135	8.801	9.569	10.464	11.514	12.107	12.754	13.459	14.230	15.075	16.002	17.023	18.148	33
34	6.609	7.060	7.572	8.157	8.829	9.609	10.518	11.587	12.193	12.854	13.577	14.368	15.237	16.193	17.247	18.411	34
35	6.617	7.070	7.586	8.176	8.855	9.644	10.567	11.655	12.272	12.948	13.687	14.498	15.390	16.374	17.461	18.665	35
36	6.623	7.079	7.598	8.193	8.879	9.676	10.612	11.717	12.347	13.035	13.791	14.621	15.536	16.547	17.666	18.908	36
37	6.629	7.087	7.609	8.207	8.900	9.706	10.653	11.775	12.415	13.117	13.888	14.737	15.674	16.711	17.862	19.143	37
38	6.634	7.094	7.618	8.221	8.919	9.733	10.691	11.829	12.479	13.193	13.979	14.846	15.805	16.868	18.050	19.368	38
39	6.638	7.100	7.627	8.233	8.936	9.757	10.726	11.879	12.539	13.265	14.065	14.949	15.929	17.017	18.230	19.584	39
40	6.642	7.105	7.634	8.244	8.951	9.779	10.757	11.925	12.594	13.332	14.145	15.046	16.046	17.159	18.401	19.793	40
41	6.645	7.110	7.641	8.253	8.965	9.799	10.786	11.967	12.646	13.394	14.221	15.138	16.157	17.294	18.566	19.993	41
42	6.648	7.114	7.647	8.262	8.977	9.817	10.813	12.007	12.694	13.452	14.292	15.224	16.263	17.423	18.724	20.186	42
43	6.650	7.117	7.652	8.270	8.989	9.834	10.838	12.043	12.738	13.507	14.359	15.306	16.363	17.546	18.874	20.371	43
44	6.652	7.120	7.657	8.276	8.999	9.849	10.861	12.077	12.780	13.558	14.421	15.383	16.458	17.663	19.018	20.549	44
45	6.654	7.123	7.661	8.283	9.008	9.863	10.881	12.108	12.819	13.605	14.480	15.456	16.548	17.774	19.156	20.720	45
46	6.656	7.126	7.664	8.288	9.016	9.875	10.900	12.137	12.855	13.650	14.535	15.524	16.633	17.880	19.288	20.885	46
47	6.657	7.128	7.668	8.293	9.024	9.887	10.918	12.164	12.888	13.692	14.587	15.589	16.714	17.981	19.415	21.043	47
48	6.659	7.130	7.670	8.297	9.030	9.897	10.933	12.189	12.919	13.730	14.636	15.650	16.790	18.077	19.536	21.195	48
49	6.660	7.131	7.673	8.301	9.036	9.906	10.948	12.212	12.948	13.767	14.682	15.708	16.863	18.169	19.651	21.341	49
50	6.661	7.133	7.675	8.305	9.042	9.915	10.962	12.233	12.975	13.801	14.724	15.762	16.931	18.256	19.762	21.482	50
51	6.661	7.134	7.677	8.308	9.047	9.923	10.974	12.253	13.000	13.832	14.765	15.813	16.997	18.339	19.868	21.617	51
52	6.662	7.135	7.679	8.310	9.051	9.930	10.985	12.271	13.023	13.862	14.803	15.861	17.058	18.418	19.969	21.748	52
53	6.663	7.136	7.680	8.313	9.055	9.936	10.996	12.288	13.045	13.890	14.838	15.907	17.117	18.493	20.066	21.873	53
54	6.663	7.137	7.682	8.315	9.058	9.942	11.005	12.304	13.065	13.916	14.872	15.950	17.173	18.565	20.159	21.993	54
55	6.664	7.137	7.683	8.317	9.062	9.947	11.014	12.319	13.084	13.940	14.903	15.990	17.225	18.633	20.248	22.109	55
56	6.664	7.138	7.684	8.319	9.065	9.952	11.022	12.332	13.101	13.963	14.932	16.029	17.275	18.698	20.333	22.219	56
57	6.664	7.139	7.685	8.320	9.067	9.956	11.029	12.344	13.117	13.984	14.960	16.065	17.322	18.760	20.414	22.327	57
58	6.665	7.139	7.686	8.322	9.070	9.960	11.036	12.356	13.132	14.003	14.986	16.099	17.367	18.819	20.492	22.430	58
59	6.665	7.140	7.687	8.323	9.072	9.964	11.042	12.367	13.146	14.022	15.010	16.131	17.410	18.876	20.567	22.528	59
60	6.665	7.140	7.687	8.324	9.074	9.967	11.048	12.377	13.159	14.039	15.033	16.161	17.450	18.929	20.638	22.623	60
61	6.665	7.140	7.688	8.325	9.075	9.970	11.053	12.386	13.172	14.055	15.054	16.190	17.488	18.980	20.706	22.715	61
62	6.666	7.141	7.688	8.326	9.077	9.973	11.058	12.394	13.183	14.070	15.075	16.217	17.524	19.029	20.771	22.803	62
63	6.666	7.141	7.689	8.327	9.078	9.975	11.062	12.402	13.193	14.084	15.093	16.242	17.558	19.075	20.834	22.887	63
64	6.666	7.141	7.689	8.327	9.079	9.978	11.066	12.409	13.203	14.098	15.111	16.266	17.591	19.119	20.894	22.968	64
65	6.666	7.141	7.690	8.328	9.081	9.980	11.070	12.416	13.212	14.110	15.128	16.289	17.622	19.161	20.951	23.047	65
66	6.666	7.142	7.690	8.329	9.082	9.981	11.073	12.422	13.221	14.121	15.144	16.310	17.651	19.201	21.006	23.122	66
67	6.666	7.142	7.690	8.329	9.083	9.983	11.077	12.428	13.228	14.132	15.158	16.331	17.679	19.239	21.058	23.194	67
68	6.666	7.142	7.691	8.330	9.083	9.985	11.079	12.433	13.236	14.142	15.172	16.350	17.705	19.275	21.108	23.263	68
69	6.666	7.142	7.691	8.330	9.084	9.986	11.082	12.438	13.243	14.152	15.185	16.368	17.730	19.310	21.156	23.330	69
70	6.666	7.142	7.691	8.331	9.085	9.987	11.084	12.443	13.249	14.160	15.197	16.384	17.753	19.343	21.202	23.394	70
71	6.666	7.142	7.691	8.331	9.085	9.988	11.087	12.447	13.255	14.169	15.209	16.400	17.776	19.374	21.246	23.456	71
72	6.666	7.142	7.691	8.331	9.086	9.990	11.089	12.451	13.260	14.176	15.219	16.416	17.797	19.404	21.288	23.516	72
73	6.666	7.142	7.691	8.331	9.086	9.990	11.090	12.455	13.265	14.183	15.230	16.430	17.817	19.432	21.328	23.573	73

See footnote at end of table.

TABLE I (continued).

Speculative interest rates

Years	4%	4½%	5%	5½%	6%	6½%	7%	7½%	8%	9%	10%	11%	12%	13%	14%	15%	Years
74	23.628	21.367	19.459	17.836	16.443	15.239	14.190	13.270	12.458	11.092	9.991	9.087	8.331	7.691	7.142	6.666	74
75	23.680	21.404	19.485	17.854	16.456	15.248	14.196	13.274	12.461	11.094	9.992	9.087	8.332	7.692	7.142	6.666	75
76	23.731	21.439	19.509	17.871	16.468	15.256	14.202	13.279	12.464	11.095	9.993	9.088	8.332	7.692	7.143	6.667	76
77	23.780	21.473	19.533	17.887	16.479	15.264	14.208	13.282	12.467	11.097	9.994	9.088	8.332	7.692	7.143	6.667	77
78	23.827	21.505	19.555	17.903	16.490	15.271	14.213	13.286	12.469	11.098	9.994	9.088	8.332	7.692	7.143	6.667	78
79	23.872	21.536	19.576	17.917	16.500	15.278	14.217	13.289	12.471	11.099	9.995	9.089	8.332	7.692	7.143	6.667	79
80	23.915	21.565	19.596	17.931	16.509	15.285	14.222	13.292	12.473	11.100	9.995	9.089	8.332	7.692	7.143	6.667	80
81	23.957	21.594	19.616	17.944	16.518	15.291	14.226	13.295	12.475	11.101	9.996	9.089	8.333	7.692	7.143	6.667	81
82	23.997	21.621	19.634	17.956	16.526	15.297	14.230	13.298	12.477	11.102	9.996	9.089	8.333	7.692	7.143	6.667	82
83	24.036	21.647	19.651	17.968	16.534	15.302	14.234	13.300	12.479	11.102	9.996	9.089	8.333	7.692	7.143	6.667	83
84	24.073	21.671	19.668	17.979	16.542	15.307	14.237	13.303	12.480	11.103	9.997	9.089	8.333	7.692	7.143	6.667	84
85	24.108	21.695	19.684	17.990	16.549	15.312	14.240	13.305	12.482	11.104	9.997	9.090	8.333	7.692	7.143	6.667	85
86	24.143	21.718	19.699	18.000	16.556	15.316	14.243	13.307	12.483	11.104	9.997	9.090	8.333	7.692	7.143	6.667	86
87	24.176	21.739	19.713	18.009	16.562	15.320	14.246	13.309	12.484	11.105	9.997	9.090	8.333	7.692	7.143	6.667	87
88	24.207	21.760	19.727	18.018	16.568	15.324	14.249	13.310	12.486	11.105	9.998	9.090	8.333	7.692	7.143	6.667	88
89	24.238	21.780	19.740	18.027	16.573	15.328	14.251	13.312	12.487	11.106	9.998	9.090	8.333	7.692	7.143	6.667	89
90	24.267	21.799	19.752	18.035	16.579	15.331	14.253	13.313	12.488	11.106	9.998	9.090	8.333	7.692	7.143	6.667	90
91	24.295	21.817	19.764	18.043	16.584	15.335	14.255	13.315	12.489	11.107	9.998	9.090	8.333	7.692	7.143	6.667	91
92	24.323	21.835	19.775	18.050	16.588	15.338	14.257	13.316	12.489	11.107	9.998	9.090	8.333	7.692	7.143	6.667	92
93	24.349	21.852	19.786	18.057	16.593	15.341	14.259	13.317	12.490	11.107	9.999	9.090	8.333	7.692	7.143	6.667	93
94	24.374	21.867	19.796	18.063	16.597	15.343	14.261	13.318	12.491	11.108	9.999	9.090	8.333	7.692	7.143	6.667	94
95	24.398	21.883	19.806	18.069	16.601	15.346	14.263	13.319	12.492	11.108	9.999	9.090	8.333	7.692	7.143	6.667	95
96	24.421	21.897	19.815	18.075	16.605	15.348	14.264	13.320	12.492	11.108	9.999	9.091	8.333	7.692	7.143	6.667	96
97	24.443	21.911	19.824	18.081	16.608	15.350	14.265	13.321	12.493	11.109	9.999	9.091	8.333	7.692	7.143	6.667	97
98	24.465	21.925	19.832	18.086	16.611	15.352	14.267	13.322	12.493	11.109	9.999	9.091	8.333	7.692	7.143	6.667	98
99	24.485	21.938	19.840	18.091	16.615	15.354	14.268	13.323	12.494	11.109	9.999	9.091	8.333	7.692	7.143	6.667	99
100	24.505	21.950	19.848	18.096	16.617	15.356	14.269	13.324	12.494	11.109	9.999	9.091	8.333	7.692	7.143	6.667	100

Equal annual amounts; payable at end of year.

TABLE II

Present Worth of Increasing and Decreasing Annuities, Straight Line Percent Changes
(Inwood Premise)
6 Percent

Years	Income annually decreasing at rate shown								
	−2%	−3%	−4%	−5%	−7%	−10%	−12%	−14%	−20%
1	0.94	0.94	0.94	0.94	0.94	0.94	0.94	0.94	0.94
2	1.81	1.81	1.80	1.79	1.77	1.74	1.73	1.71	1.66
3	2.62	2.60	2.57	2.54	2.49	2.42	2.36	2.31	2.16
4	3.37	3.32	3.27	3.22	3.12	2.97	2.87	2.77	2.48
5	4.05	3.97	3.89	3.82	3.66	3.42	3.26	3.10	2.63
6	4.69	4.57	4.46	4.34	4.11	3.77	3.54	3.31	
7	5.27	5.12	4.96	4.81	4.50	4.04	3.73	3.42	
8	5.81	5.61	5.42	5.22	4.82	4.23	3.83	3.43	
9	6.31	6.06	5.82	5.57	5.08	4.34	3.85		
10	6.77	6.47	6.18	5.88	5.29	4.40			
11	7.19	6.84	6.49	6.14	5.45				
12	7.58	7.17	6.77	6.37	5.56				
13	7.93	7.47	7.01	6.55	5.63				
14	8.26	7.74	7.23	6.71	5.67				
15	8.56	7.99	7.41	6.83	5.68				
16	8.84	8.20	7.57	6.93					
17	9.09	8.39	7.70	7.01					
18	9.32	8.57	7.81	7.06					
19	9.53	8.72	7.91	7.09					
20	9.72	8.85	7.96	7.10					

Illustration: An annuity for 5 years commencing with an initial payment of $1 and decreasing 7 cents each year, discounted at 6 percent is today worth $3.66.

Years	Income annually increasing at rate shown								
	+2%	+3%	+4%	+5%	+7%	+10%	+12%	+14%	+20%
1	0.94	0.94	0.94	0.94	0.94	0.94	0.94	0.94	0.94
2	1.85	1.86	1.87	1.88	1.90	1.92	1.94	1.96	2.01
3	2.72	2.75	2.78	2.80	2.85	2.93	2.98	3.03	3.19
4	3.56	3.61	3.66	3.71	3.81	3.96	4.06	4.16	4.45
5	4.37	4.45	4.53	4.61	4.77	5.01	5.16	5.32	5.80
6	5.15	5.26	5.38	5.49	5.72	6.06	6.29	6.52	7.21
7	5.89	6.05	6.20	6.35	6.66	7.13	7.44	7.74	8.67
8	6.61	6.80	7.00	7.20	7.60	8.19	8.59	8.99	10.18
9	7.29	7.54	7.78	8.03	8.52	9.26	9.75	10.24	11.72
10	7.95	8.25	8.54	8.84	9.43	10.32	10.91	11.50	13.28
11	8.58	8.93	9.28	9.63	10.33	11.37	12.07	12.77	14.86
12	9.19	9.59	10.00	10.40	11.21	12.42	13.22	14.03	16.45
13	9.77	10.23	10.69	11.15	12.07	13.45	14.37	15.29	18.04
14	10.33	10.85	11.36	11.88	12.91	14.46	15.50	16.53	19.64
15	10.86	11.44	12.01	12.59	13.74	15.47	16.62	17.77	21.22
16	11.37	12.01	12.64	13.28	14.55	16.45	17.72	18.99	22.80
17	11.86	12.56	13.25	13.95	15.33	17.42	18.80	20.19	24.35
18	12.33	13.09	13.84	14.59	16.10	18.36	19.87	21.37	25.89
19	12.78	13.60	14.41	15.22	16.85	19.29	20.91	22.54	27.42
20	13.21	14.09	14.96	15.83	17.58	20.19	21.94	23.68	28.91

Illustration: An annuity for 5 years commencing with an initial payment of $1 and decreasing 7 cents each year, discounted at 6 percent is today worth $3.66.

219

TABLE III

Present Worth of Increasing and Decreasing Annuities, Straight Line Percent Changes
(Inwood Premise)
7 Percent

Years	Income annually decreasing at rate shown								
	−2%	−3%	−4%	−5%	−7%	−10%	−12%	−14%	−20%
1	0.93	0.93	0.93	0.93	0.93	0.93	0.93	0.93	0.93
2	1.79	1.78	1.77	1.76	1.75	1.72	1.70	1.69	1.63
3	2.57	2.55	2.52	2.50	2.45	2.37	2.32	2.27	2.12
4	3.29	3.24	3.20	3.15	3.05	2.91	2.81	2.72	2.43
5	3.95	3.87	3.79	3.72	3.56	3.34	3.18	3.03	2.57
6	4.55	4.44	4.33	4.22	4.00	3.67	3.45	3.23	
7	5.09	4.95	4.80	4.65	4.36	3.92	3.62	3.33	
8	5.60	5.41	5.22	5.03	4.66	4.09	3.72	3.34	
9	6.05	5.82	5.59	5.36	4.90	4.20	3.74		
10	6.47	6.19	5.91	5.64	5.08	4.25			
11	6.85	6.52	6.20	5.87	5.23				
12	7.20	6.82	6.45	6.07	5.33				
13	7.51	7.09	6.66	6.24	5.39				
14	7.80	7.32	6.85	6.38	5.43				
15	8.06	7.53	7.01	6.49	5.44				
16	8.30	7.72	7.14	6.57					
17	8.51	7.88	7.26	6.63					
18	8.71	8.03	7.35	6.68					
19	8.88	8.16	7.43	6.71					
20	9.04	8.27	7.49	6.72					

Illustration: An annuity for 5 years commencing with an initial payment of $1 and decreasing 7 cents each year, discounted at 7 percent is today worth $3.56.

Years	Income annually increasing at rate shown								
	+2%	+3%	+4%	+5%	+7%	+10%	+12%	+14%	+20%
1	0.93	0.93	0.93	0.93	0.93	0.93	0.93	0.93	0.93
2	1.83	1.83	1.84	1.85	1.87	1.90	1.91	1.93	1.98
3	2.67	2.70	2.72	2.75	2.80	2.87	2.92	2.97	3.12
4	3.48	3.53	3.58	3.63	3.72	3.87	3.96	4.06	4.35
5	4.25	4.33	4.41	4.48	4.64	4.86	5.02	5.17	5.63
6	4.99	5.10	5.21	5.31	5.53	5.86	6.08	6.30	6.96
7	5.68	5.83	5.98	6.12	6.42	6.86	7.15	7.45	8.33
8	6.35	6.53	6.72	6.91	7.29	7.85	8.23	8.60	9.73
9	6.98	7.21	7.44	7.67	8.13	8.83	9.29	9.75	11.14
10	7.58	7.85	8.13	8.41	8.96	9.79	10.35	10.90	12.57
11	8.15	8.47	8.80	9.12	9.77	10.74	11.39	12.04	13.99
12	8.69	9.06	9.44	9.81	10.56	11.68	12.42	13.17	15.41
13	9.20	9.63	10.05	10.47	11.32	12.59	13.44	14.28	16.82
14	9.69	10.17	10.64	11.11	12.06	13.48	14.43	15.38	18.22
15	10.16	10.68	11.20	11.73	12.78	14.35	15.40	16.45	19.59
16	10.60	11.17	11.75	12.32	13.47	15.20	16.35	17.50	20.95
17	11.01	11.64	12.27	12.89	14.14	16.02	17.27	18.53	22.28
18	11.41	12.09	12.76	13.44	14.79	16.82	18.17	19.53	23.58
19	11.79	12.51	13.24	13.97	15.42	17.60	19.05	20.50	24.86
20	12.14	12.92	13.69	14.47	16.02	18.35	19.90	21.45	26.10

Illustration: An annuity for 5 years commencing with an initial payment of $1 and decreasing 7 cents each year, discounted at 7 percent is today worth $3.56.

220

TABLE IV

Present Worth of Increasing and Decreasing Annuities, Straight Line Percent Changes
(Inwood Premise)
8 Percent

Years	Income annually decreasing at rate shown								
	−2%	−3%	−4%	−5%	−7%	−10%	−12%	−14%	−20%
1	0.93	0.93	0.93	0.93	0.93	0.93	0.93	0.93	0.93
2	1.77	1.76	1.75	1.74	1.72	1.70	1.68	1.66	1.61
3	2.53	2.50	2.48	2.45	2.41	2.33	2.28	2.24	2.09
4	3.22	3.17	3.13	3.08	2.99	2.85	2.75	2.66	2.38
5	3.84	3.77	3.70	3.62	3.48	3.26	3.11	2.96	2.52
6	4.41	4.31	4.20	4.10	3.89	3.57	3.36	3.15	
7	4.92	4.78	4.65	4.51	4.22	3.80	3.52	3.24	
8	5.39	5.21	5.04	4.86	4.50	3.97	3.61	3.25	
9	5.81	5.59	5.38	5.16	4.72	4.07	3.63		
10	6.19	5.93	5.67	5.41	4.89	4.11			
11	6.53	6.23	5.93	5.63	5.02				
12	6.84	6.50	6.15	5.80	5.11				
13	7.12	6.73	6.34	5.95	5.17				
14	7.37	6.94	6.51	6.07	5.20				
15	7.60	7.12	6.64	6.16	5.21				
16	7.80	7.28	6.76	6.24					
17	7.99	7.42	6.86	6.29					
18	8.15	7.54	6.94	6.33					
19	8.32	7.65	7.00	6.35					
20	8.45	7.74	7.06	6.36					

Illustration: An annuity for 5 years commencing with an initial payment of $1 and decreasing 7 cents each year, discounted at 8 percent is today worth $3.48.

Years	Income annually increasing at rate shown								
	+2%	+3%	+4%	+5%	+7%	+10%	+12%	+14%	+20%
1	0.93	0.93	0.93	0.93	0.93	0.93	0.93	0.93	0.93
2	1.80	1.81	1.82	1.83	1.84	1.87	1.89	1.90	1.95
3	2.62	2.65	2.68	2.70	2.75	2.82	2.87	2.92	3.07
4	3.40	3.45	3.50	3.55	3.64	3.78	3.87	3.96	4.24
5	4.14	4.21	4.29	4.36	4.51	4.73	4.88	5.03	5.47
6	4.83	4.94	5.04	5.15	5.36	5.68	5.89	6.10	6.73
7	5.53	5.63	5.77	5.91	6.19	6.61	6.89	7.17	8.01
8	6.18	6.28	6.46	6.64	6.99	7.53	7.88	8.24	9.31
9	6.76	6.90	7.12	7.34	7.77	8.43	8.86	9.30	10.61
10	7.30	7.49	7.75	8.01	8.53	9.31	9.83	10.35	11.90
11	7.82	8.05	8.35	8.65	9.26	10.16	10.77	11.38	13.19
12	8.30	8.57	8.92	9.27	9.96	11.00	11.69	12.38	14.46
13	8.79	9.07	9.47	9.86	10.64	11.81	12.59	13.37	15.71
14	9.24	9.55	9.98	10.42	11.29	12.59	13.46	14.33	16.94
15	9.65	9.99	10.47	10.95	11.91	13.35	14.30	15.26	18.14
16	10.03	10.42	10.94	11.46	12.51	14.08	15.12	16.17	19.30
17	10.38	10.82	11.39	11.95	13.08	14.78	15.91	17.05	20.44
18	10.72	11.19	11.81	12.41	13.63	15.46	16.67	17.89	21.54
19	11.03	11.55	12.20	12.86	14.16	16.11	17.41	18.71	22.61
20	11.33	11.89	12.58	13.28	14.66	16.73	18.11	19.49	23.64

Illustration: An annuity for 5 years commencing with an initial payment of $1 and decreasing 7 cents each year, discounted at 8 percent is today worth $3.48.

TABLE V

Present Worth of Increasing and Decreasing Annuities, Straight Line Percent Changes
(Inwood Premise)
10 Percent

Years	Income annually decreasing at rate shown								
	−2%	−3%	−4%	−5%	−7%	−10%	−12%	−14%	−20%
1	0.91	0.91	0.91	0.91	0.91	0.91	0.91	0.91	0.91
2	1.72	1.71	1.70	1.69	1.67	1.65	1.64	1.62	1.57
3	2.44	2.42	2.39	2.37	2.32	2.25	2.21	2.16	2.02
4	3.08	3.04	3.00	2.95	2.86	2.73	2.64	2.56	2.29
5	3.65	3.59	3.52	3.45	3.31	3.10	2.97	2.83	2.42
6	4.15	4.07	3.97	3.87	3.68	3.39	3.19	3.00	
7	4.60	4.49	4.36	4.23	3.98	3.59	3.34	3.08	
8	5.00	4.85	4.69	4.53	4.21	3.73	3.41	3.09	
9	5.35	5.18	4.98	4.79	4.40	3.82	3.43		
10	5.67	5.46	5.23	5.00	4.54	3.86			
11	5.95	5.70	5.44	5.18	4.65				
12	6.20	5.92	5.62	5.32	4.72				
13	6.42	6.10	5.77	5.44	4.77				
14	6.61	6.26	5.90	5.53	4.79				
15	6.79	6.40	6.00	5.60	4.80				
16	6.94	6.52	6.09	5.65					
17	7.07	6.62	6.16	5.69					
18	7.19	6.71	6.22	5.72					
19	7.30	6.79	6.26	5.74					
20	7.39	6.85	6.30	5.74					

Illustration: An annuity for 5 years commencing with an initial payment of $1 and decreasing 7 cents each year, discounted at 10 percent is today worth $3.31.

Years	Income annually increasing at rate shown								
	+2%	+3%	+4%	+5%	+7%	+10%	+12%	+14%	+20%
1	0.91	0.91	0.91	0.91	0.91	0.91	0.91	0.91	0.91
2	1.75	1.76	1.77	1.78	1.79	1.82	1.83	1.85	1.90
3	2.53	2.56	2.58	2.60	2.65	2.72	2.77	2.81	2.95
4	3.26	3.30	3.34	3.39	3.48	3.61	3.70	3.78	4.05
5	3.93	4.00	4.07	4.13	4.27	4.48	4.61	4.75	5.16
6	4.55	4.65	4.74	4.84	5.03	5.32	5.52	5.71	6.29
7	5.12	5.25	5.38	5.51	5.76	6.14	6.40	6.66	7.42
8	5.66	5.82	5.98	6.14	6.46	6.94	7.26	7.58	8.54
9	6.15	6.34	6.54	6.73	7.12	7.70	8.09	8.48	9.64
10	6.60	6.83	7.06	7.29	7.75	8.43	8.89	9.35	10.72
11	7.02	7.29	7.55	7.81	8.34	9.13	9.66	10.19	11.77
12	7.41	7.71	8.01	8.31	8.91	9.80	10.40	11.00	12.80
13	7.77	8.11	8.44	8.78	9.44	10.44	11.11	11.78	13.79
14	8.10	8.47	8.84	9.21	9.94	11.05	11.78	12.52	14.73
15	8.41	8.81	9.21	9.62	10.42	11.62	12.43	13.23	15.64
16	8.69	9.13	9.56	10.00	10.87	12.17	13.04	13.91	16.51
17	8.95	9.42	9.89	10.36	11.29	12.68	13.62	14.55	17.34
18	9.19	9.69	10.19	10.69	11.68	13.17	14.17	15.16	18.14
19	9.42	9.94	10.47	11.00	12.04	13.63	14.68	15.73	18.88
20	9.62	10.18	10.73	11.29	12.40	14.06	15.17	16.27	19.60

Illustration: An annuity for 5 years commencing with an initial payment of $1 and decreasing 7 cents each year, discounted at 10 percent is today worth $3.31.

TABLE VI

Present Worth of $1
For Computing the Value of a Reversion

Years	4%	4½%	5%	5½%	6%	6½%	7%	7½%	8%	9%	10%	11%	12%	13%	14%	15%	Years
1	0.9615	0.9569	0.9524	0.9479	0.9434	0.9390	0.9346	0.9302	0.9259	0.9174	0.9091	0.9009	0.8929	0.8850	0.8772	0.8696	1
2	.9246	.9157	.9070	.8985	.8900	.8817	.8734	.8653	.8573	.8417	.8264	.8116	.7972	.7831	.7695	.7561	2
3	.8890	.8763	.8638	.8516	.8396	.8278	.8163	.8050	.7938	.7722	.7513	.7312	.7118	.6930	.6750	.6575	3
4	.8548	.8386	.8227	.8072	.7921	.7773	.7629	.7488	.7350	.7084	.6830	.6587	.6355	.6133	.5921	.5718	4
5	.8219	.8025	.7835	.7651	.7473	.7299	.7130	.6966	.6806	.6499	.6209	.5935	.5674	.5428	.5194	.4972	5
6	.7903	.7679	.7462	.7252	.7050	.6853	.6663	.6480	.6302	.5963	.5645	.5346	.5066	.4803	.4556	.4323	6
7	.7599	.7348	.7107	.6874	.6651	.6435	.6227	.6027	.5835	.5470	.5132	.4816	.4523	.4250	.3996	.3759	7
8	.7307	.7032	.6768	.6516	.6274	.6042	.5820	.5607	.5403	.5019	.4665	.4339	.4039	.3762	.3506	.3269	8
9	.7026	.6729	.6446	.6176	.5919	.5673	.5439	.5216	.5002	.4604	.4241	.3909	.3606	.3329	.3075	.2843	9
10	.6756	.6439	.6139	.5854	.5584	.5327	.5083	.4852	.4632	.4224	.3855	.3522	.3220	.2946	.2697	.2472	10
11	.6496	.6162	.5847	.5549	.5268	.5002	.4751	.4514	.4289	.3875	.3505	.3173	.2875	.2607	.2366	.2149	11
12	.6246	.5897	.5568	.5260	.4970	.4697	.4440	.4199	.3971	.3555	.3186	.2858	.2567	.2307	.2075	.1869	12
13	.6006	.5643	.5303	.4986	.4688	.4410	.4150	.3906	.3677	.3262	.2897	.2575	.2292	.2042	.1821	.1625	13
14	.5775	.5400	.5051	.4726	.4423	.4141	.3878	.3633	.3405	.2992	.2633	.2320	.2046	.1807	.1597	.1413	14
15	.5553	.5167	.4810	.4479	.4173	.3888	.3624	.3380	.3152	.2745	.2394	.2090	.1827	.1599	.1401	.1229	15
16	.5339	.4945	.4581	.4246	.3936	.3651	.3387	.3144	.2919	.2519	.2176	.1883	.1631	.1415	.1229	.1069	16
17	.5134	.4732	.4363	.4024	.3714	.3428	.3166	.2924	.2703	.2311	.1978	.1696	.1456	.1252	.1078	.0929	17
18	.4936	.4528	.4155	.3815	.3503	.3219	.2959	.2720	.2502	.2120	.1799	.1528	.1300	.1108	.0946	.0808	18
19	.4746	.4333	.3957	.3616	.3305	.3022	.2765	.2531	.2317	.1945	.1635	.1377	.1161	.0981	.0829	.0703	19
20	.4564	.4146	.3769	.3427	.3118	.2838	.2584	.2354	.2145	.1784	.1486	.1240	.1037	.0868	.0728	.0611	20
21	.4388	.3968	.3589	.3249	.2942	.2665	.2415	.2190	.1987	.1637	.1351	.1117	.0925	.0768	.0638	.0531	21
22	.4220	.3797	.3418	.3079	.2775	.2502	.2257	.2037	.1839	.1502	.1228	.1007	.0826	.0680	.0560	.0462	22
23	.4057	.3633	.3256	.2919	.2618	.2349	.2109	.1895	.1703	.1378	.1117	.0907	.0738	.0601	.0491	.0402	23
24	.3901	.3477	.3101	.2766	.2470	.2206	.1971	.1763	.1577	.1264	.1015	.0817	.0659	.0532	.0431	.0349	24
25	.3751	.3327	.2953	.2622	.2330	.2071	.1842	.1640	.1460	.1160	.0923	.0736	.0588	.0471	.0378	.0304	25
26	.3607	.3184	.2812	.2486	.2198	.1945	.1722	.1525	.1352	.1064	.0829	.0663	.0525	.0417	.0331	.0264	26
27	.3468	.3047	.2678	.2356	.2074	.1826	.1609	.1419	.1252	.0976	.0763	.0597	.0469	.0369	.0291	.0230	27
28	.3335	.2916	.2551	.2233	.1956	.1715	.1504	.1320	.1159	.0895	.0693	.0538	.0419	.0326	.0255	.0200	28
29	.3207	.2790	.2429	.2117	.1846	.1610	.1406	.1228	.1073	.0822	.0630	.0485	.0374	.0289	.0224	.0174	29
30	.3083	.2670	.2314	.2006	.1741	.1512	.1314	.1142	.0994	.0754	.0573	.0437	.0334	.0256	.0196	.0151	30
31	.2965	.2555	.2204	.1902	.1643	.1420	.1228	.1063	.0920	.0691	.0521	.0394	.0298	.0226	.0172	.0131	31
32	.2851	.2445	.2099	.1803	.1550	.1333	.1147	.0988	.0852	.0634	.0474	.0354	.0266	.0200	.0151	.0114	32
33	.2741	.2340	.1999	.1709	.1462	.1251	.1072	.0919	.0789	.0582	.0431	.0319	.0238	.0177	.0132	.0099	33

See footnote at end of table.

TABLE VI (continued).

Years	4%	4½%	5%	5½%	6%	6½%	7%	7½%	8%	9%	10%	11%	12%	13%	14%	15%	Years
34	0.2636	0.2239	0.1904	0.1620	0.1379	0.1175	0.1002	0.0855	0.0730	0.0534	0.0391	0.0288	0.0212	0.0157	0.0116	0.0086	34
35	.2534	.2142	.1813	.1535	.1301	.1103	.0937	.0796	.0676	.0490	.0356	.0259	.0189	.0139	.0102	.0075	35
36	.2437	.2050	.1727	.1455	.1227	.1036	.0875	.0740	.0626	.0449	.0323	.0234	.0169	.0123	.0089	.0065	36
37	.2343	.1962	.1644	.1379	.1158	.0973	.0818	.0688	.0580	.0412	.0294	.0210	.0151	.0109	.0078	.0057	37
38	.2253	.1878	.1566	.1307	.1092	.0914	.0765	.0640	.0537	.0378	.0267	.0189	.0135	.0096	.0069	.0049	38
39	.2166	.1797	.1491	.1239	.1031	.0858	.0715	.0596	.0497	.0347	.0243	.0171	.0120	.0085	.0060	.0043	39
40	.2083	.1719	.1420	.1175	.0972	.0805	.0668	.0554	.0460	.0318	.0221	.0154	.0107	.0075	.0053	.0037	40
41	.2003	.1645	.1353	.1113	.0917	.0756	.0624	.0515	.0426	.0292	.0201	.0139	.0096	.0067	.0046	.0032	41
42	.1926	.1574	.1288	.1055	.0865	.0710	.0583	.0480	.0395	.0268	.0183	.0125	.0086	.0059	.0041	.0028	42
43	.1852	.1507	.1227	.1000	.0816	.0667	.0545	.0446	.0365	.0246	.0166	.0112	.0076	.0052	.0036	.0025	43
44	.1780	.1442	.1169	.0948	.0770	.0626	.0509	.0415	.0338	.0225	.0151	.0101	.0068	.0046	.0031	.0021	44
45	.1712	.1380	.1113	.0899	.0726	.0588	.0476	.0386	.0313	.0207	.0137	.0091	.0061	.0041	.0027	.0019	45
46	.1646	.1320	.1060	.0852	.0685	.0552	.0445	.0359	.0290	.0190	.0125	.0082	.0054	.0036	.0024	.0016	46
47	.1583	.1263	.1009	.0807	.0647	.0518	.0416	.0334	.0269	.0174	.0113	.0074	.0049	.0032	.0021	.0014	47
48	.1522	.1209	.0961	.0765	.0610	.0487	.0389	.0311	.0249	.0160	.0103	.0067	.0043	.0028	.0019	.0012	48
49	.1463	.1157	.0916	.0725	.0575	.0457	.0363	.0289	.0230	.0147	.0094	.0060	.0039	.0025	.0016	.0011	49
50	.1407	.1107	.0872	.0688	.0543	.0429	.0339	.0269	.0213	.0134	.0085	.0054	.0035	.0022	.0014	.0009	50
51	.1353	.1059	.0831	.0652	.0512	.0403	.0317	.0250	.0197	.0123	.0077	.00488	.00309	.00196	.001252	.000804	51
52	.1301	.1014	.0791	.0618	.0483	.0378	.0297	.0233	.0183	.0113	.0070	.00440	.00276	.00174	.001098	.000697	52
53	.1251	.0970	.0753	.0586	.0456	.0355	.0277	.0216	.0169	.0104	.0064	.00396	.00246	.00154	.000963	.000606	53
54	.1203	.0928	.0717	.0555	.0430	.0333	.0259	.0201	.0157	.0095	.0058	.00357	.00220	.00136	.000845	.000527	54
55	.1157	.0888	.0683	.0526	.0406	.0313	.0242	.0187	.0145	.0087	.0053	.00322	.00196	.00120	.000741	.000458	55
56	.1112	.0850	.0651	.0499	.0383	.0294	.0226	.0174	.0134	.0080	.0048	.00290	.00175	.00107	.000650	.000398	56
57	.1069	.0814	.0620	.0473	.0361	.0276	.0211	.0162	.0124	.0073	.0044	.00261	.00157	.00094	.000570	.000346	57
58	.1028	.0778	.0590	.0448	.0341	.0259	.0198	.0151	.0115	.0067	.0040	.00235	.00140	.00083	.000500	.000301	58
59	.0989	.0745	.0562	.0425	.0321	.0243	.0185	.0140	.0107	.0062	.0036	.00212	.00125	.00074	.000439	.000262	59
60	.0951	.0713	.0535	.0403	.0303	.0229	.0173	.0130	.0099	.0057	.0033	.00191	.00111	.00065	.000385	.000228	60
61	.0914	.0682	.0510	.0381	.0286	.0215	.0161	.0121	.0091	.0052	.0030	.00172	.00099	.00058	.000337	.000198	61
62	.0879	.0653	.0486	.0362	.0270	.0201	.0151	.0113	.0085	.0048	.0027	.00155	.00089	.00051	.000296	.000172	62
63	.0845	.0625	.0462	.0343	.0255	.0189	.0141	.0105	.0078	.0044	.0025	.00139	.00079	.00045	.000260	.000149	63
64	.0813	.0598	.0440	.0325	.0240	.0178	.0132	.0098	.0073	.0040	.0022	.00126	.00071	.00040	.000228	.000130	64
65	.0781	.0572	.0419	.0308	.0227	.0167	.0123	.0091	.0067	.0037	.0020	.00113	.00063	.00035	.000200	.000113	65
66	.0751	.0547	.0399	.0292	.0214	.0157	.0115	.0084	.0062	.0034	.0019	.00102	.00056	.00031	.000175	.000098	66
67	.0722	.0524	.0380	.0277	.0202	.0147	.0107	.0079	.0058	.0031	.0017	.00092	.00050	.00028	.000158	.000085	67
68	.0695	.0501	.0362	.0262	.0190	.0138	.0100	.0073	.0053	.0029	.0015	.00083	.00045	.00024	.000135	.000074	68
69	.0668	.0480	.0345	.0249	.0179	.0130	.0094	.0068	.0049	.0026	.0014	.00075	.00040	.00022	.000118	.000064	69
70	.0642	.0459	.0329	.0236	.0169	.0122	.0088	.0063	.0046	.0024	.0013	.00067	.00036	.00019	.000103	.000056	70
71	.0617	.0439	.0313	.0223	.0160	.0114	.0082	.0059	.0042	.0022	.0012	.00061	.00032	.00017	.000091	.000049	71
72	.0594	.0420	.0298	.0212	.0151	.0107	.0077	.0055	.0039	.0020	.0010	.00054	.00029	.00015	.000079	.000042	72
73	.0571	.0402	.0284	.0201	.0142	.0101	.0072	.0051	.0036	.0018	.0010	.00049	.00025	.00013	.000070	.000037	73

TABLE VI (continued).

74	.0549	.0385	.0270	.0190	.0134	.0095	.0067	.0047	.0034	.0017	.0009	.00044	.00023	.00112	.000061	.000032	74
75	.0528	.0368	.0258	.0180	.0126	.0089	.0063	.0044	.0031	.0016	.0008	.00040	.00020	.00010	.000053	.000028	75
76	.0508	.0352	.0245	.0171	.0119	.0083	.0058	.0041	.0029	.0014	.0007	.00036	.00018	.00009	.000047	.000024	76
77	.0488	.0337	.0234	.0162	.0113	.0078	.0055	.0038	.0027	.0013	.0006	.00032	.00016	.00008	.000041	.000021	77
78	.0469	.0323	.0222	.0154	.0106	.0074	.0051	.0035	.0025	.0012	.0006	.00029	.00014	.00007	.000036	.000018	78
79	.0451	.0309	.0212	.0146	.0100	.0069	.0048	.0033	.0023	.0011	.0005	.00026	.00013	.00006	.000031	.000016	79
80	.0434	.0295	.0202	.0138	.0095	.0065	.0045	.0031	.0021	.0010	.0005	.00024	.00012	.00006	.000028	.000013	80
81	.0417	.0283	.0192	.0131	.0089	.0061	.0042	.0029	.0020	.0009	.0004	.00021	.00010	.00005	.000024	.000012	81
82	.0401	.0271	.0183	.0124	.0084	.0057	.0039	.0026	.0018	.0008	.0004	.00019	.00009	.00004	.000021	.000010	82
83	.0386	.0259	.0174	.0117	.0079	.0054	.0036	.0025	.0017	.0008	.0004	.00017	.00008	.00004	.000018	.000009	83
84	.0371	.0248	.0166	.0111	.0075	.0050	.0034	.0023	.0016	.0007	.0003	.00016	.00007	.00003	.000016	.000007	84
85	.0357	.0237	.0158	.0106	.0071	.0047	.0032	.0021	.0014	.0007	.0003	.00014	.00006	.00003	.000014	.000006	85
86	.0343	.0227	.0151	.0100	.0067	.0044	.0030	.0020	.0013	.0006	.0003	.00013	.00006	.00003	.000012	.000006	86
87	.0330	.0217	.0143	.0095	.0063	.0042	.0028	.0019	.0012	.0005	.0003	.00011	.00005	.00002	.000011	.000005	87
88	.0317	.0208	.0137	.0090	.0059	.0039	.0026	.0017	.0011	.0005	.0002	.00010	.00005	.00002	.000009	.000004	88
89	.0305	.0199	.0130	.0085	.0056	.0037	.0024	.0016	.0011	.0005	.0002	.00009	.00004	.00002	.000008	.000003	89
90	.0293	.0190	.0124	.0081	.0053	.0034	.0023	.0015	.0010	.0004	.0002	.00008	.00004	.00002	.000007	.000003	90
91	.0282	.0182	.0118	.0076	.0050	.0032	.0021	.0014	.0009	.0004	.0002	.00007	.00003	.00001	.000006	.000003	91
92	.0271	.0174	.0112	.0073	.0047	.0030	.0020	.0013	.0008	.0004	.0002	.00006	.00003	.00002	.000005	.000002	92
93	.0261	.0167	.0107	.0069	.0044	.0029	.0019	.0012	.0008	.0003	.0001	.00006	.00003	.00001	.000005	.000002	93
94	.0251	.0160	.0102	.0065	.0042	.0027	.0017	.0011	.0007	.0003	.0001	.00005	.00002	.00001	.000004	.000001	94
95	.0241	.0153	.0097	.0062	.0039	.0025	.0016	.0010	.0007	.0003	.0001	.00005	.00002	.00001	.000003	.000001	95
96	.0232	.0146	.0092	.0059	.0037	.0024	.0015	.0010	.0006	.0003	.0001	.00004	.00002	.00001	.000003	.000001	96
97	.0223	.0140	.0088	.0055	.0035	.0022	.0014	.0009	.0006	.0002	.0001	.00004	.00002	.00001	.000003	.000001	97
98	.0214	.0134	.0084	.0053	.0033	.0021	.0013	.0008	.0005	.0002	.0001	.00003	.00002	.00001	.000002	.000001	98
99	.0206	.0128	.0080	.0050	.0031	.0020	.0012	.0008	.0005	.0002	.0001	.00003	.00001	.00001	.000002	.000001	99
100	.0198	.0123	.0076	.0047	.0029	.0018	.0012	.0007	.0005	.0002	.0001	.00003	.00001	.00001	.000001	.000001	10

This is the single deposit today which, with interest, will amount to 1 in a given time; or, the present or discounted value of 1 due at a given future time.

TABLE VII

Sinking Fund Rates

For Computing Sinking Fund Requirements

Years	¾%	1%	1½%	2%	2½%	3%	3½%	4%	4½%	5%	5½%	6%	Years
1	1.00000	1.00000	1.00000	1.00000	1.00000	1.00000	1.00000	1.00000	1.00000	1.00000	1.00000	1.00000	1
2	.49917	.49751	.49628	.49505	.49383	.49261	.49140	.49020	.48900	.48780	.48662	.48544	2
3	.33222	.33002	.32838	.32675	.32514	.32353	.32193	.32035	.31877	.31721	.31565	.31411	3
4	.24875	.24628	.24444	.24262	.24082	.23903	.23725	.23549	.23374	.23201	.23029	.22859	4
5	.19867	.19604	.19409	.19216	.19025	.18835	.18646	.18463	.18279	.18097	.17918	.17740	5
6	.16528	.16255	.16053	.15853	.15655	.15460	.15267	.15076	.14988	.14702	.14518	.14336	6
7	.14143	.13863	.13656	.13451	.13250	.13051	.12854	.12661	.12470	.12282	.12096	.11913	7
8	.12355	.12069	.11858	.11651	.11447	.11246	.11048	.10853	.10661	.10472	.10296	.10104	8
9	.10964	.10674	.10461	.10252	.10046	.09843	.09645	.09449	.09257	.09069	.08884	.08702	9
10	.09851	.09558	.09343	.09133	.08926	.08723	.08524	.08329	.08139	.07950	.07767	.07587	10
11	.08940	.08645	.08429	.08218	.08011	.07808	.07609	.07415	.07225	.07039	.06857	.06679	11
12	.08182	.07885	.07668	.07456	.07249	.07046	.06848	.06655	.06467	.06283	.06103	.05928	12
13	.07539	.07241	.07024	.06812	.06605	.06403	.06206	.06014	.05828	.05646	.05463	.05296	13
14	.06989	.06690	.06472	.06260	.06054	.05853	.05657	.05467	.05282	.05102	.04928	.04758	14
15	.06512	.06212	.05994	.05783	.05577	.05377	.05183	.04994	.04811	.04634	.04463	.04296	15
16	.06095	.05794	.05577	.05365	.05160	.04961	.04768	.04582	.04402	.04227	.04058	.03895	16
17	.05727	.05426	.05208	.04997	.04793	.04595	.04404	.04220	.04042	.03870	.03704	.03544	17
18	.05400	.05098	.04881	.04670	.04467	.04271	.04082	.03899	.03724	.03555	.03392	.03236	18
19	.05107	.04805	.04588	.04378	.04176	.03981	.03794	.03614	.03441	.03275	.03115	.02962	19
20	.04843	.04541	.04325	.04116	.03915	.03722	.03536	.03358	.03188	.03024	.02868	.02718	20
21	.04605	.04303	.04087	.03878	.03679	.03487	.03304	.03128	.02960	.02800	.02646	.02500	21
22	.04388	.04086	.03870	.03663	.03465	.03275	.03093	.02920	.02755	.02597	.02447	.02305	22
23	.04190	.03888	.03673	.03467	.03270	.03081	.02902	.02731	.02568	.02414	.02267	.02128	23
24	.04009	.03707	.03492	.03287	.03091	.02905	.02727	.02559	.02399	.02247	.02104	.01968	24
25	.03842	.03541	.03326	.03122	.02928	.02743	.02567	.02401	.02244	.02095	.01955	.01823	25
26	.03688	.03387	.03173	.02970	.02777	.02594	.02421	.02257	.02102	.01956	.01819	.01690	26
27	.03546	.03244	.03032	.02829	.02638	.02456	.02285	.02124	.01972	.01829	.01695	.01570	27
28	.03413	.03112	.02900	.02699	.02509	.02329	.02160	.02001	.01852	.01712	.01581	.01459	28
29	.03290	.02989	.02778	.02578	.02389	.02211	.02045	.01888	.01741	.01605	.01477	.01358	29
30	.03175	.02875	.02664	.02465	.02278	.02102	.01937	.01783	.01639	.01505	.01381	.01265	30
31	.03067	.02767	.02557	.02360	.02174	.02000	.01837	.01686	.01544	.01413	.01292	.01179	31
32	.02966	.02667	.02458	.02261	.02077	.01905	.01744	.01595	.01456	.01328	.01210	.01100	32
33	.02872	.02573	.02364	.02169	.01986	.01816	.01657	.01510	.01374	.01249	.01133	.01027	33
34	.02782	.02484	.02276	.02082	.01901	.01732	.01576	.01431	.01298	.01176	.01063	.00960	34
35	.02698	.02400	.02193	.02000	.01821	.01654	.01500	.01358	.01227	.01107	.00997	.00897	35
36	.02619	.02321	.02115	.01923	.01745	.01580	.01428	.01289	.01161	.01043	.00937	.00839	36

Table VII (continued).

37	.02544	.02247	.02041	.01851	.01674	.01511	.01361	.01224	.01098	.00984	.00880	.00786	37
38	.02473	.02176	.01972	.01782	.01607	.01446	.01298	.01163	.01040	.00928	.00827	.00736	38
39	.02405	.02109	.01905	.01717	.01544	.01384	.01239	.01106	.00986	.00876	.00778	.00689	39
40	.02341	.02045	.01843	.01656	.01484	.01326	.01183	.01052	.00934	.00828	.00732	.00646	40
41	.02280	.01985	.01783	.01597	.01427	.01271	.01130	.01002	.00886	.00782	.00689	.00606	41
42	.02222	.01927	.01726	.01542	.01373	.01219	.01080	.00954	.00841	.00739	.00649	.00568	42
43	.02167	.01873	.01672	.01489	.01322	.01170	.01033	.00909	.00798	.00699	.00611	.00533	43
44	.02114	.01820	.01621	.01439	.01273	.01123	.00989	.00866	.00758	.00662	.00576	.00501	44
45	.02063	.01770	.01572	.01391	.01227	.01079	.00945	.00826	.00720	.00626	.00543	.00470	45
46	.02015	.01723	.01525	.01345	.01183	.01036	.00905	.00788	.00684	.00593	.00512	.00441	46
47	.01969	.01677	.01480	.01302	.01141	.00996	.00867	.00752	.00651	.00561	.00483	.00415	47
48	.01924	.01633	.01437	.01260	.01101	.00958	.00831	.00718	.00619	.00532	.00456	.00390	48
49	.01882	.01591	.01396	.01220	.01062	.00921	.00796	.00686	.00589	.00504	.00430	.00366	49
50	.01841	.01551	.01357	.01182	.01026	.00887	.00763	.00655	.00560	.00478	.00406	.00344	50
55	.01660	.01373	.01183	.01014	.00865	.00735	.00621	.00523	.00439	.00367	.00305	.00254	55
60	.01509	.01224	.01039	.00877	.00735	.00613	.00509	.00420	.00345	.00283	.00231	.00188	60
65	.01380	.01100	.00919	.00763	.00628	.00515	.00419	.00339	.00273	.00219	.00175	.00139	65
70	.01271	.00993	.00817	.00667	.00540	.00434	.00316	.00275	.00217	.00179	.00133	.00103	70
75	.01176	.00902	.00730	.00586	.00465	.00367	.00287	.00223	.00172	.00132	.00101	.00077	75
80	.01003	.00822	.00655	.00516	.00403	.00311	.00238	.00181	.00137	.00103	.00077	.00057	80
85	.01019	.00752	.00589	.00456	.00349	.00265	.00199	.00148	.00109	.00080	.00059	.00043	85
90	.00955	.00690	.00532	.00405	.00304	.00226	.00166	.00121	.00087	.00063	.00045	.00032	90
95	.00896	.00635	.00482	.00360	.00265	.00193	.00139	.00099	.00070	.00049	.00034	.00024	95
99	.00854	.00596	.00446	.00328	.00238	.00170	.00120	.00084	.00058	.00040	.00028	.00019	99
100	.00844	.00586	.00437	.00320	.00231	.00165	.00116	.00081	.00056	.00038	.00026	.00018	100

This is the annual amount which, deposited at the end of each year, with interest will amount to 1 at the end of a given time.

Bibliography

American Institute of Real Estate Appraisers; *Appraisal Terminology and Handbook;* Chicago, Illinois; 1967

American Institute of Real Estate Appraisers; *Real Estate Appraisal Practice;* 5th Ed.; Chicago, Illinois; 1967

Arnold, Ray H.; *How To Estimate Market Value in Selling Real Estate;* Englewood Cliffs, New Jersey; Prentice-Hall, Inc.; 1962

Babb, Janis, and Dordick, Beverly; *Real Estate Information Sources;* Detroit; Gale Research Co.; 1963

Casey, William; *Real Estate Investment Planning;* New York; Institute for Business Planning; 1955; A Loose-leaf Service

Curtis, Arthur and Cooper, John (Revised by McCallion, William); *Mathematics of Accounting;* 4th Ed.; Englewood Cliffs, N.J.; Prentice-Hall, Inc.; 1961

Ellwood, L. W.; *Ellwood Tables for Real Estate Appraising and Financing;* 2nd Ed.; Chicago; 1964

F. W. Dodge Co.; *Dow Building Cost Calculator and Valuation Guide;* New York; 1967; A Loose-leaf Service

Financial Publishing Co.; *Financial Compound Interest and Annuity Tables;* 3rd. Ed.; Boston; 1964

Friedman, E.; *Encyclopedia of Real Estate Appraising;* Revised and Enlarged Ed.; Englewood Cliffs, N.J.; Prentice-Hall, Inc.; 1968

Institute of Real Estate Brokers; *Percentage Leases;* Chicago; Published Periodically

Kahn, Sanders, Case, Fredrick, and Schimmel, Alfred; *Real Estate Appraisal and Investment;* New York; The Ronald Press Co.; 1963

Marshal & Stevens; *Marshal Valuation Service;* Los Angeles; Marshal & Stevens Publications Co.; A Loose-leaf Service

McMichael, S.; *McMichael's Appraising Manual;* 4th Ed.; Englewood Cliffs, New Jersey; Prentice-Hall, Inc.; 1951

McMichael, S. and P. O'Keefe, *Leases-Percentage, Short and Long Term;* 5th Ed.; Englewood Cliffs, N.J.; Prentice-Hall, Inc.; 1959

Murray, William; *Farm Appraisal and Valuation;* 4th Ed.; Ames, Iowa; Iowa State University Press; 1961

National Association of Building Owners and Managers; *Office Building Experience Exchange Report;* Chicago; Published Annually

National Cash Register Co.; *Expenses in Retail Business;* Dayton, Ohio

Nelson, Richard; *The Selection of Retail Locations;* New York; F. W. Dodge Corp.; 1958

Prentice-Hall Editorial Staff; *Encyclopedic Dictionary of Real Estate Practice;* Englewood Cliffs, N.J.; Prentice-Hall, Inc.; 1960

Ratcliff, Richard; *Real Estate Analysis;* New York; McGraw-Hill Book Co., Inc.; 1961

Reeves, C.; *Handbook of Interest, Annuity & Related Fiscal Tables;* Englewood Cliffs, N.J.; Prentice-Hall, Inc.; 1966

Ring, A.; *The Valuation of Real Estate;* Englewood Cliffs, N.J.; Prentice-Hall, Inc.; 1963

Schmutz, George L.; *Condemnation Appraisal Handbook;* revised and enlarged by Edwin M. Rams. Englewood Cliffs, N.J.: Prentice-Hall, Inc.; 1963.

Semenow, Robert W.; *Questions and Answers on Real Estate;* 6th Ed.; Englewood Cliffs, N.J.; 1966

U. S. Bureau of Census, Census of Business; *Major Retail Centers;* Current Ed.; Washington, D.C.; Government Printing Office

U. S. Bureau of Census, Census of Business; *1963 Retail Trade and Selected Services;* Government Printing Office

U. S. Bureau of Labor Statistics; *Consumer Price Index;* Washington, D.C.; Published Monthly

U. S. Corp of Engineers; *Real Property Appraisers;* Current Ed.; Washington, D.C.; Government Printing Office

U. S. Dept. of Commerce; *How to Judge a House;* Washington, D.C.; Government Printing Office

U. S. Internal Revenue Service; *Bulletin F, Tables of Useful Lives of Depreciable Properties;* Washington, D.C.; Government Printing Office

Urban Land Institute; *Community Builder's Handbook;* Executive Ed.; Washington, D.C.; 1960

Urban Land Institute; *The Dollars and Cents of Shopping Centers;* Washington, D.C.; 1963

Winstead, Robert; *Appraisal Practice Course I;* Houston, Texas; Winstead Appraisal Service; 1961

Index

DATE DUE

FE- 6 '92		
FE29 '92		
AP11 '96		
GAYLORD		PRINTED IN U.S.A.